THE
PRESIDENT'S
HEALTH
SECURITY
PLAN

THE
PRESIDENT'S
HEALTH
SECURITY
PLAN

THE COMPLETE DRAFT
AND FINAL REPORTS OF
THE WHITE HOUSE
DOMESTIC POLICY COUNCIL

TIMES 𝕿 BOOKS

RANDOM HOUSE

DEC 16 1993

This edition of The President's Health Security Plan
*contains the complete text of "Health Security: The President's Report
to the American People" by the White House Domestic Policy Council,
as published by the Government Printing Office on October 27, 1993.
Not one word has been omitted. It also contains the complete text of the
"Working Group Draft," dated September 7, 1993, by the White House
Domestic Policy Council. The White House neither authorized
nor approved its publication.*

ISBN 0-8129-2386-3

Manufactured in the United States of America

9 8 7 6 5 4 3

Contents

A NOTE TO THE READER

The President's Health Security Plan *contains*
two documents in one book: the complete text of both
the draft proposal on health-care reform and a final report
by the White House Domestic Policy Council.
For ease of comparison and reference, each report
is separately paginated.

HEALTH SECURITY:
THE PRESIDENT'S
REPORT TO
THE AMERICAN
PEOPLE

October 27, 1993

Contents

CONTENTS

October 27, 1993

MY FELLOW AMERICANS:

Every American must have the security of comprehensive health benefits that can never be taken away. That is what the Health Security Act is all about.

Americans are blessed with the world's finest doctors and nurses, the best hospitals, the most advanced medical technology, and the most promising research on the face of the earth. We cherish — and we will never surrender — our right to choose who treats us and how we get our care.

But today our health care system is badly broken.

Insurance has become a contest of finding only the healthiest people to cover. Millions of Americans are just a pink slip away from losing their health coverage, one serious illness away from losing their savings. Millions more are locked into jobs for fear of losing their benefits. And small business owners throughout our nation want to provide health care for their employees and families but can't get it or can't afford it.

Next year we will spend more than one trillion dollars on health care — and still leave 37 million Americans without health insurance, and 25 million more with inadequate coverage. Skyrocketing health care costs have forced workers to trade wage increases to maintain health benefits and crippled our nation's manufacturers in global competition. And every month that passes without health care reform adds billions to our national deficit.

In short, all the things that are wrong with our health care system threaten everything that's right. To preserve what's right and fix what's wrong, we must get the system under control — and put people first.

The Health Security Act is grounded in six basic principles: security, simplicity, savings, quality, choice and responsibility.

Security means providing every American with comprehensive health benefits that can never be taken away. We must — and we will — outlaw insurance company practices that discriminate against consumers and small businesses, and make care available to all Americans, no matter where they live or how old or sick they are.

Simplicity means reducing the paperwork that frustrates all of us and wastes countless hours and billions of dollars. We must cut through the red tape and free doctors and nurses to return to what they do best — care for patients.

Achieving savings starts with giving groups of consumers and small businesses the same buying clout as large employers to bargain for fair prices. Communities, companies and health plans across the nation are learning to discipline health costs. We must follow their lead.

Quality means improving what is already the highest quality care in the world. It means a new emphasis on keeping us healthy rather than waiting until we get sick, and giving consumers and providers the information they need to judge quality for themselves.

Choice means preserving our right to choose our doctors and increasing our choice of health plans. We must protect the doctor-patient relationship that lies at the heart of good health care.

Responsibility starts with those who profit from our current system but carries on to each and every one of us. It means every employer and employee must contribute something to the cost of health care, even if that contribution is small.

These principles are the guiding stars that we will follow on our journey toward health care reform. I am convinced that if we agree on these basic values, we can preserve all that is right with American health care, and fix what is wrong.

Our history — the history of challenges met, and obstacles over-come — teaches us that we can succeed. After decades of false starts, we must find the courage to change. And when our work is done — when we provide every American with true health security — we will know that we have answered the call of history and met the challenge of our time.

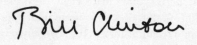

Foreword

HILLARY RODHAM CLINTON

TOGETHER, WE STAND at a unique moment in history. In the coming months, we have an opportunity to accomplish what our nation has never done before: provide health security to every American — health care that can never be taken away.

The debate over health care reform that will unfold over the next several months touches all of our lives and the lives of our children, our parents and generations to come. Because this issue is so critical to all of our futures, it is important that all of us have the opportunity to understand the complex issues and difficult choices that lie behind the design of any comprehensive reform effort.

That is why we have written this book — to lay out the dimensions of the crisis that confronts our nation, explain its elements and complexities, and state the case for comprehensive reform as proposed in the Health Security Act.

Book after book has been written about the intricacies of the health care system and the difficulties of addressing these problems. But most of them have not been written for people like you and me — people who may not be experts in health care policy but need and want to understand an issue so vital to our nation and our future.

I invite each and every American to read this book, to listen to the stories told here, to think about the issues and grapple with this complex — but solvable — problem. Then I invite every American to join in the debate.

Every month, two million Americans lose their insurance for some period of time. Every day, thousands of Americans discover that, despite years of working hard and paying for health insurance, they are no longer covered. Every hour, hundreds who need care walk into an emergency room because it is the only place they can go. And business owners, large and small, struggle to stay afloat while providing coverage for their families and employees.

Each time someone loses health coverage or is denied insurance, their experience becomes another chapter in a growing national tragedy. Anxiety and fear about the cost of health care affect tens of millions of Americans — those with health insurance and those without. Even those with the very best benefits worry that their insurance might not be there tomorrow or may no longer be affordable.

Over the past months, I have had the extraordinary opportunity of listening to thousands of Americans talk about health care. I've sat in living rooms talking to farm families. I've stood on loading docks talking to people who have worked for 10, 15, and even 20 years without insurance. I've visited hospitals, talking to doctors and nurses. I have learned firsthand about the tragedies of hard-working families who simply cannot get the health care they deserve.

I have read letter after letter of the more than 800,000 we have received at the White House from people all over our nation who took the time to sit down and share their concerns about health care. I have been moved by stories of parents who cannot afford a prescription for a child who is sick and hurting, of families barely hanging on financially and emotionally because of a health care crisis, of people trying to start a new business suffocated by skyrocketing insurance costs, of older Americans forced to choose between food and medicine, and of young people just leaving school unable to afford insurance.

I have carried their stories in my mind as we worked long and hard to devise solid answers to tough questions. The President's Health Security Act is a product of all the people who took the time to share their ideas, their research, and their personal experiences with us. And, as we move forward in this great national discussion, we must focus on these people, their health care, and their peace of mind — not solely on theories or statistics.

The concerns that were expressed again and again — from those who need care and those who give care — convinced me of one point: although America can still proudly boast the world's finest health professionals and astounding medical advances, our health care system is broken. If we go on without change, the consequences will be devastating for millions of Americans and disastrous for the nation in human and economic terms.

As a mother, I can understand the feeling of helplessness that must come when a parent cannot afford a vaccination or well-child exam. As a wife, I can imagine the fear that grips a couple whose health insurance vanishes because of a lost job, a layoff or an unexpected illness. As a sister, I can see the inequities and inconsistencies of a health care system that offers widely varying coverage, depending on where a family member lives or works. As a daughter, I can appreciate the suffering that comes when a parent's treatment is determined as much by bureaucratic rules and regulations as by doctors' expertise. And as a woman who has spent many years in the workforce, I can empathize with those who labor for a lifetime and still cannot be assured they will always have health coverage.

As an American citizen concerned about the health of our nation, I stand with you as we confront this challenge that touches all of us. We can and will achieve lasting, meaningful change.

I

Why We Need Reform

"You know, there's that old saying: If it ain't broke, don't fix it...This system is broken and desperately needs to be fixed...If I were talking about this as a patient, I would say that it is in intensive care and we're not seeing the kind of vital signs that would lead us to believe it will recover."

—*A doctor at St. Agnes Hospital*
Philadelphia, PA

In many ways, the American medical system represents our nation at its best, pioneering in the most noble of human pursuits, the healing of the sick. It is the result of five decades of national investment — investment in research into disease and prevention, training of doctors, nurses and technicians, and construction of hospitals and medical schools.

Today tens of thousands of dedicated health care professionals apply their unmatched skills to the world's most advanced technologies and procedures. They deliver some of the best health care on earth. No other health care system exceeds our level of scientific knowledge, professional skill and technical resources.

But America's health care system also presents our nation with one of its gravest challenges.

Bring together any group of citizens and the dimensions of the health care crisis emerge from their stories. Stories about insurance coverage lost, policies cancelled, fear of financial ruin, better jobs not taken, endless forms filled out. They are stories of frustration and insecurity — and, too often, pain and fear.

Today, everything that is wrong with the American health care system threatens everything that is right. That is the reality that drives the call for fundamental reform, the reality from which President Clinton's Health Security Act arises.

RISING INSECURITY

From the 1940s through the 1970s, the United States made steady progress toward broader health care coverage. Employment-based insurance and public programs expanded to reach more people and offer more benefits. Beginning in the 1980's, however, the number of Americans lacking health insurance has increased steadily — while health care costs have increased at ever-rising rates.

The result: growing insecurity. Today, according to estimates prepared by Families USA, more than two million Americans lose their health coverage every month. Many get it back within a few weeks or a few months, but every day a growing number of Americans are counted among the more than 37 million who go without health insurance — including 9.5 million children. Millions more have health coverage so inadequate that a serious illness will devastate their family savings and security.

Unlike other nations that have made health coverage a right of citizenship, the United States continues to treat it as a "fringe benefit" of employment, something that can be given or taken away. Over the course of any two-year period, one in four Americans learns how easily that privilege can be taken away, leaving them vulnerable to financial ruin. Others watch anxiously as their health benefits erode. Even those with the best benefits wonder what will happen if they lose a job or change jobs.

Americans value what health care can do for them; increasingly, many fear what the health care system can do to them.

At the root of the problem lies our health insurance system, which gives insurance companies the right to pick and choose whom to cover. Risk selection and underwriting — the practice of identifying the healthiest people, who pose the least risk — divide consumers into rigid categories used to deny coverage to sick or old people, or set high premium rates.

> *"The way the system works now, even employed, insured people are just one major illness away from financial disaster."*
>
> K.P.
> *West Lafayette, Indiana*

The result is a system that is stacked against individuals, families and small businesses. Millions of Americans have lost their insurance when they got sick and needed insurance most. People with pre-existing conditions — an insurance term for medical conditions or diseases diagnosed before people apply for coverage — either cannot obtain coverage or can often only obtain it at exorbitant prices. Many lose their insurance coverage when a spouse dies or they divorce.

Among the 37 million Americans who lack insurance, 85 percent belong to families that includes an employed adult. Those who work part-time or are self-employed, often cannot obtain group coverage. Fear of losing insurance locks millions of Americans into jobs they want to leave; changing jobs or starting a new business can mean losing health insurance. And many people stay on   welfare to get government health benefits they could not obtain if they were employed in minimum wage jobs.

For small businesses, health security has become almost impossible to achieve. Insurance companies charge small businesses higher rates than they charge major corporations, while refusing to cover some industries considered high risk. Small business owners that want to provide insurance can find themselves priced out of the market, leaving them unable to protect their families or employees.

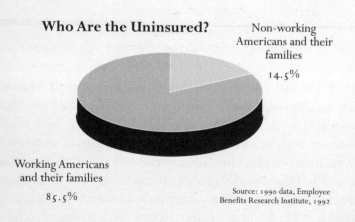

Who Are the Uninsured?

Non-working Americans and their families

14.5%

Working Americans and their families

85.5%

Source: 1990 data, Employee Benefits Research Institute, 1992

*"My husband and I own and operate a small business.
This year we will make our employees pay for any
increase in premiums and may drop [some benefits] alto-
gether. Our company cannot shop around for lower cost
health insurance because I am uninsurable."*

B.M.
Phoenix, Arizona

Prompted by ever-rising costs, employers of all sizes
have reduced health coverage benefits, raised deductibles,
limited coverage and switched to hiring more part-time
and contract workers in part to avoid paying health benefits. Sometimes without realizing it, workers sacrifice
wage increases for health benefits, making a tradeoff
between what they deserve and what they need. What
many Americans fear most about losing a job is losing
their health insurance.

Even for Americans employed by the largest corporations, rising health costs present an increasing competitive disadvantage, prompting renegotiation of benefits,
reductions in coverage, higher deductibles, limits on
choice of doctors, and attempts to shepherd employees
into one health plan. As costs continue to rise, these
trends become more pronounced — and increasing numbers of American families find health security beyond
their reach.

This growing insecurity also has a great impact on
older Americans. Any pharmacist will tell you that thousands of elderly people must decide every week between
buying medicine and buying food. Doctors who care for
the elderly know that cutting down on a dosage to stretch
a prescription or skipping a refill has become common-

place, particularly among the elderly who live only a little above the poverty line.

At the same time, a second and perhaps more daunting challenge confronts us: the growing need for security against the devastating costs of long-term care for the elderly and people with disabilities. With the number of Americans over age 85 projected to double by the year 2010, the need for long-term care is expected to rise dramatically as the next century begins, affecting not only those who need care but their families as well.

In the past, the United States has attempted to remedy the gaps in our health care system by expanding public programs or adding new programs aimed to fill specific needs. Community health centers, public health clinics, clinics for migrant workers, and public hospitals — all add up to a patchwork of services covering specific populations, but we have never met the growing need for reliable and secure health coverage.

"When my two sons were 3 and 6, Spencer and Evan were diagnosed with cystic fibrosis. In the blink of an eye, my two beautiful, healthy boys became part of our worst nightmare. We had to face the fact that we could lose them to this dreadful disease. We live in constant fear of losing our medical coverage...
Without the drug coverage that we now have, it would cost us at least $1500 a month for their medicine alone. These little boys are virtually uninsurable...As mothers we need to protect our children, and I don't want to feel frightened about this all my life."

A.B.
Pleasanton, CA

GROWING COMPLEXITY

American health care is choked by paperwork and strangled by bureaucracy. Administrative costs are higher in the American health care system than in any other country, and rising rapidly.

Confusion, complexity and increasing costs stem from the peculiarities of our health insurance system. Consumers experience it around the office or the kitchen table, when they are faced with piles of incomprehensible forms or when an insurance company refers them to the fine print in a policy to answer a question. A change in jobs or a move to another state can mean deciphering a whole new set of documents and learning a whole new set of rules.

> *"While we go about our business caring for our patients, we are being buried in paperwork. Everyday, my mailbox is filled with directives, new regulations and papers to sign. The truth is, if I read all my mail, there would be no time left to see my patients."*
>
> Dr. Jules Zysman

For small businesses, too many health care dollars go to administration not to actual care. Firms with fewer than five employees face administrative costs that absorb as much as forty cents of every premium dollar, compared to about five cents for larger companies — one reason why many small businesses do not have health insurance.

The sheer number of insurance companies and health plans also adds costs. Hospitals, clinics, doctors and other health providers must deal with hundreds of different insurance plans, each with its own benefit package, exclusions and limitations — and mountains of forms, rules, rates and payment procedures to follow. Each insurance carrier, federal program and type of policy — be it health insurance, auto insurance, or workers' compensation — has its own requirements. Hospitals have been forced to establish whole departments, create new occupational categories and hire special clerks to handle the paperwork.

In an attempt to control costs and improve quality, private insurance companies and government programs require doctors and other professionals to seek approval before providing treatment, and submit case records for reviews.

For example, a government program or insurance company considering a $30,000 hospital bill has no direct knowledge of the case or the services delivered. Reviewers want evidence that the care was necessary, that it was delivered, and that the bill is accurate and justified.

Every doctor's office and hospital must hire staff to document every service delivered, enter record codes, send out bills, and process other paperwork. They must determine whether an individual qualifies for health coverage, which company carries the primary policy, whether the services are covered, whether another policy covers the same care, how much each company is willing to pay, and how forms need to be filled out. Those staff then spend hours on the telephone with insurers arguing about what's covered and what's not. In many cases, these steps are only the beginning; receiving payment can take weeks.

Doctors, nurses and other professionals feel frustrated by bureaucracy, and worry that outside controls compromise their ability to make decisions about treatment. The relationship between doctors, nurses and their patients cannot help but be strained when the "hassle factor" and paperwork drain time and energy away from the delivery of care.

RISING COSTS

Between 1980 and 1992, American health care spending rose from 9 percent of Gross Domestic Product (GDP) to 14 percent. Without reform, spending on health care will reach 19 percent of GDP by the year 2000. If we do nothing, almost one in every five dollars spent by Americans will go to health care by the end of the decade, robbing workers of wages, straining state budgets and adding tens of billions of dollars to the national debt.

American workers already feel the impact of rising health costs in their paychecks. Had the proportion that health care makes up of workers' wages and benefits held steady since 1975, the average American worker would be making $1,000 a year more today. If current trends continue, real wages will fall by almost $600 per year by the end of this decade.

For every American family and business that purchases health coverage, the real cost of health care is substantially higher than most of us realize. We pay insurance premiums, deductibles (the amount we pay each year before insurance kicks in), plus whatever co-payments or co-insurance (the amount we pay that insurance doesn't

In 1990, the U.S. spent more on health care than on education and defense together, and the gap is widening each year.

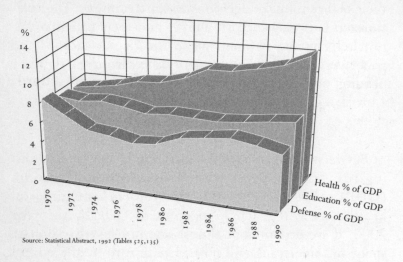

Source: Statistical Abstract, 1992 (Tables 525,135)

cover) our policies require. And ll those payments include a hidden 10 percent surcharge — in the form of higher bills — to cover the more than $25 billion in care that hospitals and doctors provide every year to people who cannot pay. Finally, we pay a payroll tax to cover the cost of Medicare, and other local, state and federal taxes to support the safety net of public programs that help fill in the gaps.

For America's employers, these costs put us at a disadvantage in international competition. Health costs in the United States, for example, add about $1,100 — about twice as much as in Japan — to the cost of every car made in America.

Rising health care costs deal the same blow to government budgets that they do to workers, families and businesses. If current rates continue, health spending will consume as much as 111 percent of the real increase in federal tax revenues during this decade. The same holds true at the state and local level, where increasing demands for public spending on health care, threaten state budgets and drain resources. For the first time in our history, state spending on health care now outstrips spending on education. Health care will consume a third of projected real increases in state and local budgets during this decade.

Rapidly escalating costs are particularly threatening to the security of two population groups — Americans

TODAY

If health care had been reformed in 1975, American workers would have over $1,000 in extra wages every year.

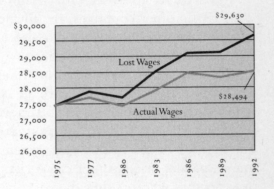

FUTURE

Without reform workers will lose almost $600 per year in wages by the year 2000

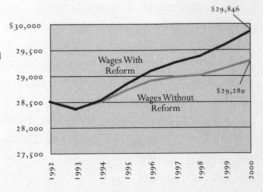

Source: Commerce Department; Office of Management and Budget

older than age 65 and the severely disabled — for whom we decided decades ago to extend health security under the Medicare program. But with growth in Medicare spending running 23 percent higher than the rate of inflation over the last decade, calls to cut Medicare have become commonplace.

The excessively high cost of health care is not the result of forces beyond our control. Other advanced countries provide coverage for all their people at lower and more stable costs and with higher levels of consumer satisfaction (and, in some cases, life expectancy). The American health care system consumes enough money to provide health security to every citizen and legal resident over time. As in other countries, the financial discipline needed to make care affordable can also keep health costs in line with the rest of the economy.

The fundamental problem in America is not that we spend too little for health care. It is that we don't get good value for the billions of dollars we spend.

Much research has demonstrated the waste and inefficiency of the health care system — as any doctor, nurse, patient or consumer can verify. First, we train too few doctors who provide the basic health care that most Americans need. Second, we neglect the basics of good medical care — such as preventive services — while investing too much in expensive, high-tech equipment that sits idle. Experts also estimate that health care fraud drains more than $80 billion each year from legitimate needs.

The incentives built into our health care system have also led to striking variations in the cost and frequency of medical treatments.

America Spends More Than Its Competitors on Health Care...

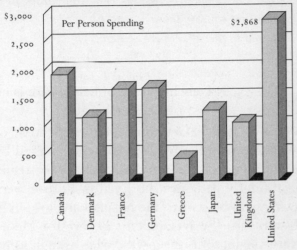

with less to show for it...
- Fewer Americans have health security

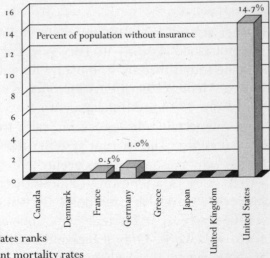

- The United States ranks
  - 19TH in infant mortality rates
  - 21ST in life expectancy for men
  - 16TH in life expectancy for women

Source: Organization of Economic Cooperation and Development; Department of Health and Human Resources

"Solutions must be found for spiraling health care costs that are eroding the competitiveness of U.S. companies in international markets and causing lower wages, higher prices for goods and services, and higher taxes here at home."

Kenneth L. Lay,
Chairman and CEO of Enron Corporation

Working at the Dartmouth Medical School, one research team compared how often patients covered by the Medicare program went into the hospital. The team discovered that elderly patients who lived in Boston were 1.5 times as likely to be sent to the hospital as those in New Haven. As a result, the average cost of care for Medicare beneficiaries living in Boston was twice as high as for those living in New Haven. But the researchers found no evidence that Medicare patients were any healthier in one city than in the other.

Other studies have documented similar variations. A study published recently in The New England Journal of Medicine found that after adjusting for differences in age and sex, Medicare payments for doctor care for patients varied from $822 in Minneapolis to $1,874 in Miami — with no discernible difference in health to justify the difference in cost. The current system offers few incentives to probe why these variations occur.

After years of attempting to slow the frightening rate of increase in health care costs by tinkering with the existing system, it is clear that only comprehensive reform will work. Only a fundamental change of direction — a change that reduces the waste and bureaucracy and turns today's upside down incentives right side up —

can bring about the savings needed to make the promise of security real. States and communities across the country arc proving that it can be done; now we must set the entire nation on this positive course.

DECREASING QUALITY

While the American health care system features some of the world's best quality care, the constant improvements in quality are now threatened. Today, we have no clear sense of what treatments work best and which treatments should be used in different situations. And our neglect of preventive care means that we are not as healthy as we could be.

Traditionally, Americans have assured medical quality by setting standards and then sending regulatory agencies to search for those who fail to meet them. In its oldest form, federal and state laws require health professionals and institutions to satisfy minimum criteria for licensing and certification. But while these procedures are necessary to protect consumers from substandard care, they have done little to improve quality or reward excellence.

Government and private sector regulators have written thousands of pages of rules governing everything from the qualifications of nurses' aides to the square footage of hospital rooms. Review agencies require doctors, nurses and hospitals to document each step in treatment and scrutinize case records. For many health professionals, quality assurance has come to mean nothing more than outside reviewers poring over records in search of errors. Too often quality programs just mean interference and punishment.

"The duplication of documentation, the authorization forms, the insurance claims forms and all of the complicated and often more contradictory instructions devised by the more than fifty insurance plans we accept are all overwhelming."

Dr. Lillian Beard
Pediatrician
Children's Medical Center
Washington, D.C.

Traditional quality systems have not produced the information that would be most valuable to doctors, nurses or consumers. Doctors and health care managers are frequently unaware of what happens where they work — for example, how often surgeons perform various operations, at what costs and with what results. They are even less likely to know how their performance compares to that of other professionals in the same community, much less across the country.

Since doctors and hospitals don't know how they measure up, patients are in the dark on most medical decisions, unaware of risks and benefits of alternative treatments or settings. Information that would allow them to make meaningful comparisons does not exist. Making this information available would give consumers a way of knowing that the care they receive is high quality and cost-effective.

DECLINING CHOICES

Free choice of doctors and other health care providers cuts to the core of the American health care system and the center of the doctor-patient relationship. For patients, the ability to keep seeing their doctor — someone familiar with their medical history and their family — can mean the difference between a good experience and a frightening one, sometimes even the difference between successful and poor outcomes. Perhaps no issue is more important to patients.

But today even patients who have good private coverage increasingly have restricted choices. Almost every practicing doctor has had patients call the office upset because they had to transfer to another physician when their employer or a job change caused them to switch them to insurance carriers. And doctors often find themselves discouraged from joining all the health plans in which they want to participate, separating them from some of their patients.

Faced with rising costs, many American employers increasingly limit the health care choices workers once took for granted. Today only one in three companies with fewer than 500 employees offers its workers a choice of health plans. Increasingly, the one plan available may limit choice of doctors, often disrupting valued relationships.

In one other sense, choices are limited in today's health care market. When the elderly or disabled need long-term care, they generally have only one place to go if they want coverage: the nursing home. Despite the fact that many would rather receive care in their homes and communities — a choice that is usually less expensive than institutional care — they are blocked from using federal health care dollars for such care. These peculiar rules and wrongheaded incentives single out for punishment those groups that deserve the security of guaranteed care.

GROWING IRRESPONSIBILITY

Irresponsible behavior in our current system begins with those who profit the most: insurance companies that search for only the healthiest people to cover while excluding the sick and the elderly; and pharmaceutical companies that sometimes charge Americans three times what they charge citizens of other nations for prescription drugs.

The medical malpractice system also fosters irresponsible behavior. Although the direct costs of medical malpractice are not great — experts estimate that they account for no more than 2 percent of health care spending — the threat of frivolous lawsuits breeds distrust and fear among doctors and other health providers. Procedures that doctors and hospitals perform to protect themselves from lawsuits adds billions more in "defensive medicine" to our bills.

This lack of responsibility can be seen throughout the system. Many people pay nothing for their health care, and in turn, contribute to skyrocketing costs. In the United States people who have no health insurance or who have inadequate coverage still receive care — but often it's the most expensive type of health care delivered in the most expensive place: the emergency room. Doctors, hospitals and clinics are forced to pass those costs along to everyone else — leading to what's known as "cost shifting" — which contributes to rapidly rising health spending.

Take the example of two businesses in a small town, a gas station and a car wash. Ever since he opened his business, the gas station owner has provided good health insurance coverage for his employees. Down the street, the owner of the car wash wants to provide insurance coverage, but he does not because he can't get a reasonable rate from an insurance company.

Not having health insurance doesn't protect the employees of the car wash from injury, of course. So when one of them gets hurt in an accident, he or she goes to the emergency room. The doctors provide treatment and the hospital sends the bill knowing full well that the patient cannot pay all or, in some cases, any of it. In turn, the hospital raises its rates for other patients to make up the difference. In effect, the gas station owner and his employees are paying for the health care of the car wash owner and his employees.

The bottom line is simple: every American pays when a company or individual fails to assume responsibility for health coverage or when insurance companies price people out of the market. Those who pay for health coverage end up paying for those who can't or don't. Restoring responsibility is vital to providing health security for every American.

AN AMERICAN CHALLENGE

Like a patient denying the symptoms of serious illness, for decades America has put off confronting the crisis in health care. Comprehensive health care reform has long seemed so formidable, complex and costly that we have denied the threat that continuing on the same course poses to our own lives, the lives of our children, and the course of our nation.

The cost of doing nothing far outweighs the cost of reform. One of every four Americans stands to lose health coverage at some point in the next two years. By the year 2000, one of every five dollars earned by Americans will go to health care. The average worker will sacrifice more than $600 in annual wages to pay for health care coverage. Rising costs will force firms to cut back further on benefits and scale back choices.

Despite its many achievements, America's health care system is threatening millions of people each year, undermining security, the ability to compete, and economic strength. The challenge of health reform is to alter that course, to reverse the harm while improving the quality of care, to replace fear with guaranteed security.

2

Principles of Reform

———————

*"Some things, like universal access, are not negotiable.
And that's exactly the way it should be."*

Former Surgeon General
C. Everett Koop, M.D.
September 1993

Six principles underlie the Health Security Act: security, simplicity, savings, quality, choice and responsibility.

SECURITY

Guaranteeing comprehensive benefits to all Americans.

1) The Health Security Act guarantees all Americans comprehensive health benefits, including preventive care and prescription drugs, and ensures they can never be taken away.

2) The Health Security Act outlaws insurance company practices that hurt consumers and small businesses. Insurers will not be able to deny anyone coverage or impose a "lifetime limit" on people who are seriously ill. And the plan outlaws charging older people more

than younger people, and sick people more than well people.

3) The Health Security Act sets limits on what consumers pay for health coverage. It limits how much health care premiums can go up each year, and sets maximum amounts that families will spend out-of-pocket each year, regardless of how much or how often they receive medical care. The Health Security Act removes "lifetime limits" on coverage, ensuring that benefits will always continue, no matter how much care you need.

4) The Health Security Act will preserve and strengthen Medicare, adding new coverage for prescription drugs. A new long-term care initiative will expand coverage of home and community-based care.

5) Access to quality care will expand, so that people know that there will always be a doctor that they can get to and a hospital that will treat them. Particular attention will be paid to the needs of underserved rural and urban areas.

SIMPLICITY

Simplifying the system and cutting red tape.

1) The Health Security Act reduces paperwork by giving everyone a Health Security card and requiring all health plans to adopt a standard claim form to replace the hundreds that exist today.

2) The plan cuts insurance company red tape by creating a uniform, comprehensive benefits package, standardizing billing and coding, and eliminating fine print.

SAVINGS

Controlling health care costs.

1) The Health Security Act increases competition, forcing health plans to compete on price and quality, instead of on who does the best job of excluding sick people or old people. Health plans will have an incentive to provide high-quality care and control costs to attract more patients.

2) The plan strengthens buying clout by bringing together consumers and businesses in "health alliances" to get good prices on health coverage. Today big businesses use their clout to get low prices; alliances will allow consumers and small businesses to get a good deal, too.

3) The plan lowers administrative costs by cutting paperwork and simplifying the system.

4) The plan places limits on how much premiums can rise, acting as an emergency brake to ensure that health care costs don't spiral out of control.

5) The Health Security Act criminalizes health-care fraud, including overbilling, and imposes stiff penalties on those who cheat the system.

QUALITY

Making the world's best care better.

1) The Health Security Act arms doctors and hospitals with the best information, latest technology and feedback as it empowers consumers with information on quality — forcing health plans to compete

on quality in order to attract patients.

2) The Health Security Act also invests in new research initiatives — into new ways to make prevention work, new treatments, and new cures for diseases.

3) The Health Security Act emphasizes preventive care — putting a new emphasis on keeping people healthy, not just treating them after they get sick. The comprehensive benefits package pays fully for a wide range of preventive services not covered by most insurance plans today. And it builds a stronger health care work force — training more primary care doctors, nurses and other health professionals to provide care into the next century.

CHOICE

Preserving and increasing the options you have today.

1) The Health Security Act ensures that you can follow your doctor and his or her team into any plan they choose to join.

2) All Americans will be able to choose from at least three and likely many more kinds of health plans offered — no matter where they work. The choice of plan will be yours — not your employer's. And every American will be able to switch plans every year if they're not satisfied with their care or service.

3) The Health Security Act makes it possible for more elderly and disabled Americans to continue to live in their homes and communities while receiving long-term care.

RESPONSIBILITY

Making everyone responsible for health care.

1) Without setting prices, the Health Security Act asks drug companies to take responsibility for keeping prices down.
2) To discourage frivolous medical malpractice lawsuits the plan requires patients and doctors to try and settle disputes before they end up in court, and it limits lawyers' fees.
3) Everybody — employers and employees alike — will be asked to pay something for health care coverage, even if the contribution is small. Low-wage small businesses and workers will get substantial discounts, but everyone must take responsibility.

3
How the New System Works

HOW REFORM WILL AFFECT YOU

After health reform goes into effect, every American citizen and legal resident will receive a Health Security card. Once you get your card, you will never lose your health coverage — no matter what. If you get sick, you're covered. If you change jobs, you're covered. If you lose your job, you're covered. If you move, you're covered. If you start a small business, you're covered.

The card guarantees you a comprehensive package of benefits that can never be taken away. Those benefits are as comprehensive as the ones that most Fortune 500 companies offer their employees. The package includes doctor and hospital care, as most insurance plans do, and also covers prescription drugs and a host of other services. [See chapter 4] You will also receive something rarely found in today's insurance plans — preventive care.

No matter which plan you choose, you will also receive something. The plan will pay 100 percent of the costs for a wide range of preventive care services, including prenatal care, well baby care; immunizations; disease screening for adults, such as mammograms, Pap smears, and cholesterol tests; and health promotion programs, like stop-smoking classes and nutrition counseling.

You will be able to choose your doctor. Every

American will have a choice of health plans — and plans will enroll everyone who applies, regardless of age, occupation or medical history. While prices will vary among plans, each health plan will charge everyone the same price for the guaranteed, comprehensive benefits package. Employers or insurance companies won't decide how or where or from whom individuals get their care — you, the consumer, will decide. You will be able to follow your doctor into a traditional fee-for-service plan, join a network of doctors and hospitals, or become a member of a health maintenance organization (HMO). For older Americans, the Medicare program will be preserved and strengthened with new coverage of prescription drugs. There will also be expanded options for home and community-based long-term care.

Like today, almost all of us will be able to sign up for a health plan where we work. Brochures will give you easy-to-understand information on several health plans — the doctors and hospitals involved, an evaluation of the quality of care, and prices. There will be regular "report cards" that measure quality and consumer satisfaction for each plan. Once a year, consumers will have a chance to choose a new plan. If you are not satisfied with your care or service, you can "vote with your feet" and pick a new plan, something most people can't do today.

If you're self-employed or unemployed, you can sign up through the health alliance in your area by phone or through the mail. Alliances, run by boards of consumers and local employers, will contract with and pay health plans, guarantee quality standards, provide information to help consumers choose plans, and collect premiums. They will, in effect, take on roles similar to major corporate benefits offices. The largest national corporations —

those employing 5,000 workers or more — have the option of continuing to self-insure their employees or joining regional alliances. For the consumer, particularly people who work, the local alliance will be largely invisible. It will help you get good prices on insurance, but you'll still sign up for health care at work.

In order to get care, most people will do what they've always done — go to the same doctors, hospitals, pharmacies, or other providers. More providers will organize into "networks" — groups of doctors, nurses, hospitals, and labs that cooperate together to coordinate the care of their patients and control costs.

Once you've picked a plan, if you need to go to the doctor for a check-up or if you get sick, you'll simply take your Health Security card, show it at the doctor's office, and they'll take care of you. Then you'll fill out one standard form, and you're done. So when you get sick, you won't be buried in forms — and neither will your doctor or hospital.

Unless your employer chooses to pay your entire premium, you will contribute about 20% of the cost. Your share of premiums will be deducted from your paycheck, the same way most people pay now. If your employer wants to pay the full cost of your premiums, that will always be an option. In addition, individuals will pay limited co-payments or deductibles to their health plans as part of their coverage. People who are either self-employed or unemployed, but still can afford to contribute, will send in a monthly check for insurance. (See charts at the end of the chapter.)

Today, most businesses offer health coverage to their workers. For these businesses, health care reform which provides universal coverage will mean a tremendous benefit. No longer will these businesses bear the costs of other businesses and their employees — through higher premiums and higher taxes to pay for people without coverage, or by covering spouses working for other businesses. And no longer will premiums continue to rise out of control. This will mean that businesses will be more competitive and be able to create more jobs.

Currently, health care costs represent an increasingly large financial burden for businesses of all sizes. Firms now pay as much as 20 percent of their total payroll just to provide health care coverage for their workers. Under the Health Security Act, no business will ever pay more than 7.9 percent of their payroll for health insurance.

> *"Successful implementation of health care reform is one of the best pieces of news American business could receive."*
>
> Henry Aaron
> Health Economist, Brookings Institute

SMALL BUSINESS IN THE NEW SYSTEM

Today's health care system is stacked against small business owners, their families and employees. Small businesses, who are too small to have benefits departments, are burdened by high administrative costs — as much as 40 cents of every dollar of their premiums — compared to only 5 cents for large companies. They are charged higher premiums because they don't have the bargaining power that large companies do to get the best prices from insurance companies. And they are the most vulnerable to sudden rate hikes if even one employee gets sick.

Despite these obstacles, most small businesses — par-

ticularly those with more than one or two employees —
do provide insurance for their workers. And most of
those that do not cover their employees want to provide
insurance but find it impossible in a health care system
that discriminates against them.

The Health Security Act creates a level playing field
that will finally allow small businesses to provide affordable coverage for their employees without being discrimi-
nated against because of their company size. The *Wall
Street Journal* has said that the Health Security Act will be
"an unexpected windfall" for many small businesses that
currently provide insurance to their employees. These
companies will likely pay substantially less under reform

Last year alone, one third of small businesses experienced
health care cost increases of more than 25%.

**Small Businesses
Face Rising
Costs Today**

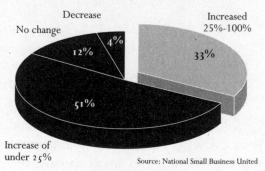

Decrease

No change

Increased
25%-100%

12%

4%

33%

51%

Increase of
under 25%

Source: National Small Business United

**Most Small
Businesses
Already Provide
Insurance**

Employees in Firms with Less than 100 Employees

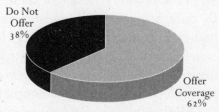

Do Not
Offer
38%

Offer
Coverage
62%

Source: Dept. of Labor; SBA Calculation of CPS Data

— because of lower premiums and reduced administrative costs. And those small businesses who are charged far too much today to provide a "bare-bones" package for their families and employees will finally be able to afford to provide a comprehensive benefits package — in many cases without spending much more than they currently pay for less coverage today. The Health Security Act will level the playing field for small businesses in the following ways:

- Small businesses will no longer face outrageous administrative costs because they will join together to get the same benefits — in terms of bargaining power and administrative simplicity — that big businesses have today.
- Small businesses will be charged the same rate as large businesses to provide coverage to their workers.
- Small businesses that now provide insurance will see their premiums decrease when they no longer have to pay for uninsured workers.
- The Health Security Act will outlaw insurance company practices — ranging from price gouging to refusing to insure entire industries — that make it impossible for small business owners to get insurance today for their families or employees.
- Reform will also streamline the workers' compensation system — which is a never-ending source of frustration, fraud, and high costs for small businesses today.
- Self-employed Americans will now be able to deduct 100% of their premiums — instead of the 25% allowed by law today.

DISCOUNTS FOR THE SMALLEST COMPANIES

Those small businesses that provide no health coverage today will have to help pay for their employees' health care. The Health Security Act is specifically designed to protect small businesses and help them make the transition to a system that guarantees their families and employees the health security they deserve. Those low-wage businesses with 75 or fewer employees will receive substantial discounts on the price of insurance, depending on the size of the company and the average wage.

- For the smallest firms that pay the lowest wages — such as restaurants — the percent of payroll devoted to health care may be as low as 3.5 percent. That amounts to $350 a year for a company with average wages of $10,000 — or less than $1 a day per employee.
- These discounts apply to most small businesses with less than 75 employees, even those that currently provide health insurance to their workers.
- The vast majority of small businesses — especially the "Mom and Pop" firms that are so vital to the American economy — will find that the savings they reap in the cost of health insurance for their own families will substantially offset any new spending required to cover employees.

AN OVERVIEW OF THE NEW SYSTEM

The Health Security Act rejects the idea of a government-run health care system. Health care will remain rooted in the private sector. Most people will get insurance through their employers, as nine out of ten people do today. The plan achieves universal coverage and recognizes that some direction from the government — including asking everyone to pay their fair share — will be necessary to achieve that goal. But it leaves the tasks of delivering care and controlling costs to the private market.

The Health Security Act seeks to build on what works best in the American economy and fix what is broken. What works best is a competitive market that provides products and services to Americans at the highest quality and lowest price.

But the competitive power of the market is not working in today's health care industry. Today, insurance companies compete not on the basis of price and quality, but by excluding people who might become sick.

The system is also broken in another fundamental way: small and mid-sized businesses, the self-employed, and average American families are powerless to bargain with insurance companies. Today, only big business has the clout to negotiate lower prices. The little guy — the local hardware store, the entrepreneur, the young family — ends up getting stuck with high prices and excessive cost increases.

The Health Security Act seeks to fix these problems so that all Americans benefit from a truly competitive health care marketplace. First, the Health Security Act outlaws insurance company discrimination based on age, sex, or medical condition. Instead, it makes insurance companies compete based on how well they cover all of us, and not how well they exclude some of us.

The Health Security Act joins consumers and small businesses together in health alliances so that they can have the same bargaining power that the largest companies get. After reform, every American will have bargaining strength to get low prices and high quality care.

For the first time, consumers will be in the driver's seat when it comes to finding quality health care. Health plans will be forced to compete on providing the best care at the most affordable prices. This will provide incentives for everyone in the health care business to operate more efficiently — incentives that don't exist today.

FLEXIBILITY

Realizing the goals of the Health Security Act requires that we build in flexibility. National reform establishes a framework within which states and local communities make their own choices. Americans cannot, and need not, come to one vision of the single best approach to health care.

Consequently the pace of reform will vary across the country. Some states are already well along in addressing the need for health reform. Some have served as models, forging paths that other states will follow as they implement reform. Under the Health Security Act states will begin implementing reform in 1996, and all states are to begin implementing reform by the end of 1997.

Reflecting the geographic diversity of our nation, the Health Security Act allows for each state to tailor health reform to its unique needs and characteristics as long as it meets national guarantees and standards for quality and access to care. Certain states, in fact, may choose to set up a single-payer system, where one agency collects and distributes all health care dollars for that state. Flexibility is essential because we know that what works in North Dakota may not work in North Carolina.

Although the Health Security Act establishes a national framework to achieve the goals of reform by spelling out standards and the comprehensive benefits that every American must receive, it does not prescribe how to deliver care or organize services. It leaves those decisions to consumers, doctors, nurses, hospitals and managers of health plans, rather than to the government. The Health Security Act establishes protection at the national level to ensure security — the solid foundation upon which American communities are free to build. Then it gets government out of the way to allow the reformed, private market to work.

What You Pay

What a Comparison Won't Tell You

Before comparing what you pay today with what you will pay under Health Security, remember this: The Health Security Act guarantees you something no amount of money can buy today — true health security, no matter what happens to you. Ask yourself these questions about your plan today:

- Do you have a comprehensive benefits package — with prescription drug coverage and preventive care at no additional cost?
- Do you have any guarantee that you won't have to pay a larger share of your premium next year?
- Do you get coverage that kicks in right away, after only a small deductible?
- Are you free from "lifetime limits" so you're guaranteed coverage no matter what happens?
- Does your insurance company charge you the same even if you are older or have a pre-existing condition?

If the answer to any of these is "no", you will get a better value for your premium under the Health Security Act.

Your Premium:	MONTHLY**			
	TODAY		REFORM	
	Range	Average	Range	Average
Two Parent Family With Children	$0-$180	$76	$0-$91	$73
Single Parent Family With Children	$0-$180	$76	$0-$80	$64
Married Couple With No Children	$0-$180	$76	$0-$80	$64
Single Person	$0-$60	$25	$0-$40	$32

** Preliminary average estimates, based on 1994 numbers; will vary from state to state.

Low-income Americans may be eligible for discounts.
This applies to:
- Two Parent Families with income below $22,200
- Single Parent Families with income below $18,400
- Married couples with income below $14,600
- Single people with income below $10,800

* Estimate of 150% of poverty in 1994. Actual cutoffs will vary by year and growth in consumer price index.

What If I Am...

 65 or older: Older Americans will continue to receive their health care through the Medicare program, as they do today. Older workers and their spouses will receive the same comprehensive coverage as other working Americans through the health alliances.

 Unemployed: Unemployed people will still have health coverage without interruption, paying only their 20% portion of the premium with discounts based on their income. Those with non-wage income — such as interest payments — may also be responsible for some or all of the employer's (80%) share.

 Part-time Worker: Part-time workers will pay for a portion of their health insurance premiums. As long as they are working, their employers will also pay part of their premiums. Depending on their income, part-time workers may receive discounts for the remainder.

 Self-employed/Independent Contractor: Today, the self-employed are only allowed to deduct 25% of their health care premiums from their taxes. Under reform, they will be able to deduct 100% of their health care costs. As with any business, they pay the employer's share, and are eligible for any discounts that apply. They also pay the individual/family share, and may be eligible for discounts on that as well, depending on their income.

 Retiree, 55-65: Faced with rising health costs, many companies have been dropping the health coverage that their retired workers depend on. Under reform, retired American workers will only be responsible for their 20% share of the premium. However, former employers may choose to cover the 20% share, or may be required to do so under collective bargaining contracts.

Financial Protection...

	TODAY	REFORM
DEDUCTIBLE The amount you pay before your insurance kicks in	Almost half of today's plans have deductibles larger than $200 per person. Some are as high as $3,000.	Many plans will have no deductible. For the plans that do, deductibles will be $200 for an individual and $400 for a family.*
LIFETIME LIMIT A limit on what insurance companies pay	In 60% of today's insurance policies, your insurance can run out if you get very sick.	There will be no limit on your total lifetime benefits.

* Preliminary estimates, based on 1994 numbers.

CO-PAYMENTS

Your co-payments — the amount you pay out-of-pocket when you go to a doctor — will be limited and uniform, protecting you financially and making it easier to choose among health plans. Co-payments will vary according to the type of plan you choose. For a wide range of preventive services, there will be no co-payments in any plan. Low-income Americans may receive discounts on their out-of-pocket costs.

FEE FOR SERVICE: Patients pay 20% of the cost of each visit after the $200 individual deductible or $400 family deductible is reached. They pay nothing after they reach the annual out-of-pocket maximum of $1,500 for an individual or $3,000 for a family.

DOCTOR NETWORK (PREFERRED PROVIDER ORGANIZATION): This plan offers low co-payments ($10) — with no deductible — if patients use the doctors within the network ("preferred providers"). If patients choose doctors outside the network, they have higher co-payments (20% of each visit) — once they've paid the $200 individual deductible or the $400 family deductible. They pay nothing once they've reached the out-of-pocket maximum ($1,500 for an individual; $3,000 for a family).

HEALTH MAINTENANCE ORGANIZATION (HMO): Patients pay no more than $10 for each doctor visit. There are no co-payments for hospital care and no deductible has to be met.

4
Security

"Six months ago, my sister-in-law, Pam, had a disabling stroke. Pam is only 39 years old, and she's a severe diabetic. Six months have passed, her short-term memory has deteriorated, her vision is leaving, and it looks as if my brother will either have to hire someone to come into their home full time to care for her, or put her in a nursing home, which his medical plan does not cover.

My brother's attorney has advised him to divorce Pam so that her medical bills don't pull him into financial ruin. My brother has two young sons that he's caring for and in order to continue to provide for them, he is giving this consideration...

A man who loves his wife must divorce her so that her misfortune (in sickness and in health) does not leave him with the inability to raise their family."

A.P.
Toledo, OH

Americans buy health insurance to provide security for themselves and their families. Security, in its full sense, is what health care reform must give us all. We must be secure that no American will face exclusion from coverage because of illness, occupation or age. We must be secure that health benefits will be comprehensive enough to keep us healthy and cover our health care needs throughout life.

COVERED BENEFITS

Benefits covered under the nationally guaranteed comprehensive package carry no lifetime limits. The package covers the following health services when they are medically necessary or appropriate:

- Hospital services, including bed and board, routine care, therapeutics, laboratory and diagnostic and radiology services and professional services.
- Emergency services.
- Services of health professionals delivered in professional offices, clinics and other sites.
- Clinical preventive services.
- Mental health and substance-abuse services (for details, see box on mental health and substance abuse).
- Family planning services.
- Pregnancy-related services.
- Hospice care during the last six months of life.
- Home health care, including skilled nursing care, physical, occupational and speech therapy, prescribed social services and home-infusion therapy after an acute illness to prevent institutional care.

- Extended-care services, including inpatient care in a skilled nursing home or rehabilitation center following an acute illness for up to 100 days each year.
- Ambulance services.
- Outpatient laboratory and diagnostic services.
- Outpatient prescription drugs and biologicals, including insulin.
- Outpatient rehabilitation services including physical therapy and speech pathology to restore function or minimize limitations as a result of illness or injury.
- Durable medical equipment, prosthetic and orthotic devices.
- Routine ear and eye examinations every two years.
- Eyeglasses for children under age 18.
- Dental care for children under age 18.

PLANNED EXPANSION OF BENEFITS

Beginning in the year 2001, the nationally guaranteed benefits package will expand to include the following:
- Preventive dental care for adults.
- Orthodontia if necessary to prevent reconstructive surgery for children.
- Expanded coverage for mental health and substance abuse treatment.

COMPREHENSIVE BENEFITS

Under the Health Security Act, all American citizens and legal residents will be guaranteed a comprehensive package of health benefits that can never be taken away. They will receive a Health Security card entitling them to enroll in a health plan. Everyone will have a choice of at least three — and, in most communities, many more — health plans. And no matter which plan people choose, they will receive the comprehensive benefits package.

The coverage provided by the comprehensive benefits package equals that provided by America's major employ-

PREVENTIVE SERVICES

The Health Security Act offers comprehensive coverage for a specific set of preventive screenings, laboratory tests and periodic checkups. Included in the benefit package, at no cost to the consumer, is coverage for preventive care such as immunizations and specific screening tests.

Some preventive services will be targeted to groups that have a high risk for certain diseases, such as men considered especially vulnerable to cardiac problems and women with a close family history of breast cancer. Children will receive a full range of prevention services, including immunizations, well-baby checkups and developmental screenings at no extra charge.

ers, such as Fortune 500 companies. It covers a full array of clinical services, from doctors' offices, to clinics, to hospitals, to rehabilitation centers, to laboratories, hospices, home-health agencies and other professional offices.

The comprehensive benefits package provides far more coverage for clinical preventive services than traditional insurance. It waives the usual co-payments and deductibles for a wide range of preventive services that are vital to keeping people healthy. Preventive services covered without co-payments include prenatal, well-baby and well-child checkups, physicals for adults, immunizations and regular screening tests such as mammograms and Pap smears.

The Health Security Act particularly expands preventive services for certain low-income women and children. By fully funding the Special Supplemental Food Program for Women, Infants and Children (WIC), more families will be able to receive nutrition counseling and get nutritious food — part of the overall strategy for keeping people healthy rather than waiting until they get sick.

"We believe reform will enhance both medical security for the nation's 65 million children and peace of mind for their parents. We are especially impressed by the commitment of yourself and the First Lady to ensuring all children have access to appropriate health care, because it is such an important investment in the nation's future."

Lawrence A. McAndrews, President and CEO
National Association of Children's Hospitals
and related institutions.
September 21, 1993

The benefit package also expands traditional coverage of mental health and substance abuse treatment. Insurance companies often tightly limit their coverage of mental health; they adopt that policy partly because they depend on the public mental health system — and the taxpayers who pick up the bills — to serve millions of people who lack coverage for even basic treatment, or who suffer from chronic or serious illness. The Health Security Act eliminates the lifetime limits on mental illness that can devastate family savings; and it provides coverage for regular clinical visits, and offers more flexible care.

For millions of Americans, the comprehensive benefits package will provide a significant expansion of coverage. Those whose current benefits are more generous — a much smaller number — will have every right to continue receiving richer benefits. Nothing in the Health Security Act prevents employers from providing more extensive benefits, with no strings attached.

Not everything is covered in the benefits package. It would just be too expensive. Examples of services that are not covered include:

- Services that are not medically necessary or appropriate
- A private room in a hospital
- Adult eyeglasses and contact lenses
- Hearing aids
- Cosmetic surgery

Individuals will be free to purchase supplementary insurance, although the comprehensive benefits package leaves little need for additional coverage. Employers are also free to offer additional benefits or absorb co-pay-

MENTAL HEALTH AND SUBSTANCE ABUSE

The Health Security Act offers Americans guaranteed coverage for mental illness and substance abuse, ending the agony that families confront when a serious mental illness occurs.

The benefit package gradually expands coverage for mental illness and substance abuse, both for inpatient and outpatient therapy. Out-patient services will include diagnostic office visits for medical management, substance abuse counseling, and relapse prevention. The benefit package also provides coverage for a wide range of new approaches, such as intensive care delivered outside the hospital.

The Health Security Act eliminates lifetime limits on mental health and substance abuse treatments. Initially it contains limits on the number of days of inpatient and outpatient treatment, but it commits to removing those limits by the year 2001.

Types of services covered:
- Inpatient care
- Alternative treatment programs which provide intensive care outside hospitals
- Outpatient therapy with requirements for patients to share part of the cost.
- Brief office visits and medical management for patients who take medication.

ments and deductibles.

However people choose to receive health care, the Health Security Act guarantees all Americans something no amount of money can buy in today's insurance market: the knowledge that they will always have comprehensive health benefits that can never be taken away — no matter what happens in their lives or their jobs. If they lose a job or change employers, coverage will continue without interruption. If they move, get married, separate from a spouse, experience a catastrophic illness or confront any other crisis, their health coverage will continue uninterrupted.

INSURANCE REFORM

The Health Security Act outlaws discriminatory insurance practices that prevent millions from obtaining health coverage today. It will return the concept of health insurance to its roots: offering protection to everyone whether they're healthy or sick, young or old. It will put an end to the practice of underwriting — searching for only the healthiest people to insure.

Under the Health Security Act, health plans will be required to:

- Enroll everyone who applies, whether they're healthy or sick, young or old;
- Charge everyone the same price for the same comprehensive benefits — no more charging higher rates to sick people, older people, or people with pre-existing conditions;
- Provide coverage without resorting to "lifetime limits" that cut off coverage when people need it most; and

- Limit deductibles in fee-for-service plans to $200 for an individual and $400 for a family.

By establishing a uniform, comprehensive benefits package, the Health Security Act no longer makes it advantageous for insurance companies to shape benefits and policies that attract the healthy and avoid the sick. Health alliances, in turn, will help organize the private market so that consumers — for the first time — can compare plans and providers and make informed choices. Their mission will be to promote competition amo⌐ health plans based on quality and price — not on ⟍ can screen out sick patients.

Limits on What Consumers and Businesses Pay

The Health Security Act also takes several important steps to protect families and businesses from rising health costs and financial ruin. To provide secure financial protection against the most devastating illnesses and injuries, it prohibits so-called "lifetime limits" and restrictions on the amount of medically necessary or appropriate care. The limits, which are included in six out of every ten insurance policies today, can mean bankruptcy for families in which catastrophic illness strikes. The Act also sets maximum annual out-of-pocket limits; even those who select the most expensive plans can spend no more than $1,500 a year for an individual, or $3,000 for a family. Insurance picks up the full cost of any medical care that exceeds those limits.

The Health Security Act also limits deductibles — the amount people pay each year before insurance kicks in, which can run into the thousands today — to $200 for individuals and $400 for families who choose traditional fee-for-service plans.

Employers will pay a maximum of 7.9 percent of their payroll for health care. Small businesses — those with fewer than 75 employees — will receive discounts of between 30 and 80 percent, compared to what the average large business pays. And the self-employed will be able to deduct from their taxes 100 percent of their health care, up from today's 25 percent.

PROTECTING OLDER AMERICANS

The Health Security Act preserves and protects the Medicare program, providing older Americans with the health security they deserve. People covered by Medi-

Older Americans and Prescription Drugs

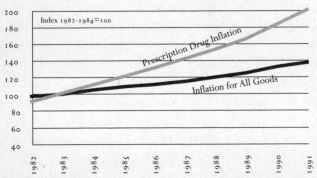

- More than 60% of those older than 65 have no insurance for drug costs.[1]
- Prescription drugs are the largest cost of daily living for 45% of all people over 65.[2]
- More than 5 million Americans over age 55 say they have to choose between buying food and paying for medication.[3]

Source: U.S. Department of Labor, Bureau of Labor Statistics

[1] USA Today, 9/25/93
[2] USA Today, 9/25/93
[3] Robert Wood Johnson Foundation

care will see little difference in how, where or from whom they receive their health care, but they will receive new prescription drug benefits.

Americans eligible for Medicare will automatically receive the new prescription drug benefit — which will cover drugs and biological products, including insulin, approved by the Food and Drug Administration — when they enroll in the Part B benefit, which covers physician and other outpatient services. Under the drug benefit, there will be a $250 annual deductible for each person. Individuals on Medicare will also pay 20 percent of the cost of each prescription up to a maximum of $1,000 over the course of a year.

Part B premiums will increase about $11 a month to cover 25 percent of the cost of this new benefit. But for seniors who have Medigap policies, which cover services not provided by Medicare, premiums for those policies should decline since they will no longer cover prescription drugs.

As Americans enrolled in health plans through alliances turn sixty-five, they can choose between remaining in their health plan or entering the Medicare system.

Older Americans will also see their long-term care options expand and improve under health care reform. The Health Security Act creates a new home and community-based care program and expands the range of choices for disabled individuals who require long-term care.

Among other things, the Health Security Act will:

- Expand home and community-based services;
- Improve Medicaid coverage for people in nursing homes;
- Improve the quality and reliability of private long-

EARLY RETIREES

When Americans over age 55 find that health problems or other events require them to stop working, they often confront the worst possibilities in the current health insurance market: because of age, or medical conditions, individual coverage is difficult to obtain or very expensive. Under health care reform, American workers who retire between the ages of 55 and 64 will never have to worry about losing their health coverage.

Under the Health Security Act, individuals over age 55 who retire before they are eligible for Medicare will pay for their coverage like other people who do not work and will be eligible for discounts based on income.

When reform is fully implemented, at the end of this decade, early retirees will become eligible for greater discounts requiring them to pay only the portion of their insurance premium that they paid as employees, unless they have an annual income higher than $100,000 for an individual, or $125,000 for a couple.

To be eligible for this greater discount, early retirees will have to have worked for ten years, the same standard used for eligibility under the Social Security Act.

The coverage for early retirees in the Health Security Act will provide a major financial benefit to employers who traditionally cover the cost of retirees' health premiums.

Employers who wish to provide coverage for any or all of the retired employee's share of the premium or for cost sharing required by health plans will continue to do so, as they do today.

When they reach age 65, retired workers have the choice of staying in their health plan or enrolling in Medicare, just as they do today.

term care insurance and provide tax incentives to encourage people to buy it; and

- Provide tax incentives to help people with disabilities work.

ACCESS TO CARE IN RURAL AND URBAN AREAS

The challenges of guaranteeing health security in rural and inner-city communities are essentially similar: both include unusually high numbers of people without health insurance, making it difficult to attract doctors. Scarce economic resources create barriers to organizing effective networks of care.

Greater incidence of poverty aggravates health problems. Many people in these areas require special services — rides to the doctor, babysitting and translators, just to get access to health care services.

Although urban and rural areas have some of the same problems, the circumstances that cause them are often very different. In rural areas, geography is the main obstacle. With a relatively small population spread over a large area and health care professionals in short supply, patients often have to travel long distances to see a doctor. Doctors are reluctant to practice in rural areas because they have no help or support from peers. Without enough doctors, nurses and health facilities, building networks of care becomes more difficult, as does the task of attracting enough health plans to foster competition.

In inner-city communities, the challenge is almost the opposite: crowded cities with culturally diverse populations. Only a few blocks away from world famous aca-

LONG-TERM CARE

Beginning in 1996, a new home and community-based care program will enable older Americans with severe disabilities to remain in their own homes or with their loved ones, yet still receive the care and assistance they need.

Medicaid nursing home coverage will be enhanced, allowing nursing home residents to keep $70 per month for living expenses. States will have the option to provide even greater financial protection by allowing individuals to retain up to $12,000 in assets, instead of today's $2,000.

The Health Security Act also provides tax incentives to encourage people to buy private long-term care insurance that meets new standards, and tax incentives to help individuals with disabilities to work.

demic health centers, residents of low-income neighborhoods contend with a laundry list of health care problems [and] too few doctors and nurses; little or no access to culturally-sensitive care; high rates of infant mortality and low-birthweight babies; frequent violence; and serious health epidemics such as AIDS.

To serve both communities, the goals of health care reform are similar: increase the economic base for health care through universal coverage, provide discounts to make care affordable, and create incentives to attract health care providers to the area.

THE MAYO CLINIC

A Model for Reform

If you went searching for the highest-quality medical care in the world, you might not immediately think to head to rural Minnesota. But there in Rochester, you'd find the Mayo Clinic, a magnet for patients all across America.

The largest managed care practice in the United States, the Mayo Clinic is known worldwide for its effectiveness at diagnosing and treating illness, and for the excellent physicians who work there. And they've proved that you can control costs and provide top-flight care, holding cost increases well below national averages.

The Mayo Clinic has led the way in encouraging the development of networks of doctors in rural areas, and linking rural physicians and regional health centers in order to increase the availability of high-quality care. These kinds of rural networks serve as the cornerstone for the Health Security plan's strategy to make care more available for residents of rural and remote areas.

The Health Security Act includes new loan programs and investments to increase the level of service available in underserved urban and rural areas. Expansion of the National Health Service Corps will send new physicians and other health professionals into underserved rural and inner-city communities, substantially increasing the supply of doctors and nurses. Successful programs, such as community and migrant health centers, will expand to increase the number of places where people can find care.

A new program of federal grants and loans will support doctors and hospitals in rural and inner-city communities form their own networks and compete with other health plans. This program will link federally funded clinics with other community providers bolstering their skills to coordinate care, negotiate with health plans, and form their own health plans.

The Health Security plan — by supporting the creation of new clinics and offices and renovating and converting existing clinics and offices — will ensure more and better places to seek care in these areas. In addition, it will improve the level of care — and reduce isolation — for urban and rural residents. This will be done by linking members of the practice networks with each other and with regional and academic health centers through the development of more sophisticated information systems.

Two new programs will overcome barriers to care for hard-to-reach, isolated, or culturally-diverse populations. One will support school health services for adolescents. Another will support transportation, child-care, translation, outreach and follow-up services for those in need of care but who are not being served by current programs.

Hospitals, clinics, doctors and health professionals who traditionally serve in these areas are also eligible for designation as "essential community providers", gaining special protections during the implementation of health reform. To help these key providers adapt to the changes in the system after reform, the Health Security Act requires health plans to contract with essential community providers for five years to enable them to continue to serve the residents in these rural and urban communities who depend on them.

5

Simplicity

---

*"Each of our medical insurance policies requires separate
and different applications for reimbursement, each of
which have to be mailed to different addresses. This
mountain of paperwork places an undue burden on older
Americans . . ."*

J.H.
Venice, FL

In order to simplify American health care, we must
move forward on two fronts. First, we must reduce
paperwork by adopting standard insurance forms and
clarifying administrative rules. Second, we must strip
away the unnecessary layers of regulation and oversight as
we hold health plans and providers accountable for
results. Streamlining administrative burdens will make
our system less daunting and frustrating for consumers
and more supportive and flexible for the doctors, nurses,
and hospitals on the front lines.

REDUCING PAPERWORK

Guaranteeing all Americans health coverage and
establishing a uniform, comprehensive set of benefits represent the first, vital steps toward simplifying health care.
If all Americans have guaranteed coverage for com-

prehensive health benefits, then doctors, hospitals and clinics have less paperwork to do when a patient walks in the door. Doctors, nurses and other health professionals will no longer have to worry which patients are covered for what services. Patients no longer will have to deal with confusing sets of insurance requirements, and will no longer be stuck with huge medical bills because they didn't read the fine print.

The Health Security Card that every citizen and legal resident receives will guarantee that health coverage travels with you as circumstances change, whether you switch jobs or move to another state. Like the cards that activate bank-teller machines, a magnetic strip will provide basic registration information, including identifying the health plan in which you are enrolled. A personal identification

PROTECTION OF PRIVACY

The Health Security Act establishes the first national privacy protection laws specifically aimed at protecting the medical records of patients.

Under reform, new security standards will protect computer information, ensuring that medical records will be available only to health professionals who have a legitimate need to see them. For example, the bill clerk in the hospital's financial department won't have access to medical information. This is an assurance that few insurers, or hospitals, can offer consumers now.

FOR OFFICIAL USE ONLY   **MEDICAL CLAIM FORM**

Health Plan Information

1) Health Plan	2) Health Plan Number

Patient Information

1) Last Name	2) First Name	3) Middle Initial	4) Patient Identification Number
5) Gender	6) Patient Signature	7) Date	8) Release Medical Information? YES ☐ NO ☐

Subscriber Information

1) Last Name	2) First Name	3) Middle Initial
4) Subscriber Identification Number		

Treatment

1) Is need for care:	a) Employment – related?	d) Auto – accident related?
	c) Other, accident – related?	e) Appointment?
	e) Emergency?	

2) Initial Diagnosis	3) Final Diagnosis

4) Description of Patient's Encounter

From	Through	Place of Service	Primary Diagnosis Code	Procedure Code	Units/Days of Service	Covered Charges	Non-Covered Charges	Co-pay Collected	Optional Field
5) Total									

Health Care Provider Information

1) Last Name	2) Identification Number
3) Signature	4) Date

number will authorize access to insurance information, reducing the process of registering and billing, but maintaining your privacy.

The Health Security Card will not be a "smart card" — which carries information in a computer chip — a national identification card, or a credit card. It does not hold sensitive information such as medical records. It's simply a way to streamline the billing process, reduce

In the last decade, the number of health administrators grew 16 times as fast as the number of doctors

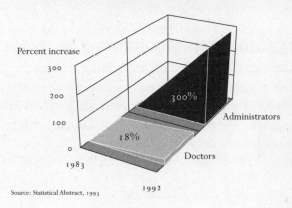

Percent increase

300

200

100

0

300%

18%

Administrators

Doctors

1983

1992

Source: Statistical Abstract, 1993

paperwork for doctors and patients, and assure people that they have a comprehensive set of benefits that can never be taken away.

All health plans will adopt a standard form that providers file for services. Replacing the hundreds of different claim and billing forms and codes insurance companies use today will allow health professionals to collect and send the same information to all health plans and alliances. Uniform claim forms will reduce the work that doctors, nurses, and hospitals must do and save an estimated 75 cents for each claim. In the long run we will save billions of dollars and free health professionals to spend more time caring for patients.

Today, different types of insurance often overlap, causing confusion, duplication, and waste. Under the Health Security Act, the health care portion of both workers compensation and auto insurance will be covered through regular health insurance. The need to coordinate benefits will decline and small businesses will be rewarded with less confusion and lower administrative costs.

> *"I know of cases where friends with insurance that covers medication will get prescriptions so that their poorer contemporaries will have the medication they need. Elderly patients try to help those without money for pre-scriptions by getting a doctor to prescribe for them in their name. We are playing Russian Roulette with med-ication because our system does not work."*
>
> M.J.
> Detroit, MI

CUTTING RED TAPE

Simplifying health care also requires aggressive steps to reduce unnecessary regulation. The Health Security Act frees hospitals and other health care institutions from excessive regulations. The federal government will develop national standards for quality which will use them as the basis for licensing hospitals and other health care institutions.

Today, dozens of public and private agencies, inspec-tors and outside groups inspect hospitals every year to make sure they meet quality standards. Although they all check the same things, they make their visits separately, and hospitals must spend time and money preparing for each visit. Under the Health Security Act, these groups will coordinate their visits, reducing preparation and follow-up time. Rather than routinely examining every hospital each year, inspections will concentrate on institutions with poor histories, following up on complaints and responding to problems.

To reduce frustration and delay, all health plans will have to make clear to participating consumers and doctors precisely how they perform "utilization review" — how the plan determines whether appropriate and effective care was given.   Health professionals and industry groups will establish new performance standards, eventually reducing reliance on obtrusive methods of control.

6

Savings

"...health care reform will be good for business. If we can stop runaway health care inflation, businesses like ours can use the dollars we save to increase capital spending and add jobs."

R. L. Crandall
Chairman and President
American Airlines

If we do nothing...

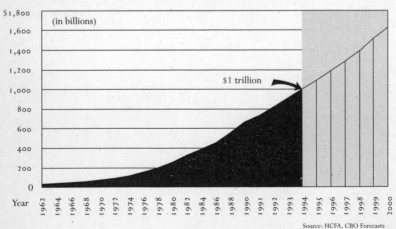

National Health Spending
The U.S. will have a $1 trillion health care bill next year

Source: HCFA, CBO Forecasts

The Health Security Act creates a new framework that will ensure all Americans secure, affordable coverage — and ensure that we spend our health care dollars wisely.

Serious health care initiatives must take aim at the waste, inefficiency, and fraud that bloat our health care system. But the key to achieving the savings that lie at the heart of health reform is to release the American spirit of competition.

Competition, after all, drives the price and quality of most products we buy. Think about a car — different companies build their automobiles, set their prices, and try to win our business. We shop around, kick the tires, make comparisons. Magazines like *Consumer Reports* help us judge what we can't see — safety records and the satisfaction of those who've driven a particular model. Armed with information, we take our pick. We buy the car that best meets our needs for quality, performance, and price.

Health care has never worked that way. Consumers often haven't had any bargaining power, they haven't had good choices, and they haven't had good information to make comparisons. Bringing competition to health care will give consumers the same buying clout in health care they've always had in other arenas. The Health Security Act will improve quality and control costs.

Bringing about savings also requires action on several fronts. Savings requires changing incentives. Savings requires streamlining and simplifying regulations and requirements. And it requires taking aggressive steps to stamp out health care fraud, which drains $80 billion each year from real health needs.

INCREASING COMPETITION

The Health Security Act controls rising costs primarily through the power of a competitive market — empowering consumers to make choices and giving health plans the incentive to compete for their business. Reform will change incentives so that health plans compete on the basis of quality, service and cost — not on screening out sick patients. Physicians, hospitals and other health professionals will be given opportunities to shape a health care system that works for patients.

Consumers will take their pick among health plans, based on what they have to offer. Which doctors are members of the plan? Are the offices and hospitals convenient? How much do they charge? Since all plans will offer the same comprehensive benefits, people will be better able to compare than they are today. Consumers will reap the savings from enrolling in health plans that deliver high-quality care most efficiently — and, therefore, charge lower premiums.

Better incentives for health plans will give consumers better value. In the current system, doctors and hospitals get paid extra for each service they perform, necessary or unnecessary. Under reform, health plans and providers make money by keeping their patients healthy — not doing more tests, but giving better care.

It will be in the interest of each health plan to operate efficiently — providing the best quality care at an affordable price. If health plans operate inefficiently, they will lose money. If they start cutting corners, they'll lose patients — and the business that those patients bring. Competition is about finding the balance — providing high-quality care while controlling costs.

CONTROLLING PRESCRIPTION DRUG PRICES

In the 1980s, the prices of prescription drug prices rose at quadruple the general rate of inflation. In recent years, several attempts have been made to control drug costs — often involving the use of buying clout to bring down prices.

For example, HMOs and managed care groups are successfully using their bargaining power to negotiate substantial discounts from drug companies. Because they often control the brand of drugs prescribed by doctors, health plans have the power to drive down prices.

Under reform, with the addition of prescription drug coverage, Medicare will become the world's largest purchaser of drugs. And the Medicare program will use its negotiating power to get discounts from the pharmaceutical companies. In addition, with competing health plans trying to become more efficient, more and more buyers will use the same successful negotiating techniques.

STRENGTHENING BUYING CLOUT

Increased buying clout can bring down costs. In today's health insurance market, for example, big companies can go to an insurance company and say, "Look, if you want the business of our 100,000 employees, you've got to give us a good deal." And they get a good deal — comprehensive benefits, high-quality care and affordable prices. But if you don't work for a large employer you're not in a position to bargain, so you're more likely to get high premiums, bare-bones coverage or nothing at all.

The Health Security Act will change that — putting consumers and small businesses in the driver's seat. It's based on the simple idea that bigger buyers get better deals. By bringing consumers and small businesses together in health alliances, the Health Security Act gives everybody else the same buying clout as the big companies.

Today, a major insurance carrier doesn't have to give any kind of deal to the Mom and Pop store in Peoria. But they will not be able to ignore 5,000 Mom and Pop stores brought together in an alliance from Central Illinois. That alliance will have more complete information on the costs of health plans, quality of care, service and consumer satisfaction than any buyer in today's market. It will keep enrollment records and collect premiums for many people, not just a few, and do it more efficiently as a result. Everyone — not just employees of large companies — will be able to get access to high-quality care at an affordable price.

LOWERING ADMINISTRATIVE COSTS

The Health Security Act simplifies the business side of health care by cutting through the paper jungle generated by some 1,500 insurance companies, and stripping away conflicting regulations imposed by a variety of federal, state, local and private agencies.

CALPERS

A Model for Reform

The state employees in California are getting a good deal on insurance — using their buying clout to bring down prices and cut administrative costs.

Adopting a role similar to the one that health alliances will play under health reform, the California Public Employees Retirement System — usually referred to as CALPERS — negotiates with health plans on behalf of almost 900,000 state and local government employees and their families in California. And CALPERS offers its members a choice of 24 different plans. Prices for health plans vary, although all plans provide coverage for the same package of health benefits — just as all plans will offer the same comprehensive benefits package under the Health Security Act.

Because they buy approximately $1.3 billion of health care each year, CALPERS — like the alliances under the Health Security Act — is in a strong position to get a good deal from health plans. Along with holding premium increases well below national averages for the last two years, CALPERS has also succeeded in reducing administrative costs.

Administrative costs take up 40 percent of every health care dollar spent by small firms and the self-employed, with only 60 percent going to buy care. Meanwhile, large purchasers pay only 5 to 7 percent for administrative overhead; 95 percent of their health dollars go to care, as they should. For all private health insurance, the cost of administration totalled $44 billion in 1991, an average of 16 percent of the benefits paid out.

"What the insurance industry burns up in commissions, marketing and claims processing costs is almost unspeakable. [President] Clinton would reduce those costs."

Professor Uwe Reinhardt
Health Economist, Princeton University

Similarly, eliminating some of the duplication among different kinds of insurance — folding the health benefits of auto insurance and workers compensation into one unified health insurance policy, for example — will produce savings. Today, doctors and hospitals often submit separate claims for payment to two or more insurers. Under the new system, everyone will have coverage, and most people will have one and only one source of insurance. Doctors and hospitals will no longer have to sort out conflicting coverage.

LIMITING PREMIUM INCREASES

The increased competition from health care reform will squeeze the waste and excess out of the health care industry that nearly every doctor, nurse, patient, consumer and insurance carrier knows exists. In order to reinforce the competitive power of the market, the Health Security Act also creates an enforceable, fail-safe limit on the growth of insurance premiums. This limit reinforces the new incentives that slow the rate of growth in costs and acts as an emergency brake to back up competition. It serves to build in some discipline and certainty so that businesses and families will know their health care costs will not suddenly spiral out of control. It also ensures that the federal government is serious about living within its means. Once American consumers and employers have reaped the gains from savings, the limits on premium growth will be reassessed, based on experience under reform.

REDUCING HEALTH CARE FRAUD

The Health Security Act makes health care fraud a specific crime. The Act takes aggressive steps to combat health care fraud, increase penalties for those who cheat the system and expand enforcement activities. It imposes new prohibitions against kickbacks and conflicts of interest, such as doctors who refer patients to laboratories in which they have a financial stake. And health care providers convicted of fraud and related crimes will be excluded from participation in health plans.

The Departments of Justice and Health and Human Services will lead the anti-fraud effort, organizing an All-Payer Health Care Fraud and Abuse Enforcement Program to coordinate federal, state and local law-enforcement activities. The effort will target practices such as overcharging for services, charging for medical care that was never delivered, giving kickbacks to doctors who refer their patients to certain clinics or pharmacies, and delivering unnecessary services. If providers file false claims against health plans, their assets can be seized and criminal penalties for health care fraud can be imposed. The revenues from seized assets will be funneled back to support anti-fraud efforts.

7

Quality

*"I am a first grade teacher in a very poor neighborhood
in North Philadelphia...Many of [my students] have
never seen a family physician; many have never even
been inside a public health clinic. I was shocked to find
that eight out of ten of their absence notes are written by
doctors in the emergency room of nearby hospitals...I feel
bad for my students who have never had an ounce of preventive medicine, but I feel angry, as do many of my
middle-income peers, who are ultimately footing the bill
for the emergency treatment these children are driven to."*

J.G.
Philadelphia, PA

In many parts of our nation, for many patients, the
quality of health care is unparalleled anywhere in the
world. The United States boasts the best technology, the
most advanced research, and the greatest number of
medical breakthroughs of any advanced nation. When it
comes to quality, we have a great deal to be proud of. The
Health Security Act protects and improves the high standards we have set for American medicine.

But the quality of our health care is uneven, and threatened by serious flaws in the way we measure and report
on which health care treatments should be used and

which work best. No clear standards define what is the best medical practice; lack of information compromises the care people get; and inadequate attention to preventive care reduces the effectiveness of treatment and services.

The Health Security Act includes specific provisions to make sure that the high-quality health care delivered in some parts of our country spreads to other areas, and becomes the standard nationwide.

This Act takes steps to arm doctors, hospitals, and health plans with the latest information on state-of-the art treatments and their effectiveness, and arm consumers with information to help them compare the quality of plans.

It measures quality and accountability, focusing on results rather than micromanagement and filling out forms.

It increases funding for health care research to keep American health care and technology state-of-the-art; and it improves health and wellness through unprecedented coverage of preventive care and steps to build a better health care workforce.

BETTER INFORMATION FOR JUDGING QUALITY

Without the information they need to reward high-quality plans with their business, consumers are powerless to force health plans to compete.

Researchers and panels of health professionals have developed new ways to measure the results of different treatments and what type of care and treatment works best. A number of medical professional groups have participated in extensive efforts to develop guidelines for effective medical care for specific conditions and illnesses. The Health Security Act will promote greater sharing and use of information, helping more practitioners benefit from the results.

Many programs around the country have begun using the new approaches to quality, building on better and more available information. Business groups are now joining with doctors, hospitals and health plans to publish information about comparative quality and price. In communities from Nashville, Tennessee to Rochester, New York, and in the state of Pennsylvania, major employers, local hospitals and state governments have begun collecting information that allows businesses and consumers to make valid comparisons among hospitals and physicians.

Under the Health Security Act, American consumers will benefit from greater access to information, which in turn will further improve quality. They will exercise not only the right to choose doctors, other health providers and health plans, but also the right to make informed choices based on meaningful information about how health plans, health professionals and hospitals perform.

Annual performance reports provided by health alliances will survey consumers and measure how their health plans, doctors and hospitals perform on a set of four critical indicators:

- Access: whether care is readily and quickly available;
- Appropriateness: whether care fits the condition;
- Outcome: whether treatments produce good results; and
- Consumer satisfaction.

These information "report cards" will compare health plans and providers, reporting how various plans performed on carefully selected indicators. Researchers know that certain medical indicators provide clues about overall performance: How many children with asthma in this plan ended up in the hospital last year? How many older people who suffered a fall didn't recover their ability to walk? How many patients who suffered heart attacks survived? On the simplest level: How many patients didn't like this plan and chose another?

Performance reports based on these types of indicators will prove valuable to consumers and health professionals. When choosing a plan or providers within a plan, consumers will be able to judge whether they can expect prompt access to treatment, how the care stacks up against competitors, and what other consumers think about the plan. Merely making this information available will force plans and providers to focus on quality.

A reformed health care system that emphasizes accountability can improve the quality of health care, improve safeguards for patients and reduce bureaucratic regulation.

The Health Security Act will replace the outmoded system for measuring quality in practice today, where government bureaucrats and insurance companies second-guess decisions made by doctors and their patients. In its place will be a quality measurement system focusing on results: Was the treatment the right one? Did it achieve the intended effect? What can we learn from the case? Focusing on results will reduce the paperwork and micromanagement that strangle doctors, nurses, hospitals and clinics. It frees health professionals from intrusive insurance companies and bureaucrats, improves morale, and creates an environment that supports what health professionals are there to do — care for patients.

Under reform, doctors, clinics and hospitals will have to examine ways to make their delivery of care more effi-cient while improving quality. "Business as usual" will no longer be profitable. Leading hospitals across the country are already moving in this direction. For example, when doctors at the Hospital of Latter Day Saints in Salt Lake City, Utah realized that post-operative wound infections were causing excessive hospital stays, they experimented with changing the timing of administering antibiotics before surgery. Patients got fewer infections, left the hospital earlier, and saved $450,000 in the first year.

INVESTING IN RESEARCH

Under the Health Security Act, there will be signifi-cant initiatives to increase research. Advances in medical science, new medications and technology, and innovations in health care delivery will improve the quality of life for all Americans.

Research related to health promotion and prevention of disease will focus on many common illnesses and other priority areas: heart disease, bone and joint disease, Alzheimer's disease, cancer, AIDS, birth defects, mental disorders, substance abuse, nutrition, and health and wellness programs.

Research regarding clinical practice will increase with an emphasis on quality and effectiveness, as well as access and financing. There will be an emphasis on "outcomes research," to help answer questions about what treatment works best for which conditions, so that doctors can provide the highest quality care for their patients. Expanded research will also measure consumer awareness, decision-making and satisfaction so that the best information is made available to the public. This will ensure that people can make well-informed decisions about their health care.

ACADEMIC HEALTH CENTERS

Academic health centers are the sites of the basic research that ushers in modern medical advances — new treatments and cures for human illnesses. They pioneer advanced techniques and procedures, from heart-lung transplants to laser surgery for brain aneurysms.

Under the Health Security Act, academic health centers will continue to train physicians and provide state-of-the-art care. The Act sets aside a portion of all health insurance premiums specifically for academic health centers. Resources will be channeled to centers by a formula that recognizes each center's contributions to education, research, and patient care.

While most Americans will not obtain regular care at an academic health center, the Health Security Act requires that everyone has access to specialized care if needed.

EMPHASIZING PREVENTIVE AND PRIMARY CARE

Prevention is the cornerstone of the Health Security Act. Incentives for patients and doctors alike to use and prescribe preventive methods are woven throughout. From free coverage of a wide range of preventive services to wellness education and increased research funding, the plan offers unprecedented focus on prevention.

The comprehensive benefits package includes a broad array of preventive services not covered by the vast majority of insurance plans — immunizations, mammograms, well-baby care, and other screenings and early detection techniques to solve health problems before they become serious illnesses. The Health Security Act covers a wide range of preventive services with no coinsurance or co-pay, no matter which plan you join.

The Health Security Act will fundamentally restructure incentives in the health care system. For the first time, every doctor, nurse and health provider will know that they can provide the services they believe are necessary — and know they will be reimbursed.

"The plan recognizes that successful disease prevention and health promotion must address the health plan of both individuals and communities. It provides for universal coverage of clinical preventive services that have been shown to be effective in preventing disease and prolonging life. All these aspects constitute an approach to prevention that is uniquely comprehensive in scope and long overdue."

Roy L. DeHart, MD, MPH
President, American College of Preventive Medicine

As the American health care system has become more complex, specialized, and technical, it has neglected some simpler and, ironically, less costly needs. The cost of treatment for acute illness has soared, but we continue to spend relatively little on preventive and public health services.

PUBLIC HEALTH

Not all health problems can be addressed by providing individual health care coverage alone. Greater public health strategies are necessary to improve public health awareness, quality of care, and the prevention of future epidemics.

Public health protects communities against infectious diseases, such as tuberculosis and measles, and helps communities discover how to control chronic disease, such as diabetes and heart disease. It also works to protect the environment and educate about health and related issues.

For too long, public health funds have been sapped to pay for individual care. Under the Health Security Act, public health dollars will reach their intended destination — targeting issues that plague entire populations rather than individuals first. These efforts promise long-term savings in lives and dol-

Good primary and preventive care is one of medicine's essential responsibilities. Meeting that need represents one of the essential requirements under health care reform. If the American health care system is to provide high-quality care at affordable prices, it must strike a better balance between physicians, nurses and other professionals who take care of basic needs and those who provide the most sophisticated and specialized treatment for serious illness.

Primary care doctors and nurses work on medicine's front line. They diagnose and treat routine medical problems, refer patients when necessary, and coordinate specialist care. Family physicians, general internists and pediatricians are the principal primary care practitioners among physicians, and many women also consistently see obstetricians and gynecologists. Advance-practice nurses and physician's assistants provide essential primary care as well.

But the number of doctors providing basic, routine care has declined and many states have prevented advance-practice nurses and other health professionals from taking on as significant a role as they might.

For decades federal policy has reinforced the trend away from training primary care doctors and toward training more specialists. Federal funding of graduate medical education averaged $70,000 for each resident in 1992, with nearly all of the money going toward training in hospitals. Little went to other health care institutions in local communities that provide more basic care. Between 1980 and 1993, American hospitals increased the number of residents in training from 82,000 to 97,000, with 94 percent of the new positions devoted to training in specialty fields of medicine.

PUGET SOUND

A Model for Reform

Chances are that if you live in the Pacific Northwest, and you belong to a health maintenance organization (HMO), you belong to Group Health Cooperative of Puget Sound. Founded in 1947 and located in Seattle, Washington, Group Health is the single largest provider of health care in the Pacific Northwest, serving 500,000 members. It offers convincing proof of the fact that emphasizing primary and preventive care can mean high-quality care, low costs, and satisfied, healthy patients.

Like the Health Security Act, Group Health covers a wide range of preventive services not covered by most insurance plans. Its efforts have brought results. In fact, Group Health formed the basis for a Rand Corporation study that concluded that providing high-quality care can go hand in hand with controlling health care costs. Another important feature of Group Health is its attention to customer satisfaction, which it measures through regular consumer surveys — much like the surveys proposed in the Health Security Act for all health plans.

Health care reform will increase the demand for primary care physicians, nurses and other health professionals, correcting the long-standing incentives that discouraged medical students from becoming family doctors. But change won't happen quickly. To encourage American teaching hospitals to switch some residency positions from specialist to primary care, the federal government must make it more worthwhile to train them.

Consequently, rather than pay for graduate medical education without regard to specialty, public and private

Doctors in the United States: An Unhealthy Mix

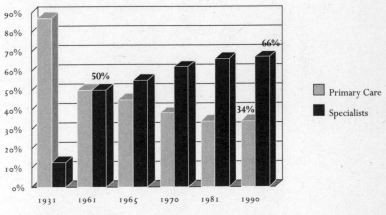

Source: Council on Graduate Medical Education, October 1992

investment will redistribute the balance between residency slots devoted to primary care and those devoted to specialty training. Other federal programs, including an expanded National Health Service Corps, will support students studying primary care and locating in underserved areas, such as rural and urban communities. Loan forgiveness programs for medical students who are trained in primary care, and re-training programs for mid-career specialists who want to work as primary care physicians will further boost the number of primary care doctors.

The Health Security Act also proposes several important steps to remove barriers to practice that currently limit the role of advanced-practice nurses. It enables qualified health professionals who participate in health plans to fully use their expertise and ability to provide care. In addition, federal funds will provide additional resources for training nurses, doubling the number of annual graduates. Support will also be provided for training in mental health and substance abuse treatment.

8

Choice

"The President's proposal guarantees stable and secure health coverage for all Americans, regardless of employment or health status. Patients can stay with the same doctor over time because patients, not employers, control their coverage choices. Patients, not their employers, choose their health plans and their physicians."

American College of Physicians

Americans value the right to decide how and where they get health care. It is a key measure and protector of quality. Yet thousands of Americans are losing that right each year, as rising health care costs force employers to cut back on the number of health plans and doctors they'll cover.

Americans will gain a new level of control over their health care choices through the Health Security Act. For many, no element of reform will be more important than the right to choose their own doctor, hospital or health plan.

CHOOSING A DOCTOR

A fundamental flaw in today's health care system is that employers — rather than employees — have the power to choose health plans and, consequently, the doctors,

CHOICE OF DOCTORS

Choice is the basis of the doctor-patient relationship. For patients, the ability to keep seeing their own doctor — someone who knows them and their family — who knows their medical history, who knows how to care for them when they are ill, someone whom patients trust, can mean the difference between a good experience and a frightening one, between a successful outcome and a poor one.

The Health Security Act ensures that consumers can follow their doctor and his or her team to any plan they might join. The Act requires every health alliance to have a point-of-service option, which gives patients the opportunity to see a doctor outside of their plan, although some plans will require extra payment for that option.

If they choose, physicians and other health providers will be able to join more than one health plan. These health care providers may also decide to remain in private practice rather than join a health plan. Patients will still have the opportunity to see their doctor even if he or she is in private practice.

hospitals and others who provide care.

The Health Security Act corrects that flaw. Through comprehensive reform, it transfers the power to choose back to individual Americans and their families. It requires both regional and corporate alliances to offer a broad choice of health plans, including at least one plan organized around the traditional fee-for-service style, where consumers visit any doctor they choose, and their health insurer pays the bill.

For patients who choose certain types of health plans, exercising the right to see a doctor who does not participate in the plan will cost more, as it does today. But that right — known as a "point-of-service" option — will always be there, even in HMOs. It reserves for every American the right to seek the care of doctors and hospitals on the leading edge of treatment if they ever confront an illness in which even specialized care available through their regular doctors and hospital is inadequate. So, if you join a plan that includes your obstetrician, your son's pediatrician, but not your daughter's dermatologist, it will cost more, but you can continue to see them all.

Health reform will also make it easier for patients to follow their doctors, even if their doctors decide to switch health plans. Because an increasing number of employers restrict the choice of plans available to employees, a patient whose doctor leaves one plan probably has little choice but to find another doctor. Under the Health Security Act, the patient will always have the option of switching plans each year, something that most people can't do today.

For doctors and other health providers, health reform also expands choice — the choice of health plans in which they practice. Under the Health Security Act, physicians and other health professionals may participate in as many, or as few, competing health plans as they wish. And because patients are guaranteed a point-of-service option in every plan, physicians will know that patients will be able to seek them out.

CHOOSING A HEALTH PLAN

Millions of Americans choose physicians and other health care providers and pay for their services one at a time through traditional indemnity insurance, a style of coverage usually described as fee-for-service. Over the last two decades, millions of other Americans have moved into so-called "managed care" health plans, including preferred provider organizations (PPOs) or Health Maintenance Organizations (HMOs).

All of those options — and other innovations that will evolve — will continue. What the Health Security Act will provide is the guarantee that a wide range of alternatives will exist and that American consumers, not their employers, will have the opportunity to choose among them.

INCREASING OPTIONS FOR LONG-TERM CARE

Expanded choice must also mean a greater set of options for Americans in need of long-term care. Today, choices are not only limited, they are costly. People either pay the full cost of home care out-of-pocket, pay the full cost of care in a nursing home, or spend themselves into poverty in order to qualify for government help, most often only for nursing home care.

Long-term care options are expanded and improved under health care reform. The Health Security Act provides a new federal program to cover home and community-based care, an option that most people prefer, and that often costs less than a nursing home.

XEROX

A Model for Reform

Most businesses pick their employees' health plan — but not the Xerox Corporation. Xerox offers its employees a choice of plans. Although it might sound like more trouble than it's worth, Xerox has managed to save money by offering choices.

Before changing the way it dealt with health benefits, annual premium increases of 20% were not unknown at Xerox. So the company started offering its employees a choice of plans at its 250 sites across the country. Xerox would pay based on the cost of the "benchmark" or average-cost plan. If the employee picks a low-cost plan, he saves money. The employee's job was to choose plans based on price and quality — and Xerox hoped that the competition among health plans would drive down costs.

It worked. Xerox's premiums have stopped spiraling higher and higher every year. And Xerox's strategy — using choice and competition to drive down costs — is central to the Health Security Act.

For those who plan ahead by purchasing private long-term care insurance, reform will provide greater protection against faulty or inadequate insurance, and tax breaks on premiums. For disabled Americans who want to work but need assistance, the Health Security Act promises help. The plan not only offers personal assistance services at home, but also personal care assistance tax credits to make working a more viable option for people with disabilities. Finally, the plan increases financial protections for those on Medicaid who receive care in nursing homes.

9

Responsibility

"My husband and I are 59 and 63 years of age, so we are not yet eligible for Medicare to help us...A brief summary of our health insurance costs over the last 4 years are:

1988- $3,578 with $500 deductible
1990- $4,607 with $2,500 deductible
1992- $10,500 with $2,000 deductible

"I have a pre-existing condition so I have to pay a penalty on the rates. Neither my husband nor myself, fortunately, has ever had a claim of any kind...

"We do not want a 'free ride.' We are more than willing to pay our share, but these amounts are just too excessive."

M.M.

Joliet, IL

Responsibility is central to every one of the principles of the Health Security Act. As the President said in his address to the Joint Session of Congress, "We need to restore a sense that we're all in this together and that we all have a responsibility to be a part of the solution."

All those involved in providing health care will, for the

first time, share collective responsibility for the quality of care patients receive, and for keeping patients healthy, not just treating them once they're sick. Health plans will have the responsibility of keeping the costs of premiums reasonable — there will be no more blank checks for

MEDICAL MALPRACTICE

Responsibility means bringing common sense to our medical malpractice system. Although experts believe that the direct cost of malpractice accounts for less than two percent of our spending on health care, reform of our existing system is badly needed. We must work to remove the threat of lawsuits that leads to so much "defensive medicine" and drives up costs for everyone. We must free doctors to do what they do best — care for patients — while protecting consumers at the same time. And we must take steps to let lawyers who profit from huge settlements know that they can no longer take advantage of the system.

In an effort to end frivolous lawsuits and protect doctors, the Health Security Act will change tort laws and develop new alternatives to resolve patients' claims against providers before they get to court. The Act will require those who believe they have been the victims of malpractice to first submit their claims to an out-of-court panel to resolve the dispute. If the patient is still unsatisfied with the resolution, the case can be taken to court, but only after obtaining a "certificate of merit," an affidavit from another doctor stating that the patient has good cause to pursue a claim.

health care. This newfound imperative for responsible health care will mean a change in the way some currently do business.

For insurance companies, responsibility means no longer denying people coverage if they get sick. For

MEDICAL MALPRACTICE

The Act will also:

- Limit attorneys' fees to one-third of an award, and allow states to impose even lower limits;
- Allow damages to be paid over a period of time rather than all at once;
- Prevent injured patients from gaming the system and getting paid twice for the same injury — once by a doctor and a second time by a health or disability insurance plan; and
- Promote progressive ideas such as a program in Maine that frees doctors from malpractice liability if they can demonstrate that they followed prescribed clinical practice guidelines.

Taken together, these steps represent the first serious national effort to take what has been learned in the states and apply it on a national level. Once implemented, these steps will help turn the incentives in our health care system right side up. By restoring responsibility to our medical malpractice system, we can also restore trust to the doctor-patient relationship which lies at the heart of health care.

unscrupulous medical companies and laboratories, responsibility means an end to fraudulent billing practices. For lawyers, responsibility means no more filing of frivolous lawsuits. "In short," as the President said, "responsibility should apply to anybody who abuses this system and drives up the cost for honest, hard-working citizens and undermines confidence in the honest, gifted health care providers we have."

For employers — both large and small — responsibility means following the lead of our nation's most successful businesses and helping contribute to the health security of every employee. For every American, responsibility means taking care of your health, rejecting behaviors that drive up health costs, and making a contribution to health coverage. "Responsibility," as the President said, "isn't just about them. It's about you, it's about me, it's about each of us."

PAYING FOR HEALTH SECURITY

Even though our nation spends nearly one of every seven dollars on health care, tens of millions of American lack health security. More than 37 million Americans have no health insurance. More than 25 million Americans have inadequate insurance — so-called "bare bones" coverage or policies that don't cover them when they need it most. And nearly every American family — even those with health insurance — live with the fear and the hard fact that only one pink slip, one seriously ill relative, one misfortune could cost them a lifetime of savings and even their independence and dignity.

Providing all Americans health security will make our nation stronger and bring down health care costs. In the short term, it will take new funds to cover the uninsured and provide those who are now covered with rock solid security and comprehensive benefits. The question is how we will pay and who will pay.

The vast majority of funding for the Health Security Act will continue to come from where it comes from today: employer and employee contributions to the cost of health insurance. New funding will be drawn from three primary sources:

- Asking all employers and the 30 million Americans who work for them but do not have health coverage to contribute to their health care;
- Increasing excise taxes on tobacco and requiring small contributions from large corporations who choose to form their own health alliance;
- Limiting the growth in federal health care programs. These are the fairest and most workable sources to yield sufficient money and guarantee health security to every American.

Expanding the Current Employer-Based System

The principal way we pay to ensure health security for all Americans is by building on our current system and asking all employers and employees to take responsibility for paying for health coverage.

Today, nine out of ten Americans who get health coverage get it through their employer. It's a system that works for the vast majority of Americans. That's why the President rejected any kind of broad-based tax to pay for a government-run system — deciding instead to leave our health care system rooted in the private sector.

85% of Uninsured Americans are in working families

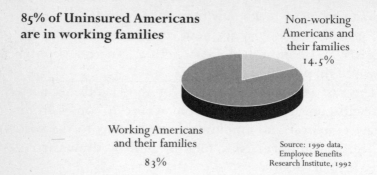

Non-working Americans and their families 14.5%

Working Americans and their families 83%

Source: 1990 data, Employee Benefits Research Institute, 1992

Today, most employers and employees contribute to the cost of health coverage, but not all do. Thirty million Americans in working families go without health coverage because they are not covered by their employers.

But these workers still get health care when they need it — often the most expensive kind of health care in the most expensive place: the emergency room. And the rest of us end up paying the bills — in higher premiums, higher taxes and inflated hospital charges.

This phenomenon — what academics call "cost shifting" — contributes to the high health care costs we all are forced to pay. This "cost-shifting" happens on every street in America where you'll find a supermarket, a dry cleaner, or a gas station that doesn't insure its workers. On the next block you'll find a supermarket, dry cleaner, or a gas station that does insure its employees. The businesses that insure pay higher premium costs because they are forced to pick up the tab for their competitors who are not paying.

The Health Security Act asks those who aren't paying to pay their fair share, lowering costs for the vast majority of companies and individuals, who will no longer see their premiums rise to pay for those without insurance.

HAWAII

A Model for Reform

Only one state in America has asked all employers to contribute to the cost of their employees' health care: Hawaii. And it has been able to achieve near-universal coverage while maintaining a thriving economy.

In many ways, the Health Security Act echoes Hawaii's experience. Hawaii passed a health reform plan in 1974 that required all employers to contribute to their workers' health care. As part of the reform, Hawaii included special programs to ease the burden for small businesses. The result? A greater percentage of Hawaiians have health insurance, far more than in any other state in the country. Health care costs are significantly lower in Hawaii than elsewhere in the U.S. And only 2% of small firms have sought out a special program for small businesses struggling to provide insurance.

In fact, since Hawaii passed health reform, the unemployment rate there has dropped to one of the lowest in the nation (2.8% in 1991). Meanwhile, small business creation rates have remained high (the number of employers grew almost 200% from 1970 to 1991).

We'll save $25 billion by providing coverage to everyone, because the government will no longer have to reimburse doctors and hospitals for the cost of caring for the uninsured.

While building on our current system ensures that 30 million working Americans will receive health coverage, requiring responsibility from all employers and employees does not alone provide true health security. Additional funding is needed to protect small businesses, provide long-term care and prescription drug coverage to older Americans, and ensure that no American — including those who lose their jobs — ever lose their health coverage.

To guarantee comprehensive benefits for all Americans, the Health Security Act requires the second and third primary sources of funding: a cigarette tax and corporate assessment, and savings from slowing the growth of federal health care programs.

The Cigarette Tax and Corporate Assessment

Cigarette taxes will increase by 75 cents a pack, raising revenue for health reform, and ensuring that those who smoke pay for the health costs that smoking causes. Higher tobacco prices may also have a significant impact in preventing teenagers from ever starting to smoke.

In addition, large corporations that form their own alliances will contribute to help support the backbone of our health care system — academic health centers, advanced medical research, as well as other elements of our health care infrastructure. Asking large corporations to pay one percent of their payroll will support those institutions that benefit every American.

Slowing the Growth of Federal Health Care Programs

The Health Security Act will also produce savings by slowing the skyrocketing growth of government spending on health care programs. Over time, the Health Security Act will slow the rate of growth in Medicare (the government program for seniors and the disabled) and Medicaid (the program that provides health care to the poor) from three times the rate of inflation to roughly two times the rate of inflation.

Upper-income people who receive Medicare — those individuals who earn more than $100,000 per year — will be asked to pay a higher percentage of the cost of coverage than they do today.

People covered by Medicare will see an increase in their benefits under the Health Security Act. Elderly and disabled Americans will receive the prescription drug coverage they need, and a new long-term care program will provide options for home and community-based care.

Most Americans who now receive health care through Medicaid will be part of the same system as other Americans, paying what they can for their care but benefitting from discounts that make coverage affordable.

By controlling costs in both the public and private sector, these savings avoid hurting privately insured people. Today, doctors and hospitals often charge more to private patients to make up for shortfalls in what they are paid to provide care to people covered by Medicare and Medicaid. The Health Security Act slows the growth in federal health care programs as part of fundamental reform that controls the cost of all health care.

These are the three primary sources of private and government funding that will help pay for health security for every American — full responsibility from businesses and individuals, cigarette taxes and a small corporate assessment, and a slowdown in the growth of Medicare and Medicaid. This is a conservative approach that doesn't count on the billions in cost savings that can be achieved from the plan's new emphasis on preventive care, encouraging real competition among health providers, and cracking down on health care fraud. It is an approach that asks responsibility of everyone. In return, it guarantees every American comprehensive health benefits that can never be taken away.

Conclusion

FOR NEARLY A century, Americans have discussed and debated how best to reform our national health care system. Since the early 1900s, commissions, committees, groups and organizations have put forth proposal after proposal to overhaul the way our nation delivers and pays for medical care.

In 1915, a group calling for health reform concluded that employers, employees and the government should contribute to the cost of health care, and recommended that the system focus on prevention.

In 1932, a commission decided that we should encourage doctors to form group practices and share responsibility for high quality, cost-effective care.

In 1933, when President Franklin Roosevelt launched the initiative that became the Social Security Act, he intended to include national health insurance.

In 1946, President Harry Truman proclaimed that health care should be a right, not a privilege, and became the first president to introduce a plan for national health reform.

And in 1972, President Richard Nixon told the American people that the only way to insure health coverage for every American was to ask employers to take responsibility and contribute to their workers' care.

Now, in 1993, with one in four of us poised to lose

health insurance in the next two years and costs expected to double by the year 2000, our nation stands ready for reform. Since President Clinton took office, more than 260 members of Congress have signed their names to some piece of legislation proposing national health care reform. Democrats and Republicans are teaming up to make history; for the first time, members of both parties have agreed that every American must be guaranteed health care.

The Health Security Act builds on what's best about the American health care system. It maintains and strengthens America's private health care. It extends the current system of employer-based coverage that works well for so many. It protects our cherished right to choose how we receive health care. It invests in improving the quality of our care. It establishes a national framework for reform, but leaves to every state, every community, every doctor, nurse and consumer the right to decide how to give and get health care.

The Health Security Act also reaches out to fix what has gone wrong with our health care system.

First and foremost, it guarantees health security for every American — a comprehensive package of benefits that can never be taken away. For those who have been victims of today's health insurance lottery — those denied insurance because of a pre-existing condition or those who have lost a job and seen their coverage disappear — nothing could be more important. And for those Americans who enjoy good health coverage today, but go to bed at night worried what might happen tomorrow, there could be no more reassuring guarantee.

The Health Security Act takes aggressive steps to bring our runaway health care system under control. It reduces the paperwork that chokes our system, the bureaucracy that forces doctors and nurses to spend hour after hour filling out forms instead of caring for patients. It promotes true competition in the health care marketplace — and reins in skyrocketing costs, making sure insurance premiums no longer rise uncontrollably. And it turns upside down incentives right side up.

The Health Security Act restores responsibility. It requires every employer and individual to pay for health coverage, even if that contribution is small. It recognizes that we can no longer afford to allow some to squeeze excess profits from health care consumers. And it promises swift and stiff penalties to those who take advantage of the system.

The Health Security Act holds the promise of strengthening our economy. It raises no new broad-based taxes, but spends our health care dollars more wisely. It levels the playing field for small businesses, making it possible for them to insure their families and their employees. It eases the tremendous burden of rising health costs on big business, helping them compete for global markets. And it sets us in the right direction of reducing our national debt.

Finally, the Health Security Act restores common sense to American health care. It protects older Americans and gives them the health benefits they deserve when they need them most. It is based on an approach that it is better to keep people healthy rather than treating them only after they get sick. It borrows from what works today, letting us phase in change at a reasonable pace and adjust our course if needed. It builds on what works best — and makes it work for everyone.

Our nation's health care system has reached a point

where change is our only option. As President Clinton said in his address to the Joint Session of Congress:

"Now it is our turn to strike a blow for freedom in this country. The freedom of Americans to live without fear that their own nation's health care system won't be there for them when they need it.

"It's hard to believe that there was once a time in this century when that kind of fear gripped old age. When retirement was nearly synonymous with poverty, and older Americans died in the street. That's unthinkable today, because over half a century ago Americans had the courage to change — to create a Social Security system that ensures that no American will be forgotten in their later years.

"Forty years from now, our grandchildren will also find it unthinkable that there was a time in this country when hardworking families lost their homes, their savings, their businesses — lost everything simply because their children got sick or because they had to change jobs. Our grandchildren will find such things unthinkable tomorrow if we have the courage to change today."

Address of the President to the Joint Session of Congress

September 22, 1993

MY FELLOW AMERICANS, tonight we come together to write a new chapter in the American story. Our forebears enshrined the American Dream — life, liberty, the pursuit of happiness. Every generation of Americans has worked to strengthen that legacy, to make our country a place of freedom and opportunity, a place where people who work hard can rise to their full potential, a place where their children can have a better future.

From the settling of the frontier to the landing on the moon, ours has been a continuous story of challenges defined, obstacles overcome, new horizons secured. That is what makes America what it is and Americans what we are. Now we are in a time of profound change and opportunity. The end of the Cold War, the Information Age, the global economy have brought us both opportunity and hope and strife and uncertainty. Our purpose in this dynamic age must be to change — to make change our friend and not our enemy.

To achieve that goal, we must face all our challenges with confidence, with faith, and with discipline — whether we're reducing the deficit, creating tomorrow's jobs and training our people to fill them, converting from a high-tech defense to a high-tech domestic economy, expanding trade, reinventing government, making our streets safer, or rewarding work over idleness. All these challenges require us to change.

If Americans are to have the courage to change in a difficult time, we must first be secure in our most basic needs. Tonight I want to talk to you about the most critical thing we can do to build that security. This health care system of ours is badly broken and it is time to fix it.

Despite the dedication of literally millions of talented health care professionals, our health care is too uncertain and too expensive, too bureaucratic and too wasteful. It has too much fraud and too much greed.

At long last, after decades of false starts, we must make this our most urgent priority, giving every American health security; health care that can never be taken away, health care that is always there. That is what we must do tonight.

On this journey, as on all others of true consequence, there will be rough spots in the road and honest disagreements about how we should proceed. After all, this is a complicated issue. But every successful journey is guided by fixed stars. And if we can agree on some basic values and principles we will reach this destination, and we will reach it together.

So tonight I want to talk to you about the principles that I believe must embody our efforts to reform America's health care system — security, simplicity, savings, choice, quality, and responsibility.

When I launched our nation on this journey to reform the health care system I knew we needed a talented navigator, someone with a rigorous mind, a steady compass, a caring heart. Luckily for me and for our nation, I didn't have to look very far.

Over the last eight months, Hillary and those working with her have talked to literally thousands of Americans to understand the strengths and the frailties of this system of ours. They met with over 1,100 health care organizations. They talked with doctors and nurses, pharmacists and drug company representatives, hospital administrators, insurance company executives and small and large businesses. They spoke with self-employed people. They talked with people who had insurance and people who didn't. They talked with union members and older Americans and advocates for our children. The First Lady also consulted, as all of you know, extensively with governmental leaders in both parties in the states of our nation, and especially here on Capitol Hill.

Hillary and the Task Force received and read over 700,000 letters from ordinary citizens. What they wrote and the bravery with which they told their stories is really what calls us all here tonight.

Every one of us knows someone who's worked hard and played by the rules and still been hurt by this system that just doesn't work for too many people. But I'd like to tell you about just one.

Kerry Kennedy owns a small furniture store that employs seven people in Titusville, Florida. Like most small business owners, he's poured his heart and soul, his sweat and blood into that business for years. But over the last several years, again like most small business owners, he's seen his health care premiums skyrocket, even in years when no claims were made. And last year, he painfully discovered he could no longer afford to provide coverage for all his workers because his insurance company told him that two of his workers had become high risks because of their advanced age. The problem was that those two people were his mother and father, the people who founded the business and still worked in the store.

This story speaks for millions of others. And from them we have learned a powerful truth. We have to preserve and strengthen what is right with the health care system, but we have got to fix what is wrong with it.

Now, we all know what's right. We're blessed with the best health care professionals on Earth, the finest health care institutions, the best medical research, the most sophisticated technology. My mother is a nurse. I grew up around hospitals. Doctors and nurses were the first professional people I ever knew or learned to look up to. They are what is right with this health care system. But we also know that we can no longer afford to continue to ignore what is wrong.

Millions of Americans are just a pink slip away from losing their health insurance, and one serious illness away from losing all their savings. Millions more are locked into the jobs they have now just because they or someone in their family has once been sick and they have what is called a preexisting condition. And on any given day, over 37 million Americans — most of them working people and their little children — have no health insurance at all.

And in spite of all this, our medical bills are growing at over twice the rate of inflation, and the United States spends over a third more of its income on health care than any other nation on Earth. And the gap is growing, causing many of our companies in global competition severe disadvantage. There is no excuse for this kind of system. We know other people have done better. We know people in our own country are doing better. We have no excuse. My fellow Americans, we must fix this system and it has to begin with congressional action.

I believe as strongly as I can say that we can reform the costliest and most wasteful system on the face of the Earth without enacting new broad-based taxes. I believe it because of the conversations I have had with thousands of health care professionals around the country; with people who are outside this city, but are inside experts on the way this system works and wastes money.

The proposal that I describe tonight borrows many of the principles and ideas that have been embraced in plans introduced by both Republicans and Democrats in this Congress. For the first time in this century, leaders of both political parties have joined together around the principle of providing universal, comprehensive health care. It is a magic moment and we must seize it.

I want to say to all of you I have been deeply moved by the spirit of this debate, by the openness of all people to new ideas and argument and information. The American people would be proud to know that earlier this week when a health care university was held for members of Congress just to try to give everybody the same amount of information, over 320 Republicans and Democrats signed up and showed up for two days just to learn the basic facts of the complicated problem before us.

Both sides are willing to say we have listened to the people. We know the cost of going forward with this system is far greater than the cost of change. Both sides, I think, understand the literal ethical imperative of doing something about the system we have now. Rising above these difficulties and our past differences to solve this problem will go a long way toward defining who we are and who we intend to be as a people in this difficult and challenging era. I believe we all understand that.

And so tonight, let me ask all of you — every member of the House, every member of the Senate, each Republican and each Democrat — let us keep this spirit and let us keep this commitment until this job is done. We owe it to the American people.

Now, if I might, I would like to review the six principles I mentioned earlier and describe how we think we can best fulfill those principles.

First and most important, security. This principle speaks to the human misery, to the costs, to the anxiety we hear about every day — all of us — when people talk about their problems with the present system. Security means that those who do not now have health care coverage will have it; and for those who have it, it will never be taken away. We must achieve that security as soon as possible.

Under our plan, every American would receive a health care security card that will guarantee a comprehensive package of benefits over the course of an entire lifetime, roughly comparable to the benefit package offered by most Fortune 500 companies. This health care security card will offer this package of benefits in a way that can never be taken away.

So let us agree on this: whatever else we disagree on, before this Congress finishes its work next year, you will pass and I will sign legislation to guarantee this security to every citizen of this country.

With this card, if you lose your job or you switch jobs, you're covered. If you leave your job to start a small business, you're covered. If you're an early retiree, you're covered. If someone in your family has, unfortunately, had an illness that qualifies as a preexisting condition, you're still covered. If you get sick or a member of your family gets sick, even if it's a life threatening illness, you're covered. And if an insurance company tries to drop you for any reason, you will still be covered, because that will be illegal.

This card will give comprehensive coverage. It will cover people for hospital care, doctor visits, emergency and lab services, diagnostic services like Pap smears and mammograms and cholesterol tests, substance abuse and mental health treatment.

And equally important, for both health care and economic reasons, this program for the first time would provide a broad range of preventive services including regular checkups and well-baby visits.

Now, it's just common sense. We know — any family doctor will tell you that people will stay healthier and long-term costs of the health system will be lower if we have comprehensive preventive services. You know how all of our mothers told us that an ounce of prevention was worth a pound of cure? Our mothers were right. And it's a lesson, like so many lessons from our mothers, that we have waited too long to live by. It is time to start doing it.

Health care security must also apply to older Americans. This is something I imagine all of us in this room feel very deeply about. The first thing I want to say about that is that we must maintain the Medicare program. It works to provide that kind of security. But this time and for the first time, I believe Medicare should provide coverage for the cost of prescription drugs.

Yes, it will cost some more in the beginning. But, again, any physician who deals with the elderly will tell you that there are thousands of elderly people in every state who are not poor enough to be on Medicaid, but just above that line and on Medicare, who desperately need medicine, who make decisions every week between medicine and food. Any doctor who deals with the elderly will tell you that there are many elderly people who don't get medicine, who get sicker and sicker and eventually go to the doctor and wind up spending more money and draining more money from the health care system than they would if they had regular treatment in the way that only adequate medicine can provide.

I also believe that over time, we should phase in long-term care for the disabled and the elderly on a comprehensive basis.

As we proceed with this health care reform, we cannot forget that the most rapidly growing percentage of Americans are those over 80. We cannot break faith with them. We have to do better by them.

The second principle is simplicity. Our health care system must be simpler for the patients and simpler for those who actually deliver health care — our doctors, our nurses, our other medical professionals. Today we have more than 1,500 insurers, with hundreds and hundreds of different forms. No other nation has a system like this. These forms are time consuming for health care providers, they're expensive for health care consumers, they're exasperating for anyone who's ever tried to sit down around a table and wade through them and figure them out.

The medical care industry is literally drowning in paperwork. In recent years, the number of administrators in our hospitals has grown by four times the rate that the number of doctors has grown. A hospital ought to be a house of healing, not a monument to paperwork and bureaucracy.

Just a few days ago, the Vice President and I had the honor of visiting the Children's Hospital here in Washington where they do wonderful, often miraculous things for very sick children. A nurse named Debbie Freiberg told us that she was in the cancer and bone marrow unit. The other day a little boy asked her just to stay at his side during his chemotherapy. And she had to walk away from that child because she had been instructed to go to yet another class to learn how to fill out another form for something that didn't have a lick to do with the health care of the children she was helping. That is wrong, and we can stop it, and we ought to do it.

We met a very compelling doctor named Lillian Beard, a pediatrician, who said that she didn't get into her profession to spend hours and hours — some doctors up to 25 hours a week — just filling out forms. She told us she became a doctor to keep children well and to help save those who got sick. We can relieve people like her of this burden. We learned — the Vice President and I did — that in the Washington Children's Hospital alone, the administrators told us they spend $2 million a year in one hospital filling out forms that have nothing whatever to do with keeping up with the treatment of the patients.

And the doctors there applauded when I was told and I related to them that they spend so much time filling out paperwork, that if they only had to fill out those paperwork requirements necessary to monitor the health of the children, each doctor on that one hospital staff — 200 of them — could see another 500 children a year. That is 100,000 children a year. I think we can save money in this system if we simplify it. And we can make the doctors and the nurses and the people that are giving their lives to help us all be healthier a whole lot happier, too, on their jobs.

Under our proposal there would be one standard insurance form — not hundreds of them. We will simplify also — and we must — the government's rules and regulations, because they are a big part of this problem. This is one of those cases where the physician should heal thyself. We have to reinvent the way we relate to the health care system, along with reinventing government. A doctor should not have to check with a bureaucrat in an office thousands of miles away before ordering a simple blood test. That's not right, and we can change it. And doctors, nurses and consumers shouldn't have to worry about the fine print. If we have this one simple form, there won't be any fine print. People will know what it means.

The third principle is savings. Reform must produce savings in this health care system. It has to. We're spending over 14 percent of our income on health care — Canada's at 10; nobody else is over nine. We're competing with all these people for the future. And the other major countries, they cover everybody and they cover them with services as generous as the best company policies here in this country.

Rampant medical inflation is eating away at our wages, our savings, our investment capital, our ability to create new jobs in the private sector and this public Treasury. You know the budget we just adopted had steep cuts in defense, a five-year freeze on the discretionary spending, so critical to reeducating America and investing in jobs and helping us to convert from a defense to a domestic economy. But we passed a budget which has Medicaid increases of between 16 and 11 percent a year over the next five years, and Medicare increases of between 11

and 9 percent in an environment where we assume inflation will be at 4 percent or less.

We cannot continue to do this. Our competitiveness,
our whole economy, the integrity of the way the government works and, ultimately, our living standards depend
upon our ability to achieve savings without harming the
quality of health care.

Unless we do this, our workers will lose almost $600
in income each year by the end of the decade. Small businesses will continue to face skyrocketing premiums. And
a full third of small businesses now covering their
employees say they will be forced to drop their insurance.
Large corporations will bear vivid disadvantages in global
competition. And health care costs will devour more and
more and more of our budget.

Pretty soon all of you or the people who succeed you
will be showing up here, and writing out checks for
health care and interest on the debt and worrying about
whether we've got enough defense, and that will be it,
unless we have the courage to achieve the savings that are
plainly there before us. Every state and local government
will continue to cut back on everything from education to
law enforcement to pay more and more for the same
health care.

These rising costs are a special nightmare for our small
businesses — the engine of our entrepreneurship and our
job creation in America today. Health care premiums for
small businesses are 35 percent higher than those of large
corporations today. And they will keep rising at double-
digit rates unless we act.

So how will we achieve these savings? Rather than
looking at price control, or looking away as the price spiral continues; rather than using the heavy hand of govern-

ment to try to control what's happening, or continuing to ignore what's happening, we believe there is a third way to achieve these savings.

First, to give groups of consumers and small businesses the same market bargaining power that large corporations and large groups of public employees now have. We want to let market forces enable plans to compete. We want to force these plans to compete on the basis of price and quality, not simply to allow them to continue making money by turning people away who are sick or old or performing mountains of unnecessary procedures. But we also believe we should back this system up with limits on how much plans can raise their premiums year in and year out, forcing people, again, to continue to pay more for the same health care, without regard to inflation or the rising population needs.

We want to create what has been missing in this system for too long, and what every successful nation who has dealt with this problem has already had to do: to have a combination of private market forces and a sound public policy that will support that competition, but limit the rate at which prices can exceed the rate of inflation and population growth, if the competition doesn't work, especially in the early going.

The second thing I want to say is that unless everybody is covered — and this is a very important thing — unless everybody is covered, we will never be able to fully put the breaks on health care inflation. Why is that? Because when people don't have any health insurance, they still get health care, but they get it when it's too late, when it's too expensive, often from the most expensive place of all, the emergency room. Usually by the time they show up, their illnesses are more severe and their mortality rates are much higher in our hospitals than those who have insurance. So they cost us more.

And what else happens? Since they get the care but they don't pay, who does pay? All the rest of us. We pay in higher hospital bills and higher insurance premiums. This cost shifting is a major problem.

The third thing we can do to save money is simply by simplifying the system — what we've already discussed. Freeing the health care providers from these costly and unnecessary paperwork and administrative decisions will save tens of billions of dollars. We spend twice as much as any other major country does on paperwork. We spend at least a dime on the dollar more than any other major country. That is a stunning statistic. It is something that every Republican and every Democrat ought to be able to say, we agree that we're going to squeeze this out. We cannot tolerate this. This has nothing to do with keeping people well or helping them when they're sick. We should invest the money in something else.

We also have to crack down on fraud and abuse in the system. That drains billions of dollars a year. It is a very large figure, according to every health care expert I've ever spoken with.

So I believe we can achieve large savings. And that large savings can be used to cover the unemployed uninsured, and will be used for people who realize those savings in the private sector to increase their ability to invest and grow, to hire new workers or to give their workers pay raises, many of them for the first time in years.

Now, nobody has to take my word for this. You can ask Dr. Koop. He's up here with us tonight, and I thank him for being here. Since he left his distinguished tenure as our Surgeon General, he has spent an enormous amount of time studying our health care system, how it operates, what's right and wrong with it. He says we could spend $200 billion every year, more than 20 percent of the total budget, without sacrificing the high quality of American medicine.

Ask the public employees in California, who have held their own premiums down by adopting the same strategy that I want every American to be able to adopt — bargaining within the limits of a strict budget. Ask Xerox, which saved an estimated $1,000 per worker on their health insurance premium. Ask the staff of the Mayo Clinic, who we all agree provides some of the finest health care in the world. They are holding their cost increases to less than half the national average. Ask the people of Hawaii, the only state that covers virtually all of their citizens and has still been able to keep costs below the national average.

People may disagree over the best way to fix this system. We may all disagree about how quickly we can do what — the thing that we have to do. But we cannot disagree that we can find tens of billions of dollars in savings in what is clearly the most costly and the most bureaucratic system in the entire world. And we have to do something about that, and we have to do it now.

The fourth principle is choice. Americans believe they ought to be able to choose their own health care plan and keep their own doctors. And I think all of us agree. Under any plan we pass, they ought to have that right. But today, under our broken health care system, in spite of the rhetoric of choice, the fact is that that power is slipping away for more and more Americans.

Of course, it is usually the employer, not the employee, who makes the initial choice of what health care plan the employee will be in. And if your employer offers only one plan, as nearly three-quarters of small or medium-sized firms do today, you're stuck with that plan, and the doctors that it covers.

We propose to give every American a choice among high-quality plans. You can stay with your current doctor, join a network of doctors and hospitals, or join a health maintenance organization. If you don't like your plan, every year you'll have the chance to choose a new one. The choice will be left to the American citizen, the worker — not the boss, and certainly not some government bureaucrat.

We also believe that doctors should have a choice as to what plans they practice in. Otherwise, citizens may have their own choices limited. We want to end the discrimination that is now growing against doctors, and to permit them to practice in several different plans. Choice is important for doctors, and it is absolutely critical for our consumers. We've got to have it in whatever plan we pass.

The fifth principle is quality. If we reformed everything else in health care, but failed to preserve and enhance the high quality of our medical care, we will have taken a step backward, not forward. Quality is something that we simply can't leave to chance. When you board an airplane, you feel better knowing that the plane had to meet standards designed to protect your safety. And we can't ask any less of our health care system.

Our proposal will create report cards on health plans, so that consumers can choose the highest quality health care providers and reward them with their business. At the same time, our plan will track quality indicators, so that doctors can make better and smarter choices of the kind of care they provide. We have evidence that more efficient delivery of health care doesn't decrease quality. In fact, it may enhance it.

Let me just give you one example of one commonly performed procedure, the coronary bypass operation. Pennsylvania discovered that patients who were charged $21,000 for this surgery received as good or better care as patients who were charged $84,000 for the same procedure in the same state. High prices simply don't always equal good quality.

Our plan will guarantee that high quality information is available in even the most remote areas of this country so that we can have high-quality service, linking rural doctors, for example, with hospitals with high-tech urban medical centers. And our plan will ensure the quality of continuing progress on a whole range of issues by speeding the search on effective prevention and treatment measures for cancer, for AIDS, for Alzheimer's, for heart disease, and for other chronic diseases. We have to safeguard the finest medical research establishment in the entire world. And we will do that with this plan. Indeed, we will even make it better.

The sixth and final principle is responsibility. We need to restore a sense that we're all in this together and that we all have a responsibility to be a part of the solution. Responsibility has to start with those who profit from the current system. Responsibility means insurance companies should no longer be allowed to cast people aside when they get sick. It should apply to laboratories that submit fraudulent bills, to lawyers who abuse malpractice claims, to doctors who order unnecessary procedures. It means drug companies should no longer charge three times more for prescription drugs made in America here in the United States than they charge for the same drugs overseas.

In short, responsibility should apply to anybody who abuses this system and drives up the cost for honest, hard-working citizens and undermines confidence in the honest, gifted health care providers we have.

Responsibility also means changing some behaviors in this country that drive up our costs like crazy. And without changing it we'll never have the system we ought to have. We will never.

Let me just mention a few and start with the most important — the outrageous cost of violence in this country stem in large measure from the fact that this is the only country in the world where teenagers can rout the streets at random with semi-automatic weapons and be better armed than the police.

But let's not kid ourselves, it's not that simple. We also have higher rates of AIDS, of smoking and excessive drinking, of teen pregnancy, of low birth-weight babies. And we have the third worst immunization rate of any nation in the western hemisphere. We have to change our ways if we ever really want to be healthy as a people and have an affordable health care system. And no one can deny that.

But let me say this — and I hope every American will listen, because this is not an easy thing to hear — responsibility in our health care system isn't just about them. It's about you, it's about me, it's about each of us.

Too many of us have not taken responsibility for our own health care and for our own relations to the health care system. Many of us who have had fully paid health care plans have used the system whether we needed it or not without thinking what the costs were. Many people who use this system don't pay a penny for their care even though they can afford to. I think those who don't have any health insurance should be responsible for paying a portion of their new coverage. There can't be any something for nothing, and we have to demonstrate that to people. This is not a free system. Even small contributions, as small as the $10 co-payment when you visit a doctor, illustrates that this is something of value. There is a cost to it. It is not free.

And I want to tell you that I believe that all of us should have insurance. Why should the rest of us pick up the tab when a guy who doesn't think he needs insurance or says he can't afford it gets in an accident, winds up in an emergency room, gets good care, and everybody else pays? Why should the small businesspeople who are struggling to keep afloat and take care of their employees have to pay to maintain this wonderful health care infrastructure for those who refuse to do anything?

If we're going to produce a better health care system for every one of us, every one of us is going to have to do our part. There cannot be any such thing as a free ride. We have to pay for it. We have to pay for it.

Tonight I want to say plainly how I think we should do that. Most of the money we will — will come under my way of thinking, as it does today, from premiums paid by employers and individuals. That's the way it happens today. But under this health care security plan, every employer and every individual will be asked to contribute something to health care.

This concept was first conveyed to the Congress about 20 years ago by President Nixon. And today, a lot of people agree with the concept of shared responsibility between employers and employees, and that the best thing to do is to ask every employer and every employee to share that. The Chamber of Commerce has said that, and they're not in the business of hurting small business. The American Medical Association has said that.

Some call it an employer mandate, but I think it's the fairest way to achieve responsibility in the health care system. And it's the easiest for ordinary Americans to understand, because it builds on what we already have and what already works for so many Americans. It is the reform that is not only easiest to understand, but easiest to implement in a way that is fair to small business, because we can give a discount to help struggling small businesses meet the cost of covering their employees. We should require the least bureaucracy or disruption, and create the cooperation we need to make the system cost-conscious, even as we expand coverage. And we should do it in a way that does not cripple small businesses and low-wage workers.

Every employer should provide coverage, just as three-quarters do now. Those that pay are picking up the tab for those who don't today. I don't think that's right. To finance the rest of reform, we can achieve new savings, as I have outlined, in both the federal government and the private sector, through better decision-making and increased competition. And we will impose new taxes on tobacco.

I don't think that should be the only source of revenues. I believe we should also ask for a modest contribution from big employers who opt out of the system to make up for what those who are in the system pay for medical research, for health education centers, for all the subsidies to small business, for all the things that everyone else is contributing to. But between those two things, we believe we can pay for this package of benefits and universal coverage and a subsidy program that will help small business.

These sources can cover the cost of the proposal that I have described tonight. We subjected the numbers in our proposal to the scrutiny of not only all the major agencies in government — I know a lot of people don't trust them, but it would be interesting for the American people to know that this was the first time that the financial experts on health care in all of the different government agencies have ever been required to sit in the room together and agree on numbers. It had never happened before.

But, obviously, that's not enough. So then we gave these numbers to actuaries from major accounting firms and major Fortune 500 companies who have no stake in this other than to see that our efforts succeed. So I believe our numbers are good and achievable.

Now, what does this mean to an individual American citizen? Some will be asked to pay more. If you're an employer and you aren't insuring your workers at all, you'll have to pay more. But if you're a small business with fewer than 50 employees, you'll get a subsidy. If you're a firm that provides only very limited coverage, you may have to pay more. But some firms will pay the same or less for more coverage.

If you're a young, single person in your 20s and you're already insured, your rates may go up somewhat because you're going to go into a big pool with middle-aged people and older people, and we want to enable people to keep their insurance even when someone in their family gets sick. But I think that's fair because when the young get older, they will benefit from it, first, and secondly, even those who pay a little more today will benefit four, five, six, seven years from now by our bringing health care costs closer to inflation.

Over the long run, we can all win. But some will have to pay more in the short run. Nevertheless, the vast majority of the Americans watching this tonight will pay the same or less for health care coverage that will be the same or better than the coverage they have tonight. That is the central reality.

If you currently get your health insurance through your job, under our plan you still will. And for the first time, everybody will get to choose from among at least three plans to belong to. If you're a small business owner who wants to provide health insurance to your family and your employees, but you can't afford it because the system is stacked against you, this plan will give you a discount that will finally make insurance affordable. If you're already providing insurance, your rates may well drop because we'll help you as a small business person join thousands of others to get the same benefits big corporations get at the same price they get those benefits. If you're self-employed, you'll pay less; and you will get to deduct from your taxes 100 percent of your health care premiums.

If you're a large employer, your health care costs won't go up as fast, so that you will have more money to put into higher wages and new jobs and to put into the work of being competitive in this tough global economy.

Now, these, my fellow Americans, are the principles on which I think we should base our efforts: security, simplicity, savings, choice, quality and responsibility. These are the guiding stars that we should follow on our journey toward health care reform.

Over the coming months, you'll be bombarded with

information from all kinds of sources. There will be some who will stoutly disagree with what I have proposed — and with all other plans in the Congress, for that matter. And some of the arguments will be genuinely sincere and enlightening. Others may simply be scare tactics by those who are motivated by the self-interest they have in the waste the system now generates, because that waste is providing jobs, incomes and money for some people.

I ask you only to think of this when you hear all of these arguments: Ask yourself whether the cost of staying on this same course isn't greater than the cost of change. And ask yourself when you hear the arguments whether the arguments are in your interest or someone else's. This is something we have got to try to do together.

I want also to say to the representatives in Congress, you have a special duty to look beyond these arguments. I ask you instead to look into the eyes of the sick child who needs care; to think of the face of the woman who's been told not only that her condition is malignant, but not covered by her insurance. To look at the bottom lines of the businesses driven to bankruptcy by health care costs. To look at the "for sale" signs in front of the homes of families who have lost everything because of their health care costs.

I ask you to remember the kind of people I met over the last year and a half — the elderly couple in New Hampshire that broke down and cried because of their shame at having an empty refrigerator to pay for their drugs; a woman who lost a $50,000 job that she used to support her six children because her youngest child was so ill that she couldn't keep health insurance, and the only way to get care for the child was to get public assistance; a young couple that had a sick child and could only get insurance from one of the parents' employers that was a nonprofit corporation with 20 employees, and so they had to face the question of whether to let this poor person with a sick child go or raise the premiums of every employee in the firm by $200. And on and on and on.

I know we have differences of opinion, but we are here tonight in a spirit that is animated by the problems of those people, and by the sheer knowledge that if we can look into our heart, we will not be able to say that the greatest nation in the history of the world is powerless to confront this crisis.

Our history and our heritage tell us that we can meet this challenge. Everything about America's past tells us we will do it. So I say to you, let us write that new chapter in the American story. Let us guarantee every American comprehensive health benefits that can never be taken away.

In spite of all the work we've done together and all the progress we've made, there's still a lot of people who say it would be an outright miracle if we passed health care reform. But my fellow Americans, in a time of change, you have to have miracles.

And miracles do happen. I mean, just a few days ago we saw a simple handshake shatter decades of deadlock in the Middle East. We've seen the walls crumble in Berlin and South Africa. We see the ongoing brave struggle of the people of Russia to seize freedom and democracy.

And now, it is our turn to strike a blow for freedom in this country. The freedom of Americans to live without fear that their own nation's health care system won't be there for them when they need it.

It's hard to believe that there was once a time in this century when that kind of fear gripped old age. When retirement was nearly synonymous with poverty, and older Americans died in the street. That's unthinkable today, because over a half a century ago Americans had the courage to change — to create a Social Security system that ensures that no Americans will be forgotten in their later years.

Forty years from now, our grandchildren will also find it unthinkable that there was a time in this country when hardworking families lost their homes, their savings, their businesses, lost everything simply because their children got sick or because they had to change jobs. Our grandchildren will find such things unthinkable tomorrow if we have the courage to change today.

This is our chance. This is our journey. And when our work is done, we will know that we have answered the call of history and met the challenge of our time.

Thank you very much. And God bless America.

Appendix 1
Existing Government Programs

MEDICARE/OLDER AMERICANS

Under the Health Security Act, people who get Medicare will receive all the benefits they do today and see little difference in how, where or from whom they receive their care. In addition, there will be an expansion of Medicare benefits to include the cost of prescription drugs. A new program will also be established to provide home and community-based long-term care. The savings from reduced growth in Medicare spending will be rechanneled into those new benefits.

Americans eligible for Medicare will automatically qualify for prescription drug coverage when they enroll in the Part B benefit, which covers physician visits and other outpatient services. Monthly Part B premiums will increase by about $11 to cover the cost of this new benefit. However, Medigap policies, the extra coverage many seniors buy to pick up where Medicare leaves off, should decline by a proportionate amount since those policies will no longer cover as much, if any, of the cost of drugs.

With the new prescription drug coverage there is a $250 annual deductible for each person. Individuals on Medicare also pay 20 percent of the cost of each prescription. The maximum amount a person can pay, however, is $1,000 over the course of a year. The prescription drug benefit covers drugs and biological products, including insulin, approved by the Food and Drug

Administration.

Today, all people covered by Medicare pay 25% of the actual cost of coverage. Under the Health Security Act, higher-income beneficiaries — those individuals who earn more than $100,000 per year — will be asked to pay 75% of the actual cost of coverage.

As health care reform moves forward, Medicare recipients will have more options — with the opportunity to join fee-for-service or other types of health plans, including health maintenance organizations and preferred provider networks. As Americans enrolled in health plans turn sixty-five, they can choose between remaining in their health plan or getting coverage through Medicare.

MEDICAID

The Health Security Act will integrate Medicaid beneficiaries into the new system, relieving pressures on state budgets and on those who need care but simply cannot afford it.

Under reform, state and federal governments will continue to pay for people receiving cash assistance. Just as private sector employers will make payments for their health coverage, state and federal governments will pay to cover the costs of providing benefits to cash assistance recipients.

Once the state where a person lives enters the new system, people who get Medicaid will enroll in health plans like other Americans, and be able to choose among plans. They will carry the same Health Security card that other Americans carry, providing [and] guaranteeing the comprehensive package of benefits. Medicaid will also offer the services it has now — such as transportation, translation and interpretation, and child care during clinic visits.

People now on Medicaid who do not receive cash assistance will no longer rely on Medicaid. They will be covered like everyone else. Families with incomes less than 150 percent of poverty — less than $22,200 for a two-parent family — will be eligible for discounts on the cost of insurance.

The Health Security Act will enable those people who now stay on welfare to keep their Medicaid benefits to seek employment.

THE DEPARTMENT OF DEFENSE

Under the Health Security Act, the Department of Defense maintains its commitment to military readiness as its first priority while fulfilling its obligation to provide health care to military personnel, their dependents and retirees.

The Secretary of Defense will develop a plan for implementing health reform and may establish military health plans centered around military hospitals and clinics in the United States. People who are now eligible for CHAMPUS will have the added choice of selected civilian health plans.

Military health plans will meet the same requirements and standards that all health plans meet. They will provide the comprehensive benefits package, and in addition, any other services they currently provide.

In areas in which a military health plan is established,

active-duty personnel will automatically enroll. Family members of active duty personnel and retirees who are under the age of 65 will have the opportunity to choose a military health plan or a civilian plan.

Employers of individuals enrolled in military health plans will pay the employer share of the premium, as they do in civilian health plans.

VETERANS HEALTH CARE

Health care reform will honor the nation's commitment to continue providing comprehensive health care to its veterans. Reform will give veterans more choices about how and where they receive care. It will also preserve veterans' benefits and increase the flexibility of the VA health care system.

Under the Health Security Act, the Department of Veterans Affairs will either organize its health centers and hospitals into health plans or allow them to act as health providers and contract with health plans to deliver services.

Health plans organized within the VA system must meet the standards for all health plans.

All veterans may choose to join a VA health plan if one exists in their area. If the health plan can serve only a limited number of people, veterans with service-connected disabilities have first priority for enrollment, followed by low-income veterans.

The Department of Veterans Affairs will continue to provide services that have become its specialty — for example, treatment of spinal cord injuries and post-traumatic stress syndrome, as well as long-term care for elderly and disabled veterans.

THE FEDERAL EMPLOYEES HEALTH BENEFITS PROGRAM

The Health Security Act is based on a principle embodied in today's FEHB program: broad consumer choice of plans. Under the Health Security Act, federal employees and retirees will join with other members of the communities where they live and choose from among the health plans offered by the regional health alliance.

Federal employees and retirees, like other Americans, will be guaranteed the security of knowing that if they change jobs, lose their job or move, they will still be covered. The benefits package provided in the Health Security Act is based on today's best plans, including several of the type now offered through FEHBP.

Under reform, government contributions will increase for federal workers to 80 percent of the average premium, up from the maximum of 75 percent today.

For current federal retirees, including those eligible for Medicare, the Office of Personnel Management (OPM) will administer a Medigap option to continue the additional protection they currently receive.

INDIAN HEALTH SERVICE

Under the Health Security Act, the Indian Health Service will operate outside the regional alliance system; tribal governments will exercise their full autonomy to devise health care delivery that works for them.

When health reform is implemented, American Indians and Alaskan Natives will have the option to choose whether they want to receive care through the Indian Health Service or through a health plan in a regional alliance.

The Indian Health Service will expand public health and prevention activities, and for the first time may provide some service to non-Indian residents living near reservations. During a five-year period, the Indian Health Service will renovate and expand its clinics to provide all of the services guaranteed in the comprehensive benefits package.

Appendix 2
Scenarios Under Reform

TODAY

Under today's system, insurance companies look at dozens of different factors to determine how much they will charge you for health care coverage. Your medical history, your family's medical history, where you live, how old you are, whether you are married, whether or not you are employed, what kind of job you have, whether you are rich or poor, how soon you are likely to have children — these are some of the circumstances they consider when making judgements about what you will pay.

Today's health care system motivates insurance companies to weed out the sick and cover the healthy. Certain populations can only obtain coverage at high prices or can't get coverage at all. Others pay artificially low prices only to find that their insurer drops them when they need health care the most. If you work for a small business or are self-employed, you may have faced the worst of these problems. Insurers may quote you different prices, and you never know what you might pay from one year to the next.

If you have been sick or injured, you could pay a lot for a "bare bones" benefits package. Or, if you are lucky, you may pay a small amount for a good benefits package. You could pay a lot because you have been labeled "high risk." Or, you could pay nothing if your employer pays 100% of your premium. You might not even know what you pay. And you cannot be sure that what you pay today will be what you'll pay tomorrow.

THE HEALTH SECURITY ACT

Under the Health Security Act, your premiums will be predictable and easy to figure out. If you are a full-time employee in a business, you and your employer will only need to know whether you are buying a policy for a single person, a married couple, a single-parent family, or a two-parent family. Employers will all contribute for their workers, and their combined payments will cover 80% of the average-priced plans in that region. Individual contributions will make up the difference — if you choose an average-priced plan, you will pay 20%. If you choose a plan that provides the same comprehensive benefits at a lower price, you will pay less. If your employer pays the entire cost of the premium, as many do today, you will pay nothing at all. If you choose a higher cost plan, you will pay more.

The following scenarios are used to show how much people will pay under reform. The individuals described are not real people, but their situations are illustrative of the impact of health reform. The national average premiums are used to represent the premiums in each alliance, although these amounts will vary by state and by region. These cases are based on average-priced plans, although consumers will be able to choose less expensive plans or more expensive plans.

National Policy Type	Family Share Premium*	Family Share (Per Month)	Family Share (Per Year)
Two-Parent Family with Children	$4,360	$73	$872
Single-Parent Family	$3,893	$65	$779
Couple	$3,865	$64	$773
Single Person	$1,932	$32	$386

* 1994 Preliminary Estimates

EMPLOYER SHARE

The employer share is a fixed amount. Employers only need to know whether their employee is buying a single, couple, or family policy to know what they will pay.*

Policy Type	Employer Share
Two-Parent Family with Children	$2,479
Single Parent	$2,479
Couple	$2,125
Single Person	$1,546

* 1994 Preliminary Estimates

For couples and families — who often have two workers — employers will pay the same amount per worker.
This method will be clear and simple for employers and
will prevent them from having to go through the complex
process of coordinating policies with a spouse's employer
or having to suddenly change contributions when there is
a divorce or a spouse is laid off.   There will be one
employer price for family policies, regardless of whether
both spouses work, or how many children they have.
This will make things simpler for employers — they
won't have to coordinate with other companies where
their employees' spouses work, or suddenly change contributions in the event of a spouse being laid-off or a couple divorcing.   Alliances will calculate the per worker
contribution based on the average number of workers in
couples and families. For example, since the average family has 1.4 workers, an individual employer's contribution
is less than 80% — in fact only 57% of the family premium. When employer contributions are totaled they will
add up to 80% of couples and family premiums in the
alliance.

TWO-PARENT FAMILY

Today:

Mary Sampson manages a small law office in San Jose, California. She makes $35,000 a year. Her husband, a minister, earns $30,000 a year. Today, they get their coverage through Mary's employer, who pays half their premium. They pay $2,940 a year, 8% of her salary, for their health care premiums alone, not including co-payments and deductibles.

Reform:

Assuming they choose an average-priced plan, the premium for Mary Sampson and her husband will be around $872 a year, or $73 a month. They could choose a higher cost plan, which would cost them more, or a lower-cost plan, which would cost them less.

	Policy Type	Premium	The Sampsons Pay (Per Year)	The Sampsons Pay (Per Month)
TODAY	Two-Parent Family	$5,880	$2,940	$245
REFORM	Two-Parent Family	$4,360	$872	$73

COUPLE

Today:

Dennis and Barbara Rutherford, who live in Hannibal, Missouri have a combined income of $21,200. Dennis was laid off from his high paying job with a large manufacturing firm in late 1990. At that time, both Rutherfords lost their health care coverage. They have been turned down for other coverage because of pre-existing conditions — Dennis' high blood pressure and Barbara's history of breast cancer. Since then, they have been unable to afford the $9,000 a year ($750 a month) premium offered by the only plan that will accept them.

Reform:

If Dennis and Barbara enrolled in an average priced plan, they would pay 20% of the $3,865 annual premium for a couple — $773 a year, or $64 a month. Under reform, insurers will no longer be allowed to use pre-existing conditions to bar the Rutherfords from coverage.

	Policy Type	Premium	The Rutherfords Pay (Per Year)	Pay (Per Month)
TODAY*	Married Couple	Uninsured	Uninsured	Uninsured
REFORM	Married Couple	$3,865	$773	$64

* Barbara and Dennis were offered a plan costing $9,000 dollars, but were unable to afford it. Today they pay nothing and are uninsured.

INDIVIDUAL

Today:

Sara Bender, a 28-year-old broadcast journalist, lives in Columbus, Ohio, and makes $34,000 a year. Because she works for a firm which gets a lower cost premium for its healthy workers, she has been paying only $300 a year, or $25 a month for her health care coverage.

Reform:

If Sara enrolled in an average cost plan she would pay 20% of the $1,932 annual premium for a single policy — $386 a year, or $32 a month. Sara will pay more, but she will have the security of knowing that her coverage will always be there, and that her costs won't rise unexpectedly as she gets older.

	Policy Type	Premium	Sara Pays (Per Year)	(Per Month)
TODAY	Single Person	$1,200	$300	$25
REFORM	Single Person	$1,932	$386	$32

SELF-EMPLOYED CONSULTANT

Today:

Susan Addington is a single parent living in Virginia. She is self-employed with an income of $40,000 a year. Because her son has a serious chronic illness, she paid $3,000 in out-of-pocket costs and $5,000 in insurance premiums in just one year. Because she is self-employed, she was only able to deduct 25% of her $5,000 premium or $1,250 of these costs.

Reform:

For the family share of her premium, for an average-priced plan, Susan will pay 20% of the $3,893 annual premium for a single parent family — $779 a year. She will also pay the employer share for a single parent — $2,479, for a total of $3,258-a-year or $272 a month. And she will be able to deduct 100% of the premium.

	Policy Type	Premium	Family Share	Employer Share	Susan Pays (Per Year)	(Per Month)
TODAY	Single Parent	$5,000	NA	NA	$5,000	$417
REFORM	Single Parent	$3,893	$779	$2,479	$3,258	$272

SMALL BUSINESS

Today:

Mr. and Mrs. Jones, who have two children, own a flower shop which is incorporated. They have three employees — Matt, Jane, and Scott. Matt is a 16-year-old high school student who comes to work part-time after school. Jane and Scott are both single and work at the shop full-time. Their average payroll, which includes the Jones's salary, is $17,000 per year per worker.

Last year, Mr. and Mrs. Jones could not afford to provide health insurance for their employees. However, they did independently purchase a policy to cover their family — at a cost of $5,200.

Reform:

Without any discounts, the flower shop will pay the employer share of $1,546 each for Scott and Jane for a single person policy, and $2,479 each for Mr. and Mrs. Jones for a two-parent policy — a total of $8,050.

As a result of discounts offered to small business, the flower shop's contribution for each employee will be limited to 5.3% of the average payroll, however. The flower shop will pay no more than $901-per-year or $75-a-month for each worker. For all four workers and their dependents, the cost will total no more than $3,604 per year.

Because Matt is covered under his parent's policy, the flower shop will not contribute towards his health insurance.

In addition to what they pay as owners of the shop, Mr.

and Mrs. Jones will pay the employee share of their family policy — $872 per year if they enroll in an average-priced plan. In total, Mr. and Mrs. Jones will have family coverage for $2,674 per year — saving $2,525 from what they are currently paying.

Another way of looking at it is that for $4,476 — $2,674 for the Jones' family coverage and $901 each for Jane and Scott — they will provide coverage for themselves and their employees.

UNION WORKER

Today:

Aleesha Maiuz is a factory worker in St. Louis, Missouri, making $36,000 a year. As a union member, she receives comprehensive benefits for which her employer pays the full amount. Her husband works at a local grocery store which does not offer health care coverage. He is covered under Aleesha's plan.

Reform:

Under the Health Security Act, Aleesha's employer will still be able to provide 100% of health benefits. Her employer's contribution for a family premium will be sharply reduced because the cost of families will be spread across all employers, and her employer will no longer be indirectly paying the unpaid medical bills of the uninsured. Lower costs for the company may mean an increase in wages for Aleesha, and will mean that Aleesha's benefits are more likely to be preserved in the future.

TEACHER

Today:

Jonathan O'Hara teaches sixth grade in Des Moines, Iowa, making $28,000 a year. Under his union contract, he receives comprehensive benefits at no personal cost. His wife, Rebecca, is a nurse, and is covered under Jonathan's plan.

Reform:

Under the Health Security Act, Jonathan and Rebecca will continue to receive the comprehensive package of benefits they receive today. They will stand a better chance for wage increases over time because the local school district, like other employers that have offered generous benefits, will see its premium costs go down. Under reform, it will no longer be indirectly paying for the unpaid medical bills of the uninsured.

In addition, the school district will see its costs go down because the hospital where Rebecca works will begin contributing to the cost of their family policy. Under reform, businesses that employ two-earner couples will no longer bear the cost of family coverage alone.

PROFESSIONAL COUPLE

Today:

Michael and Elizabeth Sands work and live in Memphis, Tennessee, and together earn almost $90,000 a year. Elizabeth is a graphic artist, making $40,000. Although Elizabeth's firm offers her health insurance, the couple chooses to receive their coverage through the architectural firm where Michael works, because it provides a more generous, comprehensive benefits package. Today, the Sands pay $720 a year, or $60 a month, for this coverage. The total premium costs $4,400 a year, and the architecture firm pays the rest.

Reform:

The Sands want to stay with their current plan. Under reform, this plan will cost less than it does today because it will no longer pay for the uncompensated care delivered to the uninsured, saving 10% of the current premium cost.

The average cost of a couple premium in the Sands' alliance is $3,865 but the Sands pick a plan that will cost $4,000. They will pay the difference between 80% of the average cost plan, which is $3092, and $4,000, or $908 a year, $75 a month.

Under reform, the Sands may pay their family share either by having it subtracted from his paycheck or from hers. For fifteen dollars more a month, the Sands will be getting the same high quality, comprehensive benefit package they do today, but with the assurance that they can never lose it.

	Policy Type	Premium	The Sands Pay (Per Year)	(Per Month)
TODAY	Married Couple	$4,400	$720	$60
REFORM	Married Couple	$4,000	$908	$75

LOW-INCOME FAMILY

Today:

Lars and Brenda Gustafson recently had a new baby, and Brenda resigned from her job shortly before the baby was born. Lars works for a messenger service in Minneapolis, Minnesota, and takes home about $250 a week, or $13,000 a year. His employer does not offer him health insurance. As a result, he and his family have been uninsured for over two years and are struggling to pay the hospital bill from the birth of the baby.

Reform:

Provided Lars and Brenda choose an average price plan, they will pay 20% of $4,360 or $872 for a two-parent family policy. However, because Lars is in a two-parent family with income less than $14,781 a year, Lars is eligible for a discount, reducing his premium to $384 a year.

	Policy Type	Premium	The Gustafsons Pay (Per Year)	(Per Month)
TODAY	Two-Parent Family	$0	$0	$0
REFORM	Two-Parent Family	$4,360	$384	$32

LOW-INCOME COUPLE

Today:

Linda Bradley, from Beaver Dam, Wisconsin, works in a local print shop making $13,570 a year. Her husband Doug is a freelance photographer but has been unable to find work in the last year. Today, they pay $50 a month for a meager benefit package they obtain through Linda's employer. Her employer, a small business, contributes $600 a year, half the premium. The policy has a high deductible and provides limited benefits.

Reform:

Because Linda and Doug select an average-priced plan and their combined income is below 150% of poverty, they are eligible for a discounted premium of $503 a year, or $42 a month, for comprehensive coverage.

	Policy Type	Premium	The Bradleys Pay (Per Year)	(Per Month)
TODAY	Married Couple	$1,200	$600	$50
REFORM	Married Couple	$3,865	$503	$42

PART-TIME WORKER WITH NO NON-WAGE INCOME

Part-time workers (defined as working more than 10 but less than 30 hours a week), who have no non-wage income, will pay 20% of the premium in their area for their policy type, assuming they enroll in an average-priced plan. Their employers will pay a pro-rated amount of the employer share based on the number of hours worked.

Today:

Lee Harris, of Cleveland, Ohio, was laid off from her job after a big downsizing at her former company. Lee was unemployed for over a year and recently took a job delivering pizzas 20 hours a week. Lee makes $10 an hour and has no non-wage income. Lee can only afford a bare bones policy which costs her $840 a year. Her employer contributes nothing towards her coverage.

Reform:

Assuming Lee picks an average-priced plan, she will pay 20% of the individual policy — $386 a year, or $32 a month. Her employer will only pay two-thirds of the employer share for a single person — $1,033 a year, or $86 a month. Since Lee has no non-wage income, federally-funded discounts will pay for one third of the employer premium.

	Policy Type	Premium	Lee Pays (Per Year)	(Per Month)
TODAY	Single Person	$840	$840	$70
REFORM	Single Person	$1,932	$386	$32

PART-TIME WORKER WITH NON-WAGE INCOME

Part-time workers with substantial non-wage income, for example those with most of their income from rental property, are liable for the remaining portion of the employer share.

If you work ...	Your employer pays	You pay ...
10 hours	1/3 of employer share	2/3 of employer share
15 hours	1/2 of employer share	1/2 of employer share
20 hours	2/3 of employer share	1/3 of employer share

Today:

Mary Wortheimer is a 45-year-old widow who receives $60,000 a year from her husband's estate. She works 10 hours a week at a local boutique. She makes an extra $6,000 a year at the shop for a total income of $66,000 a year. She buys a single policy for herself at a cost of $1,800 a year.

Reform:

The boutique will pay one third of the employer premium — $516 per year, or $43 per month. If she enrolls in an average-priced plan, Mary will pay 20% of the individual policy premium — $386 a year or $86 a month in her area. Because Mary has substantial non-wage income and works one third of the week, Mary is also responsible for two thirds of $1,549, the employer share for a single policy — $1,033 per year, or $86 per month. Mary's total health insurance premium will be approximately $1,419 per year, or $118 a month.

	Policy Type	Premium	Family Share	Employer Share	Mary Pays (Per Year)	(Per Month)
TODAY	Single Person	$1,800	NA	NA	$1,800	$150
REFORM	Single Person	$1,932	$386	$1,033	$1,419	$118

SELF-EMPLOYED FARMER

Today:

James Huggins, a self-employed family farmer in Kansas, makes $25,000 a year and has struggled to pay for health care coverage for himself, his wife and his 10-year-old son. James, like many rural residents, has had trouble getting and keeping insurance. And unlike a business, he is only able to deduct one fourth of the $4,000 he pays in premiums each year.

Reform:

If James enrolls in an average cost plan, he will pay 20% of the $4,360 annual family premium or $872 a year. Like a business, James will also pay the employer share of his premium, which would normally be $2,479. However, that amount would exceed 7.9% of James' $25,000 income, the limit on what employers are required to pay. Instead James will pay 7.9% of $25,000 or $1,975 for his employer share. James will pay a total of $2,847 a year, or $237 a month. For the first time, James Huggins will be also be able to deduct from taxable income the full cost of his health care premiums.

	Policy Type	Premium	Family share	Employer Share	James Pays (Per Year)	(Per Month)
TODAY	Two-Parent Family	$4,000	NA	NA	$4,000	$333
REFORM	Two-Parent Family	$4,360	$872	$1,975*	$2,847	$237

Capped at 7.9%

153

MEDICARE BENEFICIARY

Medicare beneficiaries will have the same guaranteed health security they have today, plus a new prescription drug benefit that will be integrated into Medicare Part B. Beneficiaries will continue to pay their Part B premium just as they do today. They will pay an additional $11-a-month for the new prescription drug benefit.

Today:

Claude and Gertrude Anderson are retired farmers living on a fixed income of about $40,000 a year in West Virginia. Today, they receive Medicare coverage and pay $36.60 for their Part B premium. They also buy a Medigap policy for $1,200 a year to help cover their prescription drug costs, co-payments and deductibles.

Reform:

Under reform, Claude and Gertrude will be covered by a new prescription drug benefit through the Medicare program. They will pay $11-a-month for this new benefit. It will provide them with coverage for 80% of their monthly $300 prescription drug costs after they meet a $250 deductible. And they will not pay more than $1,000 a year in prescription drug costs.

The Andersons will continue to pay their Medicare Part B premium just as they do today. The $100-a-month the Andersons pay for their Medigap policy will either decline to account for the new Medicare drug coverage, or cover additional services. In addition, Medicare certified managed care plans, which frequently have lower deductibles and co-payments, will be more available as an option.

	Policy Type	Part B Premium (Per Month)	Prescription Drug Premium (Per Month)	The Andersons Pay (Per Month)
TODAY	Medicare Beneficiary	$36.60	$0	$36.60
REFORM	Medicare Beneficiary	$36.60	$11	$47.60

* 1993 Medicare Part B premium; 1994 projections have not been released as of the writing of this book

WORKING MEDICARE BENEFICIARY

Working Medicare beneficiaries will join the alliances in their areas. While they are working, their employers will pay the employer share of their premium. Just like everyone else, they will pay 20% of the premium for their policy type if they enroll in an average-priced plan.

Today:

Larry Watson is a 68-year-old Medicare beneficiary who works in a law firm in Omaha, Nebraska. Today, he pays $36.60 a month for his Part B premium. His employer pays nothing towards his health care coverage.

Reform:

Under reform, Larry will be able to get his Medicare coverage through his local health alliance and receive the guaranteed comprehensive package of benefits. His employer will pay the employer share of the single person premium, and Larry will pay 20% of the average premium in his alliance assuming to enrolls in an average-priced plan — $386 a year, or $32 a month.

| | | | Larry Pays | |
Policy Type		Premium	(Per Year)	(Per Month)
TODAY	Working Medicare Beneficiary	NA	$439	$36.60
REFORM	Working Medicare Beneficiary	$1,932	$386	$32

* When Larry stops working, Medicare will pay for his benefits. Larry will pay the Part B premium and the $11-a-month for prescription drug coverage.

MEDICAID BENEFICIARIES (AFDC AND SSI)

The federal and state governments will continue to make payments for health coverage for individuals eligible for Aid to Families with Dependent Children (AFDC) and Supplemental Security Income (SSI). However, instead of paying doctors and hospitals directly, Medicaid will pay premiums to the alliance.

Today:

Pamela Johnson is a single, unemployed mother of two young children. Because she has only $300 in savings and is earning no income, she qualifies for cash assistance through the AFDC program, and she and her children receive their health insurance through the Medicaid program in their home state of Vermont. She has encountered numerous doctors who refuse to treat her because of low Medicaid reimbursement rates. In addition, Pamela would like to get off welfare and return to work, but she can't afford to lose her Medicaid coverage for herself and her two children.

Reform:

Just like everyone else, Pamela and her children will be able to enroll in a health plan through the regional alliance. For the first time, Pamela will have a choice about which health plan to enroll in. She will receive the same comprehensive package of benefits as everyone else. Medicaid will cover the cost of the average family premium in the alliance. If Pamela chooses a plan with average or below-average costs, she will be responsible only for her co-payments. If she chooses a more expensive plan, she will pay the portion of her premium that is above the average in her alliance.

Pamela and her children will continue to be eligible for supplemental services, such as non-emergency transportation, currently offered by Medicaid programs. If they join an HMO she will pay a $2-per-visit rather than the standard $10-per-visit. For the first time, Pamela will have the freedom of knowing that she will have health care coverage, making it more feasible to go to work.

MEDICAID BENEFICIARIES WHO DO NOT RECEIVE AFDC OR SSI

Today:

Alexandra Warren is single, and works as a waitress at George's Coffeehouse in rural California at minimum wage. Although her annual income is 115% of poverty, she is eligible for Medicaid because she has a chronic and costly illness which requires frequent hospitalization and which, when the costs are deducted from her income, makes her eligible for Medicaid in her state.

Reform:

Under reform, Alexandra will no longer rely on Medicaid for her health benefits. She will select a health plan through the regional alliance, and share the costs of her coverage with her employer. Since Alexandra earns only $8,256 a year — less than 150% of poverty — she will be eligible for a discounted premium. Alexandra will pay $267 a year, or $22 a month if she chooses an average-cost plan.

	Policy Type	Premium	Alexandra Pays (Per Year)	(Per Month)
TODAY	Single Person	Medicaid Pays		
REFORM	Single Person	$1,932	$267	$22

CHILD WITH DISABILITIES

Today:

Alec Moore is a 10-year-old child with severe cerebral palsy. He lives at home with his parents. Both of Alec's parents work outside the home, but because of his condition they cannot afford health insurance. Today, Alec receives Medicaid coverage because his state provides Medicaid coverage to "medically needy" individuals who, although they do not meet the normal income criteria for Medicaid, have medical expenses that are very big.

Reform:

Under reform, Alec will continue to receive all of the services he is eligible for today. His parents will obtain health insurance through their employers, and their policies will cover him for all services included in the comprehensive benefits package.

Both their employers and Alec's family will gain from health reform: Alec will have the guarantee of health security with no lifetime limits on coverage. His parents will know that they will never confront a situation in which they will be unable to obtain coverage because of his condition. Their employees will not be faced with the dilemma of unusually high premiums caused by having someone with high medical costs in their health insurance group.

Assuming they choose an average cost plan, Alec's parents will pay 20% of the premium for a family plan, $872 a year, or $73 a month.

UNDERGRADUATE STUDENT

Today:

Jason Loewith is a 19-year-old sophomore at Tulane University in New Orleans. His parents, who claim Jason as a dependent for tax purposes, live in Connecticut. He pays nothing for his health insurance because he is covered under his family's plan. Jason works for the university part-time, in the admissions office.

Reform:

Because he is a dependent student, Jason's family will continue to pay for his coverage through their alliance in Connecticut. That alliance will transfer a portion of the family's premium to an alliance in Louisiana, which will provide Jason's coverage. Neither Jason nor his employer, the university, will contribute to his premium costs, because of his status as a student and a dependent.

UNEMPLOYED INDIVIDUAL

Today:

Last year, Ann Tilson, a travel agent in a small company in Vidalia, Georgia, was diagnosed with multiple sclerosis. As a result, her employer's insurance company raised their premiums substantially. Ann later had to quit her job.

Today, Ann cannot get coverage from any other insurer for her pre-existing condition, so she elected, under the COBRA law, to remain insured by the same company that provided her coverage when she worked for the travel agency. Although she has insurance, she is responsible for paying the entire $625 monthly premium herself. Ann's parents help her with the money.

Reform:

Because Ann is unemployed and has no non-wage income other than unemployment insurance, Ann will not have to pay for her health coverage until she finds a new job. Ann will receive the guaranteed benefits package and will continue to be able to see the same doctor she sees today.

When Ann finds work, her employer will be responsible for the employer contribution and she will be responsible for the employee contribution but, unlike today, those contributions will be both predictable and affordable, and she will not pay extra for her health coverage because she has multiple sclerosis.

FEDERAL EMPLOYEE

Today:

Corinne Quigley is a 38-year-old employee of the U.S. Department of Agriculture. She and her husband and two children live in Washington DC. Corrine obtains her health insurance through the Federal Employees Health Benefits Plan (FEHBP), which combines all federal employees in the area into a large purchasing pool to offer a large number of insurance plans. All federal employees, including Corinne, have a broad range of plans to choose from, and the same premium applies to all federal employees of a given family size, regardless of age or health status. Corinne pays $1,000 a year or $83 a month.

Reform:

Under reform, federal employees like Corinne will join the regional alliance with other residents in their area. Similar to the FEHBP, an alliance will offer an array of health plans, and the same premium will be charged, regardless of age or health status. All members will have many plans to choose from, and will be able to change plans once a year. Assuming the Quigleys enroll in an average-priced plan, they will pay 20% of the average family premium in their alliance — $872 a year, or $73 a month.

	Policy Type	Premium	The Quigleys Pays (Per Year)	(Per Month)
TODAY	Two-Parent Family	$4,000	$1,000	$83
REFORM	Two-Parent Family	$4,360	$872	$73

VETERANS

Veterans with service-connected disabilities and low-income veterans will be eligible to receive the nationally guaranteed comprehensive benefit package through the Department of Veteran Affairs with no co-payments or deductibles. They will continue to be eligible for supplemental services offered by VA, such as treatment for post-traumatic stress disorder, and certain dental services.

Today:

Al Green, a 52-year-old single veteran, lives in Ann Arbor, Michigan, and works in a neighborhood store. Al lost a leg in the Vietnam War, and he receives his health care free-of-charge from the VA.

Reform:

Al will have the opportunity to choose from among several health plans offered through his alliance. If Al opts to receive his health care through another health plan and chooses an average-cost plan, he will pay 20% of the individual policy — $386 a year, or $32 a month. The store where he works will pay the employer share.

If he chooses the VA plan, Al's employer will pay the employer share of his premium, and the VA will pay his 20% share of the premium to the alliance.

THE PRESIDENT'S HEALTH SECURITY PLAN

The Draft Report

SEPTEMBER 7, 1993

Contents

CONTENTS

Introduction

ERIK ECKHOLM

AFTER A SHORT tenure in the White House that has already kept him jumping from one tightwire to another, Bill Clinton faces the most momentous battle yet as he promotes his grand strategy for overhauling American health care. Elected as a new kind of Democrat who could take on the nation's domestic ills, Clinton is all but staking his presidency on a bold and far-reaching—but complex and politically vulnerable—plan to reshape the way medical care is provided and paid for.

Clinton took office determined to solve two related crises in health care. The first was the growing number of Americans who lacked the basic security of health insurance, a trend that was increasingly seen as a national disgrace. The second was the spiral in health spending that threatened to bankrupt the government and cripple American industry. By 1993, health care absorbed 14 percent of the gross national product, far more than in any other country, and by the end of the decade it was projected to eat up an astounding 19 percent of the economy.

On paper, if not in political reality, achieving universal coverage was much the simpler of the two tasks.

Erik Eckholm is a special projects editor for *The New York Times* and is a key director of the paper's coverage of health-care issues. He is also editor of *Solving America's Health-Care Crisis* (Times Books).

Clinton came up with an unsurprising and simple answer: requiring all employers to help cover their workers and their families, building on the system of employer coverage that is already widespread. Government would provide subsidies for companies and individuals deemed too poor to bear the entire burden themselves. Clinton's promise of cradle-to-grave security for all, regardless of health or employment status, is a central selling point of his plan—the one feature the President, the First Lady, Hillary Rodham Clinton, and their supporters are driving home every chance they get. At the same time, the mandated employer payment could prove to be the Achilles' heel of his proposal, for it has aroused the opposition of hundreds of thousands of small-business owners who say they cannot pay the price, and whose dire predictions of bankruptcies and lost jobs are hard for politicians to ignore.

Taming the dragon of medical spending was more daunting to contemplate. Yet without cost control, any solution to the first problem, providing coverage to all, was doomed because as premiums soared, ever more people would be flung into the ranks of the uninsured. Clinton rejected as politically infeasible the approach favored by some liberals, a complete government takeover of medical insurance with national spending limits, as exists in Canada. He rejected the approach favored by some conservatives, promotion of a wide-open market in health care, as insufficient to the task. His plan—set forth in detail in the current document—would combine elements of both approaches. He has proposed a major restructuring of medical care that would both promote market competition and establish vast new powers of government regulation.

This new synthesis, or mishmash, depending on who is doing the describing, was the product of a remarkable process of policy development that, like the end product itself, was seen by some as brilliant and others as hopelessly naive and chaotic. The First Lady, Hillary Rodham Clinton, was in charge and even as she toured the country in the spring and summer of 1993 gathering information about health care she began the job of selling the unfinished proposals. A brain trust presided over by Ira C. Magaziner, the first couple's longtime friend and a management whiz, worked in secret on the nitty-gritty, for a time assembling some 500 experts who labored day and night to clarify alternatives and spell out details. Though the plan's release was delayed several times its development had to be considered quick, given the complexity of the topic.

As a self-imposed September 1993 deadline approached, the main outlines of the plan were set and President Clinton made choices among the winnowed options, preparing for a prime-time address to Congress late in the month. White House officials began showing key Congressmen and their staffs secret copies of their report—the present document—and copies soon found their way to the press. With all the parts of the proposal finally available for viewing in one place, the national debate began even before the President's official unveiling.

The measure of success will not be how well the plan hangs together on paper, of course, but whether it can make it through the Congress. Bowing to political reality, and with the possibility of gaining support from moderate Republicans, Clinton made it clear that he was ready to deal. Indeed, hardly had the report been circulated before serious questions were raised about its financing provisions in particular. If the thinking on some details was soon undergoing revision, the report still remains the essential statement of the Clinton strategy, the basis for a national debate that seems certain to carry on well into 1994 at least.

Drawing on the "managed competition" proposal developed by market-oriented health economists, the President would have most people obtain their health insurance through a new system of regional purchasing cooperatives, or "health alliances," run by the states. These would set standards, under federal guidelines, for local health plans and make a range of plans available to consumers, all offering the same basic package of benefits. Large corporations could join the alliances or establish their own array of plans, but would have to offer the same benefits package under the same basic rules.

The theory is that the health plans—affiliated groups of physicians and hospitals, often organized by insurers—would compete for customers on the basis of price and quality. But the White House is clearly worried that this elaborate, untried structure may not drive down spending quickly enough. To the consternation of some economists and many health providers, it proposes that the federal government impose caps on the growth in health premiums, keeping it in line with the general inflation rate. Overseeing national spending trends, and setting national standards for care and required benefits, would be a powerful new National Health Board.

In a field rife with special interests, nearly every organized group has complained, even those that stand to gain from the proposals. Large corporations welcome the prospect of strong cost controls, but bemoan the new regulations to which they would have to adhere. The larger insurance companies, which have already begun developing managed-care plans, would presumably thrive under the system but they attack the proposed budget caps as pernicious. Doctors support extending generous insurance to everyone, which means 37 million new paying patients. But they lament the pressures that will push most of them and their patients into managed-care plans, which limit their autonomy, they resent proposed restrictions on fees and they fear the impact of overall budget limits.

In Congress, the President's most immediate challenge was to come up with a credible means of financing the large new subsidies required to extend universal coverage and to offer new benefits, such as a prescription drug plan for the elderly. For such a huge and noble cause, he had to work under a harsh 1990's restraint: no new general taxes. The President was prepared to propose increased taxes on cigarettes and possibly alcohol, but to achieve the desired ends he also, in the initial plan, posited draconian cuts in Medicare and Medicaid among other measures. Among Democrats and Republicans alike there was wide agreement that the financing proposals as written were unrealistic, and the White House was searching for other ways to raise funds or cut costs.

Republicans attack the requirement that all employers offer health coverage and the proposed budget caps. But they have struggled to come up with credible alternative answers to the crisis, and many have signalled a willingness to talk with the President and bargain over specifics.

In the end, it may be the views of citizens around the country that make or break the President's proposals. Polling results in the months before the release of the plan indicated widespread confusion and uncertainty about the direction the country should take with health care, with many consumers anxious about the future but unwilling to pay much of a price for a solution.

For the 37 million Americans who lack health insurance, and the tens of millions more who may find themselves in jeopardy in the coming years when they lose or change jobs or develop a serious disease, the appeal of the Clinton proposal and its guaranteed life-long coverage is obvious. The majority of Americans who are decently insured already and happy with their own doctors may have a harder time deciding how they feel about the plan.

As administration officials describe it, the plan would leave nearly everyone better off. In return for generous benefits and peace of mind, most would pay little more, if any, than they do now. But the heart of the Clinton strategy for curbing medical spending is to make people become acutely aware of the true cost of their health care, and that may be jarring for many Americans who have long received generous medical benefits at work. In the structure outlined by the White House, many people may find themselves choosing among unfamiliar new health plans and accepting new limits on their freedom to choose doctors or hospitals, or paying extra to use the system as freely as they are accustomed to.

Under the proposal, everyone would be required to carry health insurance and to contribute to its cost, with subsidies to help the poor. All employers would be required to contribute for workers and their families, with employers paying 80 percent of the cost of premiums and workers 20 percent. But in a departure, individuals and most companies would sign up with the purchasing cooperatives, or health alliances, which would present their members with a choice of health plans.

The proposal envisions three basic kinds of plans: "low cost-sharing" plans, HMOs in which patients pay only $10 per office visit to make use of affiliated doctors and hospitals who have received preset fees to care for patients; "high cost-sharing" plans, which allow familiar freedom to visit any doctors and facilities that are paid on a fee-for-service basis, but require families to pay their first $400 in bills and pay 20 percent of all subsequent bills, with maximum family spending of $3,000 per year; and "combination" plans in which patients pay little to use affiliated doctors and more to use others.

Any patient could choose any plan. But the system is designed to use financial incentives to nudge more people into the most cost-effective HMOs. Through stiffer deductibles and copayments patients would pay heavily to keep the traditional freedom to choose any doctor. The extra amount, officials say, would fairly represent the extra cost of unmanaged care, but some consumers may find the cost difference oppressive.

For many in the public and for many doctors too, the freedom to choose doctors is one of the hottest issues raised by the Clinton strategy. Critics attack the plan as curbing choice, while the White House says it will be opening more choices to Americans. Both are right. More than 41 million Americans are already in HMOs. To the extent that more people are pushed against their preference into HMOs, they will certainly face new limits. These groups usually allow a choice of primary physician among affiliated doctors, but patients must go through this "gatekeeper" to visit a specialist who is also in the group.

The specter is raised of chronically ill patients ripped from a trusted doctor. This may happen, but the chances would be reduced if virtually all doctors sign up with health plans, as the proposal envisages; most patients could follow their doctor into a plan. Administration officials also point out, correctly, that large numbers of Americans do not now enjoy the hallowed freedom of choice. Many are uninsured and lucky to find a doctor; they would gain access to the same alliance and health plans as everyone else. The 30 million people on Medicaid, the program for the poorest of the poor, often have trouble finding a doctor who will see them and they, too, would gain mainstream care through the regional alliances. Also, officials note, a growing number of employers have restricted their workers to a single managed-care plan.

Whether the lower-cost HMOs into which many people may be pushed would offer long lines and second-class medical care, as some critics fear, or efficient, prudent, top-flight care, as officials confidently predict, could only be known with time. HMOs save money not only by negotiating lower fees with doctors, hospitals and other suppliers but also by scrutinizing medical decisions and discouraging wasteful or unnecessarily costly services. At best, this can produce fine care and weed out useless and harmful procedures that are common in American medicine. At worst, groups working for a preset fee can be tempted to scrimp on costly care, jeopardizing health, and on personnel and facilities, producing long waits.

Administration officials say their proposal is designed to assure high-quality care. As they make their annual selection of health plans, consumers would vote with their feet, shunning plans that perform poorly. Equally important, a national program would develop ways to measure quality of care offered by health plans. Annual performance reports, covering both consumer satisfaction and medical indicators for all health plans, would be published and made available to consumers, creating a higher level of public knowledge and accountability than now exists in the health system. Critics question whether methods exist for adequately comparing medical performance, and fear that the lower-priced plans into which many Americans would be pushed would cut corners.

A crucial longer term issue of medical quality is not mentioned in the White House document. Assuming competition does not do the job, by late in this decade the government would act to end inflation in medical spending. In contrast, spending in recent years has growth at close to twice the rate of the economy as a whole, driven not only by rising prices but also increases in use of medical services, new technologies and the gradual growth and aging of the population.

White House officials, backed by many medical experts argue that the current system carries so much waste—in duplicated technology and facilities, in unneeded medical procedures and excess paperwork, in use of unnecessarily costly drugs or procedures, in profiteering and fraud—that huge sums can be wrung out over time without impairing care. But some new costs also reflect advances in technology that reduce suffering and disease, advances that will continue at a furious pace.

At some point, the demand for useful forms of care could press against cost controls, forcing a kind of rationing that few Americans support. Many medical experts think efficiency gains could stave off such bitter choices for many years at least. But many experts also say that the nation will at some point have to come to grips with divisive issues of medical limits—restricting access to the costliest technologies, for example, to patients who have a good chance of benefitting. This is a sensitive matter on which the White House is not anxious to foster discussion, but critics are already starting to voice their concern. The emerging health-care debate, it seems clear, will force Americans to confront basic questions of life, death, and economics in a way they rarely have before.

The American
Health Security Act

THE PROBLEM

All Americans, those who have health insurance and those who do not, understand that serious problems exist in the health care system:

• **Americans lack security.** One out of four people—or 63 million people—will lose health insurance coverage for some period during the next two years. Thirty-seven million Americans have no insurance and another 22 million lack adequate coverage.

Losing or changing a job often means losing insurance. Becoming ill or living with a chronic medical condition can mean losing insurance coverage or not being able to obtain it.

• **Health care costs are rising faster than other sectors of the economy.** Precipitous growth in health care costs robs workers of wages, fuels the growth of the federal budget deficit and puts affordable care out of reach for millions of Americans.

Left unchecked, rising health care costs will consume almost two-thirds of the increase in Gross Domestic Product for each American for the rest of the decade.

Health care costs will grow from 14 percent of GDP to 19 percent even without an expansion of coverage to insure all Americans.

• **Bureaucracy overwhelms consumers and health providers.** Excessive paperwork confuses and frustrates doctors, nurses, patients and their families.

Bureaucracy also drives up costs. Studies document that administrative costs contribute a steeply rising portion of the expenses involved in running a typical doctor's office or hospital.

• **Quality is uneven.** Because no clear standards define best medical practice, lack of information and inadequate attention to prevention make the quality of health care across America uneven. Consumers have no reliable information with which to measure the quality of their health care or coverage.

• **Coverage for long-term care is inadequate.** Many elderly and disabled Americans enter nursing homes and other institutions when they would prefer to remain at home. Families exhaust their resources trying to provide for disabled relatives.

• **Many Americans cannot obtain quality care.** In many rural and inner-city areas, shortages of doctors, clinics and hospitals form barriers to care.

• **Fraud and abuse cheat everyone.** Many Americans believe that exorbitant charges, fraud and abuse undermine both quality and access to care.

OVERVIEW

The American Health Security Act guarantees comprehensive health coverage for all Americans regardless of health or employment status. Health coverage continues without interruption if Americans lose or change jobs, move from one area to another, become ill or confront a family crisis.

Through a system of regional and corporate health alliances that organize the buying power of consumers and employers, the American Health Security Act stimulates market forces so that health plans and providers compete on the basis of quality, service and price.

Under the Act health plans must meet national standards on benefits, quality and access to care but each state may tailor the new system to local needs and conditions. Thus the program encourages local innovation within a national framework.

It frees the health care system of much of the accumulated burden of unnecessary regulation and paperwork, allowing doctors, nurses, hospitals and other health providers to focus on providing high-quality care.

Creating Security

The American Health Security Act enhances the security of the American people by extending universal coverage in a environment that improves quality and controls rising costs:

• All employers contribute to health coverage for their employees, creating a level playing field among companies.
• Everyone shares the responsibility to pay for coverage.
• Limits on out-of-pocket payments protect American families from catastrophic costs, while subsidies

ease the burden on low-income individuals and small employers.

• A comprehensive benefit package with no lifetime limits on medical coverage guarantees access to a full range of medically necessary or appropriate services.

• Elderly and disabled Americans receive coverage for outpatient prescription drugs under Medicare for the first time.

• Guaranteed choice of health plans and providers enhances choice for many Americans.

• No health plan may deny enrollment to any applicant because of health, employment or financial status nor may they charge some patients more than others because of age, medical condition or other factors related to risk.

• All health plans meet national quality standards and provide useful information that allows consumers to make valid comparisons among plans and providers.

• Separate programs increase federal support for long-term care and improve the quality and reliability of private long-term care insurance.

Controlling Costs

The American Health Security Act brings growth in health care costs in line with growth in Gross Domestic Product by 1997. It accomplishes this goal by increasing competition in health care, reducing administrative costs and imposing budget discipline:

• A standard, universal package of health benefits and reliable information about the price and performance of health plans encourages informed choices.

• Consumers pay less for low-cost plans and more for high-cost plans, creating incentives for cost-conscious choice.

• Health plans receive fixed premiums based on risk characteristics of their patients. Working under a fixed budget, they have incentives to spend resources cost effectively.

If savings attained through effective competition and reductions in administrative costs do not achieve the spending goals, the national health care budget provides a backstop, ensuring that health care spending is in line with economic growth.

Like the private sector, major government programs, including Medicare and Medicaid, also operate under a budget restraining the growth of federal and state spending for health care.

Enhancing Quality

The American Health Security Act improves the quality of health care by creating standards and guidelines for practitioners, reorienting quality assurance to measuring outcomes rather than regulatory process, increasing the national commitment to medical research and promoting primary and preventive care.

• Explicit quality goals and standards shape the health care system.

• Health plans are held accountable for quality improvement.

• Regular publication of accessible information about quality and cost allows consumers to make informed choices among health care plans.

- Increased investment in research advances medical knowledge.
- A special funding mechanism ensures that academic health centers continue their vital role in research, training and specialty care.
- New investments support training for primary care physicians and other health professionals; federal action helps remove artificial barriers to practice that hinder nurses and other non-physicians.
- Investments in public health enhance the level of protection for all Americans.
- Changes in Medicare rate schedules and in the allocation of federal funds supporting graduate medical education provide new incentives for primary care physicians.
- Preemption of state laws limiting the scope of practice and new funding for the education of health professionals who are not physicians enhance opportunities for nurses, social workers and other non-physician providers.

Expanding Access to Care

The American Health Security Act invests in the development of an adequate health care system in areas with inadequate service. Those investments hold the promise of improving the availability and quality of health care in rural communities and urban neighborhoods.

- Health alliances assume responsibility for building health networks in rural and urban areas with inadequate access.
- National loan programs support the efforts of local health providers to develop community-based plans.

- Investments in new health programs such as school-based clinics and community clinics expand access to care for underserved populations.
- Financial incentives attract health professionals to areas with inadequate care.

Reducing Bureaucracy

The American Health Security Act reduces the burden of paperwork and administration; regulatory, billing and reporting requirements decline, and consumers experience a streamlined and simpler system:

- A single, comprehensive benefit package that covers every eligible person eliminates confusion about coverage.
- Administrative costs caused by multiple policies with different benefits and risk selection disappear.
- Standard forms for insurance reimbursement, the submission of claims and clinical encounter records simplify paperwork and reduce administrative costs.
- The cost of administering coverage in small companies declines because they purchase through health alliances that benefit from economics of scale.
- Federal regulatory requirements for Medicare, Medicaid and other programs are simplified.
- Health care services covered by workers' compensation and automobile insurance merge into the new health system, reducing duplication and waste.
- Malpractice reform reduces incentives in the current system to perform excessive tests or unnecessary procedures.

Reducing Fraud and Abuse

The American Health Security Act cracks down on health care providers and institutions that impose excessive charges or engage in fraudulent practices, setting tough standards and imposing stiffer penalties including:

• New criminal penalties for fraud related to health care and for the payment of bribes or gratuities to influence the delivery of health services and coverage.

• New civil monetary penalties against providers who submit false claims.

• Tighter restrictions eliminate referral "kickbacks" in the private sector, and new standards prohibit physicians from prescribing services delivered at institutions in which they hold financial interests.

• Accountability standards make provider fraud and other misbehavior automatic grounds for exclusion from all health plans.

2

Ethical Foundations
of Health Reform

THE VALUES AND principles that shape the new health care system reflect fundamental national beliefs about community, equality, justice and liberty. These convictions anchor health reform in shared moral traditions.

Universal Access: Every American citizen and legal resident should have access to health care without financial or other barriers.

Comprehensive Benefits: Guaranteed benefits should meet the full range of health needs, including primary, preventive and specialized care.

Choice: Each consumer should have the opportunity to exercise effective choice about providers, plans and treatments. Each consumer should be informed about what is known and not known about the risks and benefits of available treatments and be free to choose among them according to his and her preferences.

Equality of Care: The system should avoid the creation of a tiered system providing care based only on differences of need, not individual or group characteristics.

Fair Distribution of Costs: The health care system should spread the costs and burdens of care across the entire community, basing the level of contribution required of consumers on ability to pay.

Personal Responsibility: Under health reform, each individual and family should assume responsibility for protecting and promoting health and contributing to the cost of care.

Intergenerational Justice: The health care system should respond to the unique needs of each stage of life, sharing benefits and burdens fairly across generations.

Wise Allocation of Resources: The nation should balance prudently what it spends on health care against other important national priorities.

Effectiveness: The new system should deliver care, and innovation that works and that patients want. It should encourage the discovery of better treatments. It should make it possible for the academic community and health care providers to exercise effectively their responsibility to evaluate and improve health care by providing resources for the systematic study of health care outcomes.

Quality: The system should deliver high quality care and provide individuals with the information necessary to make informed health care choices.

Effective Management: By encouraging simplification and continuous improvement, as well as making the system easier to use for patients and providers, the health care system should focus on care, rather than administration.

Professional Integrity and Responsibility: The health care system should treat the clinical judgments of professionals with respect and protect the integrity of the provider-patient relationship while ensuring that health providers have the resources to fulfill their responsibilities for the effective delivery of quality care.

Fair Procedures: To protect these values and principles, fair and open democratic procedures should underlie decisions concerning the operation of the health care system and the resolution of disputes that arise within it.

Local Responsibility: Working within the framework of national reform, the new health care system should allow states and local communities to design effective, high-quality systems of care that serve each of their citizens.

3

Coverage

ALL AMERICANS and legal residents are guaranteed access to health services in a nationally defined, comprehensive package of benefits with no lifetime limits on coverage. Categories of eligible individuals:

- American citizens
- Nationals
- Citizens of other countries legally residing in the United States
- Long-term non-immigrants.

Sources of Health Coverage

A health security card provided to each eligible person entitles him or her to obtain coverage through a health plan that delivers services covered in a nationally defined, comprehensive benefit package.

Eligible individuals enroll in a health plan through a health alliance unless they are covered under government-sponsored health programs that continue, including:

- Medicare
- Military personnel covered by the Department of Defense

- Department of Veterans Affairs
- Indian Health Service

Individuals eligible for those programs continue to receive care through them, although the Department of Defense, Department of Veterans Affairs and the Indian Health Service may gradually integrate some of their services into the new health care system. (See section on Government Programs.)

Individuals eligible for Medicaid receive coverage through regional health alliances. (See Medicaid Section.)

All employed persons choose a health plan through a corporate or regional health alliance. Employees of firms with 5,000 or fewer workers become members of a regional alliance established to serve the area in which they reside. Employees of firms with more than 5,000 employees obtain coverage through a corporate alliance established by their employer unless the employer chooses to purchase coverage through regional alliances.

Members of Taft-Hartley plans with more than 5,000 covered workers obtain coverage from an alliance formed by the Taft-Hartley plan. Employees of rural electric and telephone cooperative plans that include more than 5,000 covered workers may receive coverage through a corporate alliance formed by the cooperative.

Employees of government, including federal, state, local, and special-purpose agencies, obtain coverage through the regional alliance where they live. All individuals who are self-employed or not employed obtain coverage through regional alliances unless they are eligible for Medicare. The United States Postal Service may operate as a corporate alliance.

Obtaining Coverage

Individuals obtain health coverage by enrolling in a plan through a regional or corporate health alliance. The national health security card serves as proof of eligibility.

An individual eligible for cash assistance (AFDC or SSI), whether employed or unemployed, has coverage purchased from the regional alliance by the Medicaid program.

Individuals over age 65 continue to enroll in the Medicare program. The Medicare secondary payer program remains for Medicare eligible individuals who continue to work. Individuals over the age of 65 but not eligible for Medicare receive coverage through regional alliances, into which they pay premiums. Depending on income, they may be eligible for subsidies to pay all or part of the cost of premiums and required cost sharing. Individuals who are eligible for Medicare because of disability continue to receive Medicare coverage.

Retired workers under 65 are eligible for health care coverage through regional alliances, and pay only the 20 percent share they would have paid if employed. Retirees who receive health coverage through former employers or through pension funds continue to be eligible for payment for their share of the premium from those sources.

Assurance of Coverage

It is the obligation of every eligible individual to enroll in a health plan. Anyone who does not meet the established deadline for enrollment automatically is enrolled in a health plan when he or she seeks medical care. Regional alliances assign patients who do not seek enrollment to a health plan; they automatically assign any newborn infant who is not enrolled through his or her parents to a plan.

No health plan may cancel an enrollment until the individual enrolls in another plan.

Employer Obligation

All employers contribute to the purchase of health coverage for their employees. All employers pay 80 percent of the weighted-average premium for health insurance coverage in the regional alliances which serve their employees or in their corporate alliance. The required employer contribution in regional alliances is capped at a percentage of payroll, with lower caps for small and low-wage employers. (See section on Financing Health Coverage.)

Firms that employ more than 5,000 workers ensure that their employees are enrolled in health plans that meet federal guidelines and report information about enrollment. Employers with more than 5,000 employees that choose to operate corporate alliances may be required to continue to pay for health insurance coverage for their terminated employees for six months following termination or may have to pay 1 percent of payroll to cover unemployed workers.

Large employers may fulfill their obligation to provide coverage by operating a program of self-insurance through a corporate alliance, contracting with a certified health plan or joining the regional alliance. If a large employer merges with a firm in the regional alliance, it may continue as a corporate alliance. If the number of employees falls below 4,800, the employer joins the regional alliance.

Individual Obligations

Families and individuals pay 20 percent of the weighted-average premium for an average cost health plan chosen through an alliance. An individual or family who chooses a less expensive plan pays less, and someone who chooses a more expensive plan pays more.

An employer also may elect to pay some or all of the employee's portion of the premium.

Self-employed and unemployed individuals are responsible for paying the family share of the premium as well as the employer share, unless they are eligible for assistance based on income.

Enforcement

The Secretary of Labor ensures that all employers fulfill the obligation to make contributions or provide coverage through a qualified health plan.

Coordination of Coverage

When an individual obtains necessary medical services outside the geographic area served by his or her regional or corporate alliance, the plan pays for care under arrangements established among alliances.

Undocumented Persons

Undocumented persons are not eligible for guaranteed health benefits. However, employers are required to pay health insurance premiums for all of their employees, regardless of immigration status.

Alliances do not share information related to health insurance premiums paid by employers with the Immigration and Naturalization Service.

Individuals living in the United States without proper documentation may continue to use emergency and other health services as provided under current federal law. Health care institutions that serve a large number of patients who are not eligible for coverage continue to receive federal funding to compensate for their care.

Any individual not eligible for the national benefit package may purchase coverage from a private insurance plan to the extent such plans are available.

Territories

Individuals who reside in territories of the United States receive the comprehensive benefit package through their existing health care systems.

Others

States with migrant labor populations are required to address the needs of migrant workers and their families in state plans for the implementation of health reform. States may extend coverage to migrant workers through regional alliances or propose alternative programs tailored to the specific needs of the migrant population.

Students who are dependents are covered by their parents' health policies, but may obtain coverage through the regional alliance where they attend school. Students who are not dependents enroll in the regional alliance where their school is located.

Employees are defined to include not only those workers defined as employees under Internal Revenue Service rules but broadly enough to discourage employers from designating employees as independent contractors in order to avoid payment of health insurance premiums. For purposes of health insurance, independent contractors who earn more than 80 percent of their annual incomes from one employer are covered as an employee of that employer.

Employers make contributions toward health care premiums for part-time employees (generally individuals working more than 10 hours but less than 30 hours per week) on a pro-rated basis.

Prisoners remain the financial responsibility of the various prison systems.

4

Guaranteed National
Benefit Package

THE HEALTH BENEFITS guaranteed to all Americans provide comprehensive coverage, including mental health
services, substance-abuse treatment, some dental services and clinical preventive services.

The guaranteed benefit package contains no lifetime
limitations on coverage, with the exception of coverage
for orthodontia.

Medical Services Covered

Each health plan must provide coverage for the following categories of services as medically necessary or
appropriate with additional limitations and cost sharing
only as specified in the American Health Security Act
of 1993 or by the National Health Board. Covered
health services are:

- Hospital services
- Emergency services
- Services of physicians and other health professionals
- Clinical preventive services
- Mental health and substance abuse services
- Family planning services
- Pregnancy-related services
- Hospice

- Home health care
- Extended-care services
- Ambulance services
- Outpatient laboratory and diagnostic services
- Outpatient prescription drugs and biologicals
- Outpatient rehabilitation services
- Durable medical equipment, prosthetic and orthotic devices
- Vision and hearing care
- Preventive dental services for children
- Health education classes.

Definition of Services

Hospital services:

- Inpatient hospital, including bed and board, routine care, therapeutics, laboratory, diagnostic and radiology services and professional services specified by the National Health Board when furnished to inpatients.
- Outpatient hospital services
- 24-hour-a-day emergency department services
- Definition: A hospital is an institution meeting the requirements of §1861(e) of the Social Security Act.

Services of physician and other health professionals:

- Includes inpatient and outpatient medical and surgical professional services, including consultations, delivered by a health professional in home, office, or other ambulatory care settings, and in institutional settings.

- Definitions
  — A health professional is someone who is licensed or otherwise authorized by the State to deliver health services in the State in which the individual delivers services.
  — Covered services are those that a health professional is legally authorized to perform in that state. No state may, through licensure requirements or other restrictions, limit the practice of any class of health professionals except as justified by the skill or training of such professional.

The benefit package does not require any plan to reimburse any particular provider or any type or category of provider. However, each plan is expected to provide a sufficient mix of providers and specialties and appropriate locations to provide adequate access to professional services.

Clinical preventive services:

- Specified in Table I.
- Limitation: Must be provided as consistent with the periodicity schedule specified in Table I or as specified by the National Health Board in regulations.
- Targeted screening tests and immunizations required for high-risk patients, as defined by the National Health Board, are covered under outpatient laboratory and diagnostic services and outpatient prescription drugs and biologicals.
- Periodic medical examinations: every 3 years for individuals ages 20 to 39, every 2 years for adults ages 40 to 65, and annually for adults ages 65 or more.

Table I. Covered Clinical Preventive Services

Age	Immunizations	Tests
0–2	4 DTP, 3 OPV, 3–4 HiB, 1 MMR, 3 HBV	1 Hematocrit, 2 Lead*, 7 Clinician visits***
3–5	1 DTP, 1 OPV, 1 MMR	1 Urinalysis, 2 Clinician visits***
6–19	1 Td	Pap/pelvic** every 3 years after menarche, 5 Clinician visits***
20–39	1 Td every 10 years	Cholesterol every 5 years; Pap/pelvic** every 3 years*** †
40–49	1 Td every 10 years	Cholesterol every 5 years; Pap/pelvic** every 3 years*** †
50–64	1 Td every 10 years	Cholesterol every 5 years; Pap/pelvic and Mammogram†† every 2 years
65 +	1 Td every 10 years Pneumococcal—once Annual influenza	Cholesterol every 5 years Mammogram†† every 2 years

Preventive coverage includes coverage for women of any age presenting for prenatal care.

* = *For children at high risk for lead exposure only.*

** = *Papanicolaou smears and pelvic exam for females who have reached child-bearing age and are at risk of cervical cancer.*

*** = *Once three annual negative smears have been obtained.*

† = *For females of childbearing age at risk for sexually transmitted disease, an annual Pap smear and screening for chlamydia and gonorrhea.*

†† = *Females only.*

††† = *Visits for tests and immunizations include blood pressure check, risk assessment and appropriate health guidance.*

DTP = *Diphtheria, tetanus, pertussis vaccine*

OPV = *Oral polio vaccine*

HiB = *Haemophilus influenzae type B vaccine*

HBV = *Hepatitis B vaccine*

MMR = *Measles, mumps, rubella vaccine*

Td = *Tetanus diphtheria toxoid*

Family planning services

Pregnancy-related services

Hospice care:

- Covered services (as under Medicare):
  — Nursing care provided by or under the supervision of a registered professional nurse.
  — Medical social services under the direction of a physician.
  — Physicians' services.
  — Counseling services for the purposes of training the individual's family or other caregiver to provide care and for the purpose of helping the individual and those caring for him or her to adjust to the individual's death.
  — Short-term inpatient care, although respite care is provided only on an occasional basis and may not be provided for more than five days.
  — Medical supplies and the use of medical appliances for the relief of pain and symptom control related to the individual's terminal illness.
  — Home health aide and homemaker services.
  — Physical or occupational therapy and speech-language pathology.
- Limitations
  — Only for terminally ill individuals
  — Only as an alternative to continued hospitalization.
- Definition:
  — An individual is considered terminally ill if the individual has a medical prognosis of a life

expectancy of 6 months or less if the terminal illness runs its normal course.

Home health care:

- Same services as under the current Medicare program (including skilled nursing, physical, occupational and speech therapy, prescribed social services) with the addition of prescribed home infusion therapy and outpatient prescription drugs and biologicals.
- Limitations
  — Only as an alternative to institutionalization (i.e., inpatient treatment in a hospital, skilled nursing or rehabilitation center) for illness or injury.
  — At the end of each 60 days of treatment, the need for continued therapy is re-evaluated. Additional periods of therapy are covered only if the risk of hospitalization or institutionalization exists.

Extended-care services:

- Inpatient services in a skilled nursing or rehabilitation facility.
- Limitations
  — Only after an acute illness or injury as an alternative to continued hospitalization.
  — Maximum of 100 days per calendar year.

Ambulance services:

- Ground transportation by ambulance; air transportation by an aircraft equipped for transporting an injured or sick individual.

- Limitations
  — Ambulance service is covered only in cases in which the use of an ambulance is indicated by the individual's condition.
  — Air transport covered only in cases in which other means of transportation are contra-indicated by the patient's condition.

Outpatient laboratory and diagnostic services:

- Prescribed laboratory and radiology services, including diagnostic services provided to individuals who are not inpatients of a hospital, hospice or extended care facility.

Outpatient prescription drugs and biologicals:

- Drugs, biological products, and insulin.
- Limitations:
  — Must be prescribed for use in an outpatient setting.
  — No frequency or quantity limitations other than reasonable rules for amount to be dispensed and number of refills. Health plans are permitted to establish formularies, drug utilization review, generic substitution, and mail order programs.

Outpatient rehabilitation services:

- Outpatient occupational therapy, outpatient physical therapy, and outpatient speech-pathology services for the purpose of attaining or restoring speech.
- Limitations
  — Coverage only for therapies used to restore functional capacity or minimize limitations on

physical and cognitive functions as a result of an illness or injury.

— At the end of each 60 days of treatment, the need for continued therapy is reevaluated. Additional periods of therapy are covered only if function is improving.

Durable medical equipment, prosthetic and orthotic devices:

- Covered services:
  — Durable medical equipment.
  — Prosthetic devices (other than dental) which replace all or part of an internal body organ.
  — Leg, arm, back and neck braces.
  — Artificial legs, arms and eyes (including replacements if required due to a change in physical condition).
  — Training for use of above items.
- Limitations
  — Items must improve functional abilities or prevent further deterioration in function.
  — Does not include custom devices.

Vision and hearing care:

- Covered services:
  — Routine eye exams, including procedures performed to determine the refractive state of the eyes
  — Diagnosis and treatments for defects in vision
  — Routine ear examinations.
- Limitations
  — Eyeglasses and contact lenses limited to children under the age of 18.

— Routine eye examinations limited to one every 2 years for persons 18 years of age or more.

Preventive dental services for children:

• For children under age eighteen, treatment for prevention of dental disease and injury, including maintenance of dental health, and emergency dental treatment for injury.

Health education classes:

Participating health plans are permitted to cover health education or training for patients that encourage the reduction of behavioral risk factors and promote healthy activities. Such courses may include smoking cessation, nutritional counseling, stress management, skin cancer prevention, and physical training classes. Cost sharing is determined by the plan.

Mental Health and Substance Abuse

Mental health and substance abuse services form an integral component of a national system of health care. Scientific evidence and societal attitudes have coalesced to support a benefit structure that represents a significant departure from past approaches.

A comprehensive array of services, along with the flexibility to provide such services based on individual medical and psychological necessity through effective management techniques, produces better outcomes and better cost controls than traditional benefits. By the year 2001, a comprehensive, integrated benefit structure with appropriate management replaces prescribed limits on individual services.

That change of direction requires a phase-in period to allow health plans time to develop the service system capacity to deliver and manage a more comprehensive mental health and substance abuse benefit. The phase-in allows states, health alliances, and health plans sufficient time to develop appropriate quality assurance programs essential to a managed comprehensive benefit.

It also provides incentives for states to implement a fully comprehensive, integrated system by combining state and local funds now supporting the separate public system with health care reform to reduce duplication and inefficiency, assure cost savings and maximize resources. During the phase-in of the more comprehensive mental health and substance abuse benefit, the federal government supports state demonstrations to prove the efficacy of a comprehensive, integrated system of care with improved benefits.

By the year 2001, all states are required to submit to the National Health Board a plan detailing steps it is undertaking to move from the traditional two-tier structure for separate public and private mental health and substance abuse services and develop an integrated, comprehensive managed system of care.

Definition of Benefit

Inpatient and residential treatment:

• Inpatient hospital, psychiatric units of general hospitals, therapeutic family or group homes or other types of residential treatment centers, community residential treatment and recovery centers for substance abuse, residential detoxification services, crisis residential services, and other residential treatment services.

- Limitations
  - By the year 2001, management of benefit determines lengths of stay.

    Initially, a maximum of 30 days per episode of inpatient or residential treatment, with 60 days annually for all settings in this category. Health plans upon special appeal may grant an exception waiver of the episode maximum (but only up to the annual limit) for the limited number of individuals for whom hospitalization or continued residential care is medically necessary because the patient continues to make or is at serious risk of making an attempt to harm him- or herself.

    By the year 1998, the annual maximum rises to 90 days.
  - Inpatient hospital substance abuse treatment covers only medical detoxification as required for the management of psychiatric or medical complications associated with withdrawal from alcohol or drugs.
  - Inpatient hospital care for mental and substance abuse disorders is available only when less restrictive nonresidential or residential services are ineffective or inappropriate.
- Definitions:
  - A hospital is an institution meeting the requirements of §1861(e) or (f) of the Social Security Act.
  - A residential treatment facility is one which meets criteria for licensure or certification established by the state in which it is located.

- Eligibility

Individuals are eligible for mental health and substance abuse services other than screening and assessment and crisis services if they have, or have had in the past year, a diagnosable mental or substance abuse disorder, which meets diagnostic criteria specified within DSM-III-R, and that resulted in or poses a significant risk for functional impairment in family, work, school, or community activities.

— These disorders include any mental disorder listed in DSM-III-R or their ICD-9-CM equivalents, or subsequent revisions, with the exception of DSM-III-R "V" codes (conditions not attributable to a mental disorder) unless they co-occur with another diagnosable disorder.

— Persons who are receiving treatment but without such treatment would meet functional impairment criteria are considered to have a disorder.

Family members of an eligible participant receiving mental or substance abuse services may receive medically necessary or appropriately related services in conjunction with the patient (so-called collateral treatment).

Professional and outpatient treatment services:

- Professional services, diagnosis, medical management, substance abuse counseling and relapse prevention, outpatient psychotherapy.
  - Limitations
    — By the year 2001, limits on outpatient treatment and cost sharing are eliminated, making this benefit comparable to other health services; management of the benefit determines availability of

services. Initially, a limit of 30 visits per year for outpatient psychotherapy visits (and variation in cost sharing described later). Medical management, crisis management, evaluation and assessment, and substance abuse counseling are not limited.

— Licensed or certified substance abuse treatment professionals must provide substance abuse and relapse counseling.

• Eligibility criteria specified above for inpatient mental health and substance abuse treatment services apply, except that all persons are eligible for screening and assessment and 24-hour crisis services.

• Definitions for services of physicians and other health professionals apply.

• Coverage for case management with no cost sharing.

Intensive non-residential treatment services:

• Partial hospitalization, day treatment, psychiatric rehabilitation, ambulatory detoxification, home-based services, behavioral aide services.

• Limitations

— By the year 2001, benefit limits are replaced by management of the comprehensive benefit to determine availability of benefit.

Initially, a limit of 120 days per year apply.

— Provided only for the purpose of averting the need for, or as an alternative to, treatment in residential or inpatient settings, or to facilitate the earlier return of individuals receiving inpatient or residential care, or to restore the functioning of individuals with mental or substance abuse disorders, or to assist individuals to develop the skills and access the supports needed to achieve their maximum level of functioning within the community.

• Eligibility: As specified for inpatient mental health and substance abuse treatment services.

Integration of Public and Private Mental Health Care Systems

Through the end of this decade, the structure of the mental health and substance abuse benefit package requires continuation of the existing public system that provides mental health and substance abuse treatment. It also requires maintenance of the existing block grant program to the states, which supplements spending on mental and addictive disorder programs.

To promote the eventual integration of the public and private systems, states are encouraged to use the flexibility allowed under health reform to fold their expenditures for public mental health and substance abuse programs into funding available to regional health alliances to require integrated care for all health needs, including mental and addictive disorders. States adopting this direction may obtain a waiver from limits in the benefit package and are eligible for federal matching funds to develop integrated service systems.

Exclusions

The benefit package does not cover services that are not medically necessary or appropriate, private duty nursing, cosmetic orthodontia and other cosmetic surgery, hearing aids, adult eyeglasses and contact lenses, in vitro fertilization services, sex change surgery and related services, private room accommodations, custodial care, personal comfort services and supplies and investigational treatments, except as described below.

Coverage of Investigational Treatments

The comprehensive benefit package includes coverage for medically necessary or appropriate medical care provided as part of an investigational treatment during an approved research trial. The intention of this provision is to cover routine medical costs associated with an investigational treatment that would occur even if the investigational treatment were not administered.

• An investigational treatment is a treatment the effectiveness of which has not been determined and which is under clinical investigation as part of an approved research trial.

• An approved research trial is a peer-reviewed and approved research program, as defined by the Secretary of the Department of Health and Human Services, conducted for the primary purpose of determining whether or not a treatment is safe, efficacious, or having any other characteristic of a treatment which must be demonstrated in order for that treatment to be medically necessary or appropriate.

Coverage is automatically available if the research trial is approved by the National Institutes of Health, the FDA, the Department of Veterans Affairs, Department of Defense or a qualified non-governmental research entity as identified in NTH guidelines.

Expansion of Other Benefits

The initial benefit plan provides comprehensive preventive coverage for all patients and focuses comprehensive dental, mental health and substance abuse coverage on priority concerns including preventive dental services for children and treatment for seriously mentally ill adults, seriously emotionally disturbed children and individuals with substance-abuse disorders.

The National Health Board has discretion to introduce additional benefits earlier if savings from reform and budget resources permit. Additional benefits included in planned expansion include:

Dental Services:

- Preventive dental care extended to adults
- Restorative services
  — Low cost sharing: $20 per visit
  — High cost sharing: 40 percent co-insurance, $50 deductible, and $1,500 annual maximum benefit for prevention and restoration
- Orthodontia in cases in which it is necessary to avoid reconstructive surgery
  — Low cost sharing: $20 per visit
  — High cost sharing: 40 percent co-insurance, $50 deductible, and $2,500 lifetime maximum benefit.

Cost Sharing

Consumer out-of-pocket costs for health services in the comprehensive benefit package are limited, to ensure financial protection, and standardized to ensure simplicity in choosing among health plans.

Health plans use standard consumer cost sharing requirements. Health plans may offer consumers one of three cost sharing schedules:

• **Low cost sharing:** $10 co-payments for outpatient services; no co-payments for inpatient services; may offer point of service option with 40 percent coinsurance.

• **Higher cost sharing:** $200 individual/$400 family deductibles; 20 percent coinsurance; $1,500/3,000 maximum on out-of-pocket spending.

• **Combination:** Plan provides low cost sharing if participants use preferred providers and higher cost sharing (20 percent coinsurance) if they use out-of-network providers.

Low Cost Sharing

	Cost-sharing	Limitations
Overall		
—Deductible	None	
—Coinsurance	$10 per visit	
—Out-of-pocket max		
Individual	$1,500	
Family	$3,000	
Inpatient hospital	Full coverage	Private room only when medically necessary
Professional services, outpatient hospital services	$10 per visit	
Emergency services	$25 per visit	Waived in emergency
Preventive services, including well-baby, prenatal	Full coverage	Services limited to periodicity in Table 1
Hospice	Full coverage	As hospital alternative for terminally ill
Home health care	Full coverage	As inpatient alternative; coverage reassessed at 60 days; added coverage only to prevent institutional care
Extended care facilities (SNFs, rehab facility)	Full coverage	As hospital alternative; 100 day limit
Outpatient physical, occupational, speech therapy	$10 per visit	Only to restore function or minimize limitations from illness or injury; reassessment at 60 days; additional coverage only if improving
DME, outpatient lab, ambulance	Full coverage	
Routine eye and ear exams, eyeglasses	$10 per exam or 1 set glasses	Eyeglasses limited to children only

Low Cost Sharing (Cont.)

	Cost-sharing	Limitations
Dental services		
—Initial: Prevention	$10 per visit	For <18 only
—Additions in 2001:		Remove age limit on prevention
Restoration	$20 per visit	
Orthodontia	$20 per visit	Only to avoid reconstructive surgery
Prescription drugs	$5/prescription	
Mental health/ substance abuse		
Initial		
Inpatient services:	Full coverage	30 day/episode; 60 day/year max
Hospital alternatives:	Full coverage	120 days maximum
Brief office visits for medical management:	$10 per visit	no limits
Psychotherapy:	$25 per visit	30 visits maximum
2001		
Inpatient services:	Full coverage	
Hospital alternatives:	Full coverage	no limits
Outpatient incl. 1–12 psychotherapy visits:	$10 per visit	

High Cost Sharing

	Cost-sharing	Limitations
Overall		
—Deductible	$200/400 indiv/family	
—Coinsurance	20%	
—Out-of-pocket max (oop max)		
Individual	$1,500	
Family	$3,000	
Inpatient hospital	20% co-ins	Private room only when medically necessary
Professional services, outpatient hospital services including emergency	20% co-ins	
Preventive services, including well-baby, prenatal	Co-ins and deductible do not apply	Services limited to periodicity in Table 1
Hospice	20% co-ins	As hospital alternative for terminally ill
Home health care	20% co-ins	As inpatient alternative; coverage reassessed at 60 days; added coverage only to prevent institutional care
Extended care facilities (SNFs, rehab facility)	20% co-ins	As hospital alternative; 100 day limit
Outpatient physical, occupational, speech therapy	20% co-ins	Only to restore function or minimize limitations from illness or injury; reassessment at 60 days; additional coverage only if improving
DME, outpatient lab, ambulance	20% co-ins	
Routine eye and ear exams, eyeglasses	20% co-ins	Eyeglasses limited to children only

High Cost Sharing (Cont.)

	Cost-sharing	Limitations
Dental services		
—Initial: Prevention	20% co-ins	For <18 only
—Additions in 2001:		Remove age limit on prevention
Restoration	$50 deduc + 40% co-ins	
Orthodontia	40% co-ins	Only to avoid reconstructive surgery; $2500 lifetime max
Prescription drugs	$250/year deduc 20% co-ins oop max applies	
Mental health/ substance abuse		
Initial		
Inpatient services:	20% co-ins; oop max applies	30 day/episode; 60 day/year max
Non-residential intensive services:	20% co-ins	120 days maximum
All outpatient:	20% co-ins	no limits
Psychotherapy:	50% cost sharing	30 visits maximum
2001		
Inpatient services:	20% co-ins; oop max applies	
Non-residential intensive services:	20% co-ins	no limits
Outpatient including psychotherapy visits:	20% co-ins	

Combination Cost Sharing

Services (with same limitations as above)	In network	Out of network
Overall		
—Deductible	None	$200/400 indiv/family
—Coinsurance	$10 per visit	20%
—Out-of-pocket max		
Individual	$1,500	$1,500
Family	$3,000	$3,000
Inpatient hospital	Full coverage	20% co-ins
Professional services, outpatient hospital services	$10 per visit	20% co-ins
Emergency services	$25 per visit	20% co-ins
Preventive services, including well-baby, prenatal	Full coverage	Full coverage
Hospice	Full coverage	20% co-ins
Home health care	Full coverage	20% co-ins
Extended care facilities (SNFs, rehab facility)	Full coverage	20% co-ins
Outpatient physical, occupational, speech therapy	$10 per visit	20% co-ins
DME, outpatient lab, ambulance	Full coverage	20% co-ins
Routine eye and ear exams, eyeglasses	$10 per exam or 1 set glasses	20% co-ins

Combination Cost Sharing (Cont.)

Services (with same limitations as above)	In network	Out of network
Dental services		
—Initial: Prevention	$10 per visit	20% co-ins
—Additions in 2001:		
Restoration	$20 per visit	$50 deduc + 40% co-ins
Orthodontia	$20 per visit	40% co-ins
Prescription drugs	$5/prescription	$250/year deduc 20% co-ins oop max applies
Mental health/ substance abuse		
Initial		
Inpatient services:	Full coverage	20% co-ins; oop max applies
Hospital alternatives:	Full coverage	20% co-ins
All outpatient:	$10 per visit	20% co-ins
2001		
Inpatient services:	Full coverage	20% co-ins; oop max applies
Non-residential intensive services:	Full coverage	20% co-ins
Outpatient	$10 per visit	20% co-ins

5

National Health Board

THE AMERICAN Health Security Act creates an independent National Health Board responsible for setting national standards and overseeing the establishment and administration of the new health system by states.

The National Health Board and existing executive agencies divide responsibility for administration of the new health care system at the national level.

Authority of the National Health Board

The Board undertakes the following functions:

- **Oversight of the state system**

The Board establishes requirements for state plans, monitors compliance with those requirements, provides technical assistance, and ensures access to health care for all Americans.

- **Comprehensive benefit package**

The Board interprets and updates the nationally guaranteed benefit package and issues regulations. The Board may recommend to the President and Congress appropriate adjustments to the nationally guaranteed benefit package to reflect changes in technology, health care needs and methods of service delivery.

• Budgets

The Board issues regulations concerning implementation of the national budget for health care spending and enforces the budget.

The board establishes baseline budgets for alliances by allocating national spending among alliances to reflect regional variations.

The Board certifies compliance with the budget. (See section entitled Budget Development and Enforcement.)

• National quality management system

The Board establishes and manages a performance-based system of quality management and improvement described in the section entitled "Quality Management and Improvement." The Board develops measures reported in the annual quality performance report of health plans. In developing these measures, the Board consults with appropriate parties, including providers, consumers, health plans, states, purchasers of care, and experts in law, medicine, economics, public health, and health services research including appropriate agencies such as AHCPR, NIH and HCFA.

To measure quality, the Board develops and implements standards to establish a National Health Information System as described in the section on Information Systems and Administrative Simplification.

• Breakthrough drug committee

To encourage reasonable pricing of breakthrough drugs, a committee of the National Health Board has the authority to make public declarations regarding the reasonableness of launch prices.

The committee could address new drugs that represent a breakthrough or significant advance over existing therapies. The committee could also address all drugs subject to a "reasonable price" clause in a contract with the National Institutes of Health.

The committee could investigate drug prices only in those cases where available evidence suggests that the price may be unreasonable. The committee could make an initial determination about the reasonableness of a drug price based on a comparison of prices for therapeutically similar drugs in the United States and seven other industrialized countries.

If the drug price exceeds what the committee thinks to be reasonable based on the information available, or if there is insufficient data, the committee would have the authority to obtain information from the company about the drug's price. The committee could then issue a report regarding the reasonableness of the drug price. The committee would have no authority to set or control drug prices.

National Health Board decisions related to benefits, standards of performance and accountability apply to health plans operating through both regional and corporate alliances.

Membership

The National Health Board consists of seven members appointed by the President by and with the advice and consent of the Senate. At least one of the members represents the interests of states.

The President designates one member as chairman. The chairman serves a term concurrent with that of the President and serves at the pleasure of the President. The chairman may serve a maximum of three terms.

The other members serve staggered four-year terms. These members may be reappointed for one additional term. The President may remove a member for neglect of duty or malfeasance in office.

When a vacancy occurs, the President appoints a successor to serve the remainder of the term. A vacancy in the membership of the Board does not impair the right of the remaining members to exercise all powers of the Board. The Board designates a member to act as chairman during any period when no chairman is designated by the President.

Upon expiration of a term of office, a member continues to serve until a successor is appointed and qualified. The President has the power to fill all vacancies that occur during the recess of the Senate by granting commissions that expire with the next session of the Senate.

Qualifications

The President nominates Board members on the basis of their experience and expertise in relevant subjects, including health care finance and delivery, state health systems, consumer protection, business, law or delivery of care to vulnerable populations. Members of the National Health Board must be citizens of the United States.

During the term of appointment, Board members serve as employees of the federal government and may hold no other employment. A member of the Board may not have a pecuniary interest in or hold an official relation to any health care plan, health care provider, insurance company, pharmaceutical company, medical equipment company or other affected industry. Before assuming an appointment to the National Health Board, the prospective member must certify under oath that he or she has complied with this requirement.

After leaving the Board, former members are subject to post-employment restrictions applicable to comparable federal employees.

Operation of the Board

The National Health Board appoints and sets the compensation of an executive director. The Board also appoints additional officers and employees, subject to applicable civil service rules, as necessary to carry out its functions. The Board hires sufficient staff to carry out the functions described above.

The Board establishes advisory committees that include representatives of states, health providers, employers, consumers and affected industries.

The Board may contract with the Department of Health and Human Services and other governmental and nongovernmental bodies to conduct research and analysis as required to execute its responsibilities. The Board has access to all relevant information and data available from appropriate federal departments and agencies. It coordinates its activities, particularly the conduct of original research and associated studies, with the activities of appropriate federal agencies.

The Board prepares and sends to the President and Congress an annual report addressing the implementation of the health care system, including federal and state action, data related to quality improvement and other issues. The annual report includes recommendations for changes in the administration, regulation and laws related to health care and coverage, as well as a full account of Board decisions and activities during the previous year.

The Office of Management and Budget reviews the Board's budget, which is submitted to Congress in conjunction with the President's budget. The Office of Management and Budget does not review regulations issued by the Board or its annual report to Congress prior to publication.

The General Accounting Office conducts periodic audits of the Board.

Responsibilities of Department of Health and Human Services

The Department of Health and Human Services continues to administer existing programs, such as Medicaid, Medicare and the Public Health Service. The Department of Health and Human Services also administers and implements those aspects of the new health care system not delegated to the National Health Board or any other federal department.

NATIONAL ADMINISTRATION

The National Health Board reviews plans submitted by the states for the implementation of the new health care system. Corporate alliances are supervised through ERISA and the Department of Labor. (See Corporate Alliances/ERISA.)

In the event that a state fails to meet the deadline for establishing regional health alliances or fails to operate the alliance system in compliance with federal requirements, the National Health Board ensures that all eligible individuals have access to services covered in the comprehensive benefit package.

To induce a state to act, the National Health Board informs the Secretary of the Department of Health and Human Services of a state's failure to comply. The Secretary has the authority to order the withholding of federal health appropriations.

If a state persists in its failure to comply with federal requirements, the National Health Board informs the Secretary of Health and Human Services. The Secretary is required to take one of the following actions to ensure that all eligible individuals have access to nationally guaranteed health benefits:

- Dissolve an existing health alliance and establish one or more regional alliances in compliance with federal requirements.
- Contract with private parties or others to establish and operate regional alliances.
- Order regional alliances or health plans to comply with specific federal requirements.
- Take other steps as needed to assure coverage.

When the National Board notifies the Secretary of Health and Human Services that a state has failed to comply with federal requirements, the National Board shall also notify the Secretary of the Treasury. The Secretary of the Treasury will impose a payroll tax on all employers in the state. The payroll tax shall be sufficient to allow the federal government to provide health coverage to all individuals in the state and to reimburse the federal government for the costs of monitoring and operating the state system.

An alliance operating under the supervision of the Secretary of the Department of Health and Human Services is responsible for meeting all requirements imposed on regional health alliances.

When a state demonstrates to the National Health Board that it is prepared to resume its statutory responsibilities, the state may establish its own alliances or take over management of alliances established under federal supervision.

6

State Responsibilities

STATES ASSUME primary responsibility for ensuring that all eligible individuals have access to a health plan that delivers the nationally guaranteed comprehensive benefit package.

State Plans

Each state submits to the National Health Board a plan for implementation of health reform, demonstrating that its health care system meets requirements under federal law. States periodically update their plans, as required by the National Health Board.

State plans designate an agency or official to coordinate the state responsibilities under federal law and delegate those responsibilities to state agencies or entities.

The plan also describes how the state intends to perform each of the following functions:

• Administration of subsidies for low-income individuals, families and employers.
• Certification of health plans.
• Financial regulation of health plans.
• Administration of data collection and quality management and improvement program.

• Establishment and governance of health alliances, including a mechanism for selecting members of the boards of directors and advisory boards for alliances.

Establishment of Alliances

No later than January 1, 1997, each state must establish one or more regional health alliances responsible for providing health coverage to residents in every area of the state.

The state ensures that all eligible individuals enroll in a regional alliance and that all alliances offer health plans that provide the comprehensive benefit package. The state also ensures that each alliance enrolls all eligible persons in the geographic area covered by the alliance.

Alliance Size and Population

The geographic area assigned to each regional alliance must encompass a population large enough to ensure that it controls adequate market share to negotiate effectively with health plans. States may establish one, and only one, regional alliance in each area.

States may not establish boundaries for health alliances that concentrate racial or ethnic minority groups, socio-economic groups or Medicaid beneficiaries. An alliance may not subdivide a primary metropolitan statistical area, but an alliance that covers a Consolidated Statistical Metropolitan Area within a state is presumed to be in compliance with these requirements.

An alliance may not cross state lines, but two or more contiguous states may coordinate the operation of alliances. Coordination may include adoption of joint operating rules, contracting with health plans, enforcement activities and negotiation of fee schedules with health providers.

Risk Adjustment

States ensure that each alliance establishes a risk-adjustment mechanism that meets federal standards and accounts for differences in patient populations related to age, gender, family size and health status. (See section on Risk Adjustment.)

Incentives to Serve Disadvantaged Groups

States may determine that financial incentives are needed to ensure that health plans enroll disadvantaged groups and provide appropriate extra services, such as outreach to encourage enrollment, transportation and interpreting services to ensure access to care for certain population groups that face barriers to access because of geographic location, income levels, racial or cultural differences.

State Regulation of Plans

States qualify health plans to participate in alliances. Each state establishes a mechanism to assess the quality of health plans, their financial stability and capacity to deliver the comprehensive benefit package to the proper geographic market of each plan. States will disclose the criteria that each health plan must satisfy to become qualified. Health plans which satisfy those criteria shall be qualified. Only plans qualified by the state may offer health coverage through regional alliances.

States define requirements related to levels and geographic distribution of services required of health plans to ensure adequate access for all eligible participants, including residents of low-income areas and areas in which the health care system is inadequate. States must ensure that all consumers have the opportunity to purchase coverage under a qualified health plan at a price equal to or less than the weighted-average premium. To fulfill that obligation, states may either require at least some plans to cover the entire alliance area, or sub-alliance service areas, or may provide a subsidy that allows consumers to pay only the weighted-average premium.

Where no plan applies, the state must assure that at least one health plan is available for every eligible individual residing within an area.

States may establish requirements for health plans to assure access to services, including the requirement to reimburse or contract with designated specialty providers and centers of excellence.

States may not discriminate against health plans on the basis of their domicile.

A state may not regulate premium rates charged by health plans, except when necessary to meet budget requirements or to ensure plan solvency. (See section on Budget Development and Enforcement.)

Solvency and Fiscal Oversight

Each state establishes capital standards for health plans that meet federal requirements established by the National Health Board in consultation with the states.

The minimum capital requirement consists of $500,000. Additional capital may be required for factors likely to affect the financial stability of health plans, including:

- Projected enrollment, number of providers and rate of growth.
- Market share and strength of competition.
- Degree and approach to risk sharing with providers and financial stability of providers.
- Structure of the plan and degree of integration.
- Prior performance of plan, risk history and liquidity of assets.

Each state defines financial reporting and auditing requirements and requirements for fund reserves adequate to monitor the financial status of plans.

States designate an agency that assumes control if a health plan fails. Procedures established by states to handle the failure of health plans assure continuity of coverage for consumers enrolled in the plan.

Guaranty Funds

Each state operates a guaranty fund to provide financial protection to health care providers and others if a health plan becomes insolvent. States may use existing guaranty fund arrangements provided that the arrangement meets national standards.

Guaranty funds pay health providers and others if a health plan is unable to meet its obligations. Guaranty funds cover liability for services rendered prior to health plan insolvency and for services to patients after the insolvency but prior to their enrollment in other health plans. Guaranty funds are liable at least for payment of all services rendered by a health plan for the comprehensive benefit package, including any supplemental coverage for cost sharing provided by the health plan.

If a health plan cannot meet its financial obligations to health care providers, providers have no legal right to seek payment from patients for any services covered in the comprehensive benefit package other than the patients' obligations under cost sharing.

If a health plan fails, health providers are required to continue caring for patients until they are enrolled in a new health plan.

All health plans must participate in a guaranty fund, and the fund is liable for all claims against the plan by health care providers, contractors, employees, governments or any other claimants. The guaranty fund stands as a creditor for any payments made on behalf of a plan.

If a health plan fails, the state may assess payments of up to 2 percent of premiums on other plans within the alliance to generate sufficient revenue to cover outstanding claims against the failed plan. The failure of a health plan is defined as the imminent inability to pay legitimate claims.

A guaranty fund has the ability to borrow funds against future assessments in order to meet the obligations of the failed plan.

Additional Benefits

Any state may provide health benefits in addition to those guaranteed under the comprehensive national package. However, in order to expand benefits, a state must appropriate revenue from sources other than those established by the American Health Security Act to support delivery of the nationally guaranteed benefit. A state may not rely on a payroll mandate on employers or another revenue source applicable solely to corporations or payroll.

Single-Payer Option

A state may establish a single-payer health care system rather than an alliance system offering multiple plans. A state may establish a single-payer alliance that serves a portion of the state.

A single-payer system is one in which the state or its designated agency makes all payments to health care providers with no intermediaries, health plans or other entities assuming financial risk. However, providers, such as HMOs, networks of physicians and hospitals may assume risk by accepting capitated payments to cover the health needs of individuals.

A single-payer system provides, at a minimum, the health services defined in the comprehensive benefit package and imposes requirements for co-insurance, co-payments, deductibles and out-of-pocket limits no greater than those charged by regional alliance health plans. Single-payer systems also must comply with requirements for quality management and improvement, the collection of health data and other guidelines for health plans and alliances.

If a state chooses to establish a single-payer health system, the federal government may waive any of the following requirements under the alliance system:

- ERISA rules governing corporate alliances
- Rules delineating participation in regional and corporate alliances
- Rules continuing Medicare as a separate program outside the alliance structure consistent with requirements for the protection of Medicare beneficiaries
- Guaranty fund rules

A single-payer system established by a state may eliminate cost-sharing requirements; however, a state must appropriate revenue from sources other than those established by this Act to support delivery of the benefits equal to or in excess of the nationally guaranteed benefit package.

Regional Health Alliances

REGIONAL HEALTH alliances assume the following responsibilities:

• Representing the interests of consumers and purchasers of health care services.
• Structuring the market for health care to encourage the delivery of high-quality care and the control of
costs.
• Assuring that all residents in an area who are covered through the regional alliance enroll in health plans
that provide the nationally guaranteed benefits.

Operation of Alliances

A regional alliance may operate as a non-profit corporation, an independent state agency or an agency of the
state executive branch. A board of directors, composed
of representatives of consumers and employers who
purchase coverage through the alliance, governs
alliances that are non-profit corporations. States establish a mechanism for selecting members of alliance
boards.

The board of each alliance includes an equal number of employer and consumer representatives, plus one additional member to serve as chairman. The board must include the following:

- Employers who purchase health coverage through the alliance.
- Employees who purchase through the alliance.
- Self-employed individuals who purchase through the alliance.
- Other individuals who obtain coverage through the alliance.

The board of an alliance may not include members of the following groups or their immediate families:

- Health care providers or their employees, owners of health plans or their employees, or other persons who derive substantial income from health plans or the provision of health care.
- Members of associations, law firms or other institutions or organizations that represent the interests of health care providers, health plans or others involved in the health care field, or who practice as a professional in an area involving health care.
- Owners, employees, board members or individuals who derive substantial income from pharmaceutical companies and suppliers of medical equipment, devices and services.

To ensure that alliances are accountable to consumers and employers, states may establish statewide councils composed of representatives of employer and consumer organizations to prepare lists of nominees for alliance boards.

States require each alliance to provide an ombudsman to assist consumers in dealing with problems that arise with health plans and the alliance. States may also permit consumers at annual enrollment to check off a $1 contribution from their premium payment to support the office of the ombudsman or other consumer representatives.

In addition to a Board of Directors or Advisory Board, each regional alliance establishes a Provider Advisory Board made up of representatives of health care professionals who practice in health plans administered by the alliance.

In the case of a health alliance that is a state agency or an independent state entity administered by a state-appointed authority, an advisory board consisting of representatives of the same groups is appointed to provide advice to the agency.

Enrollment

Each regional alliance enrolls all eligible persons, including low-income and non-working persons, who reside in the geographic area it serves into a health plan that provides the comprehensive benefits.

Alliances hold an annual open enrollment period during which each individual and family participating in the alliance has the opportunity to choose among health plans offered through the alliance. Enrollments made during the annual open season become effective on a date established by law.

Alliances also provide a mechanism for promptly enrolling individuals and families who become eligible for coverage between open-enrollment periods. Individuals and families who move into the region served by an alliance notify the alliance within 30 days. If the individual is employed, the employer notifies the alliance. If the individual is not employed, he or she notifies the alliance.

Within 10 days of receiving notification that an eligible person has moved into its service area, regional alliances provide enrollment materials. Within 30 days of receiving enrollment materials, eligible individuals are responsible for choosing a health plan and applying to the alliance for enrollment.

An application for coverage submitted by the fifteenth day of any month becomes effective on the first day of the following month. An application made after the fifteenth of the month becomes effective on the first day of the second month following application.

Alliances establish a mechanism for enrolling individuals who have not chosen a health plan or purchased insurance when they seek health services. The point-of-service mechanism follows these guidelines:

• Within 10 days of enrollment at a point of service, the alliance provides an individual with materials describing health plans.

• If the individual does not choose a health plan within 30 days, the alliance assigns the individual to the lowest-cost plan available.

• Using the fee-for-service schedule adopted by the alliance, the health plan to which the patient is assigned reimburses the provider who brought the uninsured individual into the system for services rendered prior to enrollment.

Managing Access to Plans

In the event that more consumers apply to enroll in a particular health plan than its capacity allows, alliances develop a process of random selection for use in determining which new applicants may enroll. Consumers already enrolled in the plan continue their coverage without interruption.

Marketing

Alliances control direct marketing to consumers by health plans. Marketing rules include at least the following requirements:

• The alliance must approve marketing materials used by health plans.
• If a health plan uses direct marketing, it may not limit distribution to an area smaller than the geographic area it serves within the alliance.
• Health plans and their agents are prohibited from attempting to influence an individual's choice of plans in conjunction with the sale of any other insurance.

Information

Alliances publish (or otherwise make available to consumers) easily understood, useful information, including brochures, computerized information and interactive media, that allows them to make valid comparisons among health plans. The following information must be included:

- Cost to consumers, including premiums and average out-of-pocket expenses.
- Characteristics and availability of health care professionals and institutions participating in the plan.
- Any restrictions on access to providers and services.
- The annual Quality Performance Report, which contains measures of quality presented in a standard format.

Insurance Risk

An alliance may not bear insurance risk.

Relations with Plans

Each regional alliance negotiates with health plans to provide the comprehensive benefit package to all eligible persons in the alliance area through a choice of plans. Only health plans that enter into contracts with the appropriate regional or corporate alliance are authorized to provide the guaranteed benefit package.

Alliances contract with health plans on at least an annual basis but may enter into multi-year contracts. Multi-year contracts may not specify premium increases for future years in excess of the projected inflation factor for the alliance budget.

Contracting Requirements and Exclusion of Plans

Alliances write uniform contracts with health plans, including all certification requirements imposed by federal or state law. Alliances must offer a contract to each qualified health plan seeking to serve its area unless:

- The proposed premium exceeds the weighted-average premium within the alliance by more than 20 percent.
- The health plan's quality of service or care are unsatisfactory as determined by the state.
- The plan engages in practices that have the effect of discriminating against one or more classes of persons based on race, ethnicity, gender, income or health status.
- The plan fails to comply with contract requirements.
- The plan is a fee-for-service plan that is not a successful bidder. Through a competitive bidding process, an alliance may limit to three the number of plans that pay any willing provider on a fee-for-service basis and have no network of providers operating under a contract with the plan.

An alliance may decline to enter into a contract with a health plan if the health plan's proposed premium would cause the alliance to exceed its budget target.

Alliances may not discriminate against health plans or providers on the basis of race, gender, ethnicity, religion, mix of health professionals or organizational arrangement.

Areas with Inadequate Health Services

Alliances may use financial incentives to encourage health plans to expand into areas that have inadequate health services.

Alliances may organize health providers to create a new health plan targeted at such an area, providing assistance with setting up and administering the plan. An alliance may not assume risk on behalf of a new health plan but may arrange favorable financing to encourage a health plan to operate in an area with inadequate health services.

Risk Adjustment

Alliances use a risk-adjustment mechanism to account for variations in enrollment across health plans with respect to the health status and risk of participants and access to basic health services. (See section on Risk Adjustment.)

Fee-for-Service Plans

Each Alliance includes among its health plan offerings at least one plan organized around a fee-for-service system. A fee-for-service system is one in which patients have the option of consulting any health provider subject to reasonable requirements. Reasonable requirements may include utilization review and prior approval for certain services but do not include a requirement to seek approval through a gatekeeper.

Under certain conditions, with approval from the National Health Board, a state may waive the requirement for each alliance to offer a fee-for-service health plan if the alliance demonstrates that:

- A fee-for-service plan is not financially viable in the area.
- There is insufficient provider interest in participating in a fee-for-service plan.
- There is insufficient enrollment to sustain a fee-for-service plan.

Each alliance, after negotiations with providers, establishes a fee schedule for the fee-for-service component of health plans in that alliance. Each health plan uses the same schedule and must reimburse health providers under its fee-for-service option up to the level of the fee schedule. Providers may collectively negotiate the fee schedule with the alliance. A state may choose to adopt a state-wide fee schedule.

Balance Billing

A provider may not charge or collect from a patient a fee in excess of the fee schedule adopted by an alliance. A plan and its participants are not legally responsible for payment of any amount in excess of the allowable charge.

Prospective Budgeting of Fee-for-Service

States have the authority to impose prospective budgeting on fee-for-service plans offered through health alliances.

Under prospective budgeting:

• The alliance chooses or develops one fee-for-service plan as the designated plan for its service area. The alliance negotiates with health providers annually to develop a budget for the plan.
• The negotiated budget establishes spending targets for each sector of health expenditures.
• The fee-for-service plan periodically reviews service utilization and adjusts payments to providers to assure compliance with the negotiated budget.
• Provider groups may establish fee-for-service plans. A board composed of representatives of providers may manage fee-for-service plans, developing a utilization review system and other procedures to assure the financial viability of the plan.

Portability

Health plans pay for urgent care delivered outside the plan's service area. An eligible individual who intends to establish residence in an area for longer than six months registers with the local health alliance.

An eligible individual who establishes residence in an area for more than three months but less than six months may choose to:

• Continue coverage through the regional alliance and health plan in which he or she is enrolled, limiting the use of health care to emergency services and urgent care.
• Register with the alliance serving the temporary residence and choose a local health plan.

- Enroll in a health plan with a fee-for-service component that covers care provided outside the alliance service area.

Enforcement

The Department of Labor oversees the financial operations of the alliance. The Department of Labor conducts audits of management and financial systems, and may recommend to the National Board that remedial action is required.

8

Corporate Alliances and the Employment Retirement Income Security Act

---

THE FOLLOWING organizations and firms must either form corporate health alliances or join regional health alliances:

- Employers with more than 5,000 employees.
- Existing plans formed pursuant to collective bargaining with more than 5,000 covered employees, (or a group of plans within the same union structure) such as Taft-Hartley plans, although certain limitations apply to the ability of such plans to provide coverage to associate union members
- Plans formed by rural electric and telephone cooperatives with more than 5,000 covered employees.

The term employer is defined as it is under the ERISA statute.

The threshold of 5,000 employees is applied calculating the number of workers employed by firm nationally. The common control test defines whether separate trades or businesses are treated as a single employer.

Employers whose primary occupation is employee leasing are required to participate in regional health alliances regardless of the number of employees. Federal, state, local and special purpose units of governments are required to participate in regional alliances regardless of their size. The United States Postal Service may operate as a corporate alliance.

A firm or organization that is certified as a corporate alliance must discontinue as a corporate alliance if the number of full-time employees of the firm or the number of full-time employees covered by the organization falls below 4,800.

The Department of Labor regulates employers and determines whether a corporate alliance may continue to operate in the case of mergers, acquisitions and bankruptcies.

A state adopting a single payer approach may require all employers and individuals to participate in the single payer system.

Election to Form a Corporate Alliance

Large employers eligible to form corporate alliances elect to exercise that option or to purchase health coverage through a regional alliance.

During the implementation of the new health system a large employer has a one-time opportunity to enroll in regional alliances at community rates workers residing in regional alliances where less than 100 of the employer's workers reside.

Large employers periodically have the opportunity to switch to regional alliances, according to the following terms:

• The employer pays a risk-adjusted, weighted-average premium for a period of four years, after which the rates charged to that employer adjust to obtain a community rate over four years.

- The election applies to all employees of the employer, nationwide.
- Employers or establishments that join regional alliances must continue to purchase coverage through them.

Taft-Hartley Plans and Rural Cooperatives

The board of directors of an existing Taft-Hartley plan or rural cooperative elects whether to form a corporate alliance. If it elects not to form a corporate alliance, its member employers purchase health coverage through regional alliances like any other employer. These new rules regarding Taft-Hartley plans do not affect and are in addition to current rules governing the collective bargaining process.

If an employer that participates in a Taft-Hartley plan or rural cooperative leaves the arrangement, it purchases coverage through the regional alliance like any other employer.

Enrollment

Each corporate alliance offers all eligible persons health plans that provide the nationally guaranteed comprehensive benefits.

Corporate alliances hold annual open enrollment periods during which individuals and families choose among health plans. The open enrollment period for the corporate alliance coincides with the enrollment period for regional alliances.

Enrollment of Newly Eligible Persons

Corporate alliances provide a mechanism for promptly enrolling individuals and families who become eligible for coverage between open enrollment periods.

Over-Subscription in a Plan

A health plan may become over-subscribed, meaning that the plan does not have sufficient capacity to serve everyone who wants to enroll. When a plan is over-subscribed, existing members of the plan have preference to continue in the plan. In determining which new members join an over-subscribed plan, a corporate alliance uses a process of random selection.

Health Plans

Corporate alliances provide health benefits to eligible employees and dependents either through a certified self-funded employee benefit plan or through contracts with state-certified health plans.

Contracts between health plans and corporate alliances comply with the following requirements:

• Premium rates charged to the corporate alliance may be based on community rating, adjusted community rating or experience rating.

For corporate alliances composed of more than one employer, such as Taft-Hartley plans and rural electric or telephone cooperatives, premium rates charged to individual employers must be community rated.

• Health plans that contract with corporate alliances must accept all eligible employees and their dependents, regardless of individual characteristics, health status, anticipated need for health services, occupation, affiliation with any person or entity (except for affiliation with another alliance or health plan).

• Health plans may not terminate, restrict or limit coverage for the nationally guaranteed comprehensive benefit package.

— Exclusions for existing medical conditions and waiting periods or riders that exclude certain individuals are prohibited.

— Health plans may not cancel coverage for eligible employees and dependents until they enroll in another health plan.

Failure to Pay Premiums

If a corporate alliance fails to make premium payments to a health plan, the plan may terminate coverage after reasonable notice. If coverage is terminated, the corporate alliance is responsible for providing coverage to individuals previously insured under the contract.

A health plan that notifies a corporate alliance of its intention to terminate coverage also sends a copy of the notice to the Secretary of Labor.

Information

Corporate alliances assure that employees have ready access to comparative information about health plans. Information is obtained through a brochure published annually. At a minimum, the brochure must include the following information about health plans:

- Cost to consumers, including premiums and average out-of-pocket expenses.
- Characteristics and availability of health providers.
- Restrictions on access to providers and services.
- The annual Quality Performance Report for each health plan containing measures of quality presented in a standard format.

Corporate alliances are responsible for assuring that employees are aware of information they may obtain from participating plans.

Choice of Plans

Each corporate alliance contracts with at least one fee-for-service health plan. A corporate health plan has a fee-for-service component if a participant has the option of consulting any health provider, subject to reasonable plan requirements.

Reasonable plan requirements include utilization review and requirements to obtain approval for certain service before they are obtained but does not involve primary care physicians or networks acting as gate-keepers.

A corporate alliance may be excused from the requirement to offer a fee-for-service option in a geographic area in which the regional alliance obtains a waiver from the requirement.

In addition to a fee-for-service plan, a corporate alliance contracts with at least two other health plans offering the comprehensive benefits. A corporate alliance may be excused from this requirement if an insufficient number of state-certified plans exist in a particular geographic area, or if the plans are unwilling to contract with the corporate alliance.

Contracts with Health Plans

Corporate alliances contract with health plans on at least an annual basis but may enter into multi-year contracts.

Contracts include certification requirements outlined in federal and state law, as well as a statement regarding the maximum capacity the plan is willing to serve. A corporate alliance may set additional requirements for contracting health plans.

Risk Adjustment

A corporate alliance may, but is not required to, use a risk adjustment system to account for variations in enrollment among health plans with respect to risks and access to basic health services among participants.

Payments and Ratings

A corporate alliance makes direct payments to health plans.

A corporate alliance has the option of using any type of rating arrangement with health plans, including full or partial self-funding, prospective or retrospective experience rating, adjusted community rating, community rating by class, or community rating. In a Taft-Hartley plan or a rural cooperative, participating employers are charged on a community rated basis within the plan.

Employees covered in all corporate alliances pay a community rate for their portion of premiums, however.

Plan of Operation

Corporate alliances submit plans of operation to the Department of Labor. The Secretary of the Department of Labor determines whether the plan meets all statutory and regulatory requirements.

ERISA

The American Health Security Act amends the Employee Retirement Income Security Act of 1974 (ERISA) to create a new chapter governing employee health benefit plans and modifying the current ERISA preemption section.

Requirements Related to Employee Health Benefit Plans

A new chapter or title of ERISA establishes fiduciary and enforcement requirements for employers and others sponsoring health benefit plans in corporate alliances. Current provisions of ERISA do not apply to health benefits except by specific reference. Provisions address:

• Ensuring that everyone enrolled in corporate health alliances obtains coverage providing at least the nationally guaranteed benefit package

- Establishing fiduciary requirements for employers, plan sponsors and plan fiduciaries
- Setting requirements related to information and notification made available to employees
- Ensuring compliance with national standards with respect to uniform claims form, data reporting, electronic billing and other areas
- Applying grievance and benefit dispute procedures to self-funded health benefit plans
- Establishing financial reporting requirements for self-funded health benefit plans and for corporate alliances
- Setting financial reserve requirements for self-funded health benefit plans.

The new title or chapter also sets fiduciary requirements for employers in regional alliances governing the withholding of employee contributions from wages. The Department of Labor may enter into agreements with states to enforce these requirements.

Financial Reserve Requirements

New requirements for financial reserves apply to self-funded health plans. Self-funded health plans establish a trust fund that is maintained at a level equal to the estimated amount that the plan owes providers at any given time. The plan pays claims from the trust fund. Trust funds are protected by special status in bankruptcy proceedings if the sponsoring employer fails.

Reserve requirements may be met through letters of credit, bonds or other appropriate security rather than establishing the trust fund.

A new national guaranty fund for self-funded health plans provides financial protection for health providers in case of financial failure of a plan. The Department of Labor oversees the national guaranty fund; it operates in a manner similar to state insurance guaranty funds.

The Department of Labor may inspect the books and records of self-funded health plans and assume control over plans if they fail to meet reserve requirements. Health benefit plans notify the Department of Labor if they fail to meet requirements.

Preemption of State Laws

The ERISA preemption provision is modified to:

• Apply the preemption only with respect to employers and health benefit plans in corporate alliances.

• Permit taxes and assessments on employers or health benefit plans in corporate alliances if the assessments are nondiscriminatory in nature.

• Permit states to develop all-payer hospital rates or all-payer rate setting.

• States also may require all payers, including health benefit plans in corporate alliances, to reimburse essential community providers.

9

Health Plans

HEALTH PLANS provide coverage for the nationally guaran
teed comprehensive benefit package through contracts
with regional or corporate alliances. Only state-certified
health plans are allowed to provide health insurance and
benefits in regional alliances.

Enrollment

Health plans accept every eligible person enrolled by an
alliance without regard to individual characteristics,
health status, anticipated need for health care, occupation, affiliation with any person or entity (except affiliation with a corporate alliance or health plan).

Health plans may not terminate, restrict or limit
coverage for the comprehensive benefit package for any
reason, including non-payment of premiums. They may
not cancel coverage for any individual until that individual is enrolled in another health plan.

Health plans may not exclude participants because of
existing medical conditions or impose waiting periods
before coverage begins. Riders that serve to exclude certain illnesses or health conditions also are prohibited.

With the approval of the state, health plans may limit enrollment because of restrictions on the plan's capacity to deliver services or to maintain financial stability.

Community Rating

Health plans use community rating to determine premiums, establishing separate rates to reflect family status.

Beginning in August of each calendar year, alliances negotiate premium rates with each health plan contracting for coverage through that alliance. Negotiations set individual and family premiums for each health plan within the alliance. During an annual open enrollment period, alliances publish the negotiated rates for all health plans.

Employers and employees pay a community-rated premium. However, payments to health plans by alliances are adjusted to account for the level of risk associated with individuals enrolled in plans. The adjustment is made using a formula developed by the National Health Board.

Reinsurance

Health plans may purchase reinsurance to cover disproportionate costs beyond those predicted by risk adjustment formulas.

Information

Each health plan provides to the alliance and makes available to consumers and health care professionals information concerning:

- Costs
- Qualifications and availability of providers
- Procedures used to control utilization of services and expenditures
- Procedures for assuring and improving the quality of care
- Rights and responsibilities of consumers and patients.

Health plans are responsible for the accuracy of information submitted and may be disqualified from participating in an alliance if information is inaccurate.

In keeping with the overall goal of increased consumer knowledge about health care issues and choices, health plans are expected to encourage patients to participate in decisions about treatment options and to offer consumers up-to-date information regarding potential benefits, risks, and costs of various medical and surgical procedures.

Health plans in states that allow advance directives and surrogate decision making related to medical treatment are required to provide information about those legal options at the time of enrollment in the plan.

Grievance Procedure

Health plans offering coverage through both regional and corporate alliances are required to establish a benefit claims dispute procedure. The new health care system relies on the development of alternative dispute resolution procedures to reduce costs and increase the efficiency of the grievance process by setting specific deadlines for resolution and providing for early review of disputes by neutral third parties. If the grievance procedure fails to resolve a complaint, consumers have the option of pursuing the issue with the alliance ombudsman or pursuing other legal remedies.

The Department of Labor will ensure that both regional and corporate alliance health plans establish grievance procedures and monitor the performance of such procedures.

Health Plan Arrangements with Providers

Health plans enter into agreements with health care providers to deliver services. Not withstanding state laws to the contrary and except for services provided under a fee-for-service component, a health plan is authorized to:

- Limit the number and type of health care providers who participate in the health plan.
- Require participants to obtain health services other than emergency services from participating providers or from providers authorized by the health plan.
- Require participants to obtain a referral for treatment by a specialized physician or health institution.
- Establish different payment rates for participating health providers and providers outside the plan.
- Create incentives to encourage the use of participating providers.
- Use single-source suppliers for pharmacy, medical equipment and other health products and services.

In addition, state laws related to corporate practice of medicine and to provider ownership of health plans or other providers do not apply to arrangements between integrated health plans and their participating providers.

Health plans cover emergency and urgent care provided to members outside of its service area. Reimbursement is based on the fee-for-service rate schedule in the alliance where the services are provided.

During a transitional period, health plans must cover services provided to their members by designated essential community providers. Payments to essential providers are based on the Medicare method for community health centers.

A state has the authority to waive the obligation to reimburse essential community providers for a particular health plan operating in a particular area. To obtain a waiver, a health plan demonstrates that it has the capacity to deliver a comparable range and level of services to consumers in the area served by the essential community provider.

Health plans may not discriminate against providers on the basis of race, ethnicity, gender, religion, mix of health professionals or patient population.

Provider Participation in Plans

Each health plan in each regional alliance has an advisory board composed of providers participating in the health plan. The providers will select the membership of the advisory board.

The health plan consults frequently with the advisory board, and must respond to concerns raised by the advisory board. The advisory board has access, under rules established by the National Board, to health plan information that relates to the delivery of health care by that health plan.

Loans to Community-Based Health Plans

A loan program will be established in HHS to assist the development of community-based health plans. The program may provide direct loans to health plans or guarantee loans made by private financial institutions.

Additional Requirements for Plans

In addition to the requirements discussed above, health plans must meet national, uniform Conditions of Participation established by the National Health Board, including:

Fiscal soundness, including minimum standards for financial reserves, and disclosure of financial condition to all purchasers.

Truth in marketing, including standards for fair marketing practices and disclosure to consumers of all material information regarding the plan and its performance.

Verifying credentials of practitioners and facilities, including bi-annual checks of providers against national databases, investigating and resolving consumer complaints and dropping providers who consistently fail to meet quality standards or are responsible for fraud or mismanagement. Health plan must ensure that all practitioners and health institutions meet state licensing standards.

Consumer protection, including disclosure of all material information regarding the plan and their rights and responsibilities, providing due process for patients to appeal denial, termination or reduction of coverage and resolving appeals of complaints.

Confidentiality, including maintaining a policy for protecting patient privacy and confidentiality in compliance with law and allowing patients to obtain copies of their medical records upon request. (See Information Systems and Administrative Simplification.)

Complaints, including investigating and attempting to resolve complaints about practitioners, providers, treatments, access to care and health plan policies and procedures.

Disenrollment for cause, including permitting consumers to resign from health plans at any time for good cause.

Utilization management, including disclosure of protocols for controlling utilization and costs.
— Methods used to manage the network of providers, such as the selection criteria and internal performance standards.
— Compensation methods for providers, such as capitation;
— Incentives to providers to control utilization;
— Utilization review criteria—criteria by which health care services are determined to be inappropriate; and
— Protocols for managing the care of high-cost patients.

Data management and reporting, including maintaining encounter data and required quality data electronically and reporting the data to the national network. (See Information Systems and Administrative Simplification, and Quality Management and Improvement.)

SUPPLEMENTAL INSURANCE

Supplemental insurance to cover both cost sharing and additional health benefits is allowed.

A supplemental benefit policy may cover all or some portion of benefits not included in the comprehensive package, such as long-term rehabilitation services and cosmetic surgery. A policy covering cost sharing might pay a portion of co-payments and co-insurance required by a health plan.

Any entity that offers supplemental policies must abide by the rules for supplemental insurance. However, the following types of insurance policies are not subject to these rules:

- Long-term care insurance
- Insurance against specific diseases
- Hospital or nursing home indemnity insurance
- Medigap insurance
- Insurance against accidents.

Cost Sharing

The National Health Board develops two standard, supplemental cost-sharing policies. One model provides standard coverage; the other maximum coverage. Once developed, only the model policies may be offered, and every health plan that uses the high cost sharing model (described under Guaranteed National Benefit Package) is required to offer both.

Limitations on pre-existing medical conditions are prohibited, and supplemental policies must be available to every participant in a health plan at the same price. Policies may not exclude cost-sharing coverage for specific diseases or conditions.

Only qualified health plans with the high cost sharing option (see section on Guaranteed National Benefit Package) may offer supplemental insurance for cost sharing under the comprehensive benefit package. A member of a health plan may purchase supplemental insurance for cost sharing only during the annual enrollment period.

The price of any insurance policy covering cost sharing includes the cost of additional benefits plus any expected increase in utilization caused by the insurance.

No plan may sell coverage for cost sharing at a price that results in a loss-ratio less than 90 percent. (The loss ratio is the ratio of the premium returned to the consumer in payout relative to the total premium collected.)

The National Health Board develops rules for the coverage of cost sharing in corporate alliances. The rules may require that only one standard, supplemental policy is offered, or that no policy is offered if an employer already substantially covers cost-sharing.

Additional Benefits

No health plan, insurer, or any other person may offer anyone eligible for the guaranteed benefit package a supplemental insurance policy that duplicates coverage in the national benefit package.

Any health plan that sells duplicate coverage is disqualified from participating in alliances. Any firm or individual who offers such policies is subject to loss of the license to sell insurance.

No policy covering additional health services may fail to cover for a period longer than six months, limit or restrict coverage for any illness, disease, or other condition that existed prior to the purchase of the policy. All policies covering additional benefits must be offered at a single price to all individuals in an alliance.

Insurance policies providing coverage for additional benefits must be available to any purchaser, subject to the capacity and financial limits of the insurer. Coverage available only through membership in fraternal, religious, professional and other organizations and policies sold to employers to cover benefits for their employees are exceptions.

The National Health Board develops, in consultation with the states, minimum standards that prohibit marketing practices by insurance companies and agents that involve:

• Tying or otherwise conditioning the sale of supplemental insurance to the purchase of the comprehensive benefit package.

• Providing compensation to an agent selling supplemental benefits for promoting or otherwise encouraging the purchaser of supplemental benefits.

• Using or disclosing to any party information about the health status or claims experience of participants in the plan for the purpose of marketing supplemental benefits.

Risk Adjustment

ALLIANCES ADJUST premium payments to health plans to reflect the level of risk assumed for patients enrolled in comparison to the average population in the area. The adjustment mechanism takes into account factors such as age, gender, health status and services to disadvantaged populations.

Development of Federal Model System

Nine months before the date on which states first enroll consumers in regional alliances, the National Health Board promulgates a risk-adjustment system.

Regional alliances are required to use the risk-adjustment system unless an alliance obtains a waiver from the National Health Board. The Board provides technical assistance to states and alliances in implementing the federal system.

The federal system takes into account the following:

• Appropriate compensation for health plans that enroll individuals with higher or lower-than-average health costs.
• Variations in health costs and utilization such as demographic characteristics and health status.

- Factors that impede access to health care, such as geographic location, prevalence of poverty, language and cultural barriers.
- Factors related to the unique problems of mental illness.

The risk adjustment system uses prospective adjustment of payments to health plans and reinsurance to protect health plans that have a disproportionate share of high cost cases. Greater reliance may be placed on reinsurance in the first years, until a more sophisticated risk adjustment system is fully implemented.

Incentives to Enroll and Serve Disadvantaged Groups

Certain population groups face barriers to care due to their geographic location (rural or inner city), to poverty, or to other factors such as language or cultural differences. States may determine that financial incentives are needed to insure that health plans enroll disadvantaged groups and provide appropriate outreach services for them.

Advisory Committee

The National Health Board creates an advisory committee to provide technical advice and recommendations regarding the development of the risk-adjustment system. The advisory committee is composed of fifteen representatives of health plans, alliances, consumers, experts, employers and health providers. Once it is adopted, the committee makes recommendations for updating the risk-adjustment system.

The National Health Board may conduct research and undertake demonstration projects to support the development of the system.

Risk Adjustment System Required

States are required to assure that alliances use the federal risk-adjustment system.

A state that wishes to modify the system or substitute another risk-adjustment mechanism applies to the National Health Board. The Board grants a waiver if the alliance demonstrates that its proposed system is at least as effective and accurate as the model system.

Rural Communities in the New System

ECONOMIC AND demographic characteristics of many rural communities result in a larger number of uninsured and underinsured citizens in rural areas. Under the American Health Security Act, access to care is ensured for Americans who live in rural areas through:

- Alliance requirements to serve rural areas
- Investment in infrastructure
- Creation of incentives to expand rural community-based networks and plans
- Investments for the development of the health workforce
- Expansion of the rural public health system.

Guaranteed Universal Access

Alliances have the capacity to ensure adequate health services in rural areas by:

- Creating alliance-sponsored plans
- Fostering cooperative relationships among rural and urban providers
- Requiring urban health plans to serve rural areas in the alliance

- Developing an information and referral infrastructure to link academic health centers and rural health providers
- Offering long-term contracts to health plans serving rural areas.

Infrastructure Development During Transition

As described in the section on Public Health Service Access Initiatives, qualifying community-based organizations in rural areas have access to federal loan guarantees for capital improvements.

Rural Community-Based Networks and Plans

Federal funding and technical assistance become available to support local planning and development of primary care systems in areas with inadequate health services, such as rural areas. Grants support the development of telecommunications capacity to link rural providers with health care centers and institutions as well as continuing education and professional support. In addition, grants to Academic Health Centers assist in the development of an information and referral infrastructure to support rural health networks.

Workforce

The National Health Services Corps and related programs expand to reduce the shortage of health care providers in rural areas. Incentives are provided to attract and retain health professionals in rural areas.

Tax incentives encourage practice in rural areas. Incentives include:

• A non-refundable personal tax credit of $1,000 per month that can be recaptured during the first five years of practice by a physician in a rural area with a shortage of health professionals ($500 for physician assistants and nurse practitioners).

• The exclusion from gross income of National Health Service Corps Loan Repayments received under section 338B.

• An allowance of up to $10,000 annually (depreciation not required) for the purchase of medical equipment used in areas with a shortage of health professionals.

• Deductibility of up to $5,000 in annual student loan interest for physicians, physician assistants, advanced practice nurses and registered nurses performing services under agreements with rural communities.

The allocation of residency positions in new health care systems involves special attention to geographic factors.

Increased relative compensation for primary care physicians also encourages practice in rural areas. (See section on Creating a New Health Workforce.)

Public Health System

To assure access to health care in rural areas, supplemental services are provided for low-income populations. These services include: transportation, outreach, non-medical case management, translation, child care during clinic visits, health education, nutrition, social support and home visiting services. (See section on Public Health Initiatives.)

Workers' Compensation
Insurance and Automobile
Insurance

HEALTH PLANS provide treatment for individuals with work-related injuries covered under workers' compensation insurance.

Workers' compensation insurers (including self-funding employers) continue to be responsible for the costs of treatment based on current law and reimburse health plans for services provided. Reimbursement is based on a fee schedule or on an alternative arrangement established by alliances or negotiated between workers' compensation insurers and health plans.

To obtain state certification, a health plan demonstrates its ability to provide or arrange for comprehensive medical benefits for work related-injuries and illnesses, including rehabilitation and long-term care services.

• Health plans employ or enter into contracts with specialists in industrial medicine and occupational therapy.

• Health alliances are responsible for coordinating access to specialized health providers or centers of excellence in industrial medicine and occupational therapy.

• Alliances may designate as subcontractors health care professionals and institutions that provide specialized services for the treatment of work-related injuries and illnesses on behalf of all health plans serving the alliance region.

Individuals enrolled in health plans within the alliance receive treatment for work-related injuries or illnesses from their health plans, although emergency treatment may be obtained from any provider.

State laws regarding choice of provider for workers' compensation cases are overridden with respect to individuals covered through health alliances. Exceptions may be necessary in cases of disputes.

Each health plan designates a workers' compensation case manager to coordinate the treatment and rehabilitation of injured workers. The case manager ensures that:

• The plan of treatment for an injured worker meets appropriate protocols and is designed to assure rapid return to work.

• The plan of treatment is coordinated with the workers' compensation insurance carrier and/or the employer to facilitate rapid return to work.

• The health plan complies with medical and legal requirements related to workers' compensation.

• If the health plan is unable to provide a needed service to treat a work-related injury or illness, the workers' compensation case manager, in consultation with the workers' compensation carrier, refers the worker to an appropriate provider.

Health plans are reimbursed by workers' compensation insurance carriers or self-funded employers for work-related medical benefits in accordance to the fee-for-service schedule in the alliance.

• Alliance fee schedules include rehabilitation, long-term care and other services commonly used for the treatment of work-related injuries and illnesses.

• Alliances are permitted to adopt varying arrangements with health plans for providing work-related medical benefits, including negotiating per case capitation payments.

• Health plans are permitted to negotiate fees that vary from the fee-for-service rate schedule with workers' compensation insurers and employers.

Information related to provider and health plan performance in treating work-related injuries and illnesses (including the health plan performance in facilitating injured workers' returning to work) are included in reporting information about the quality of care provided by the health plan.

Nothing in this policy alters or diminishes the effects of state workers' compensation laws as the exclusive remedy for work-related injuries or illnesses. Disputes related to whether an injury or illness is work-related are resolved in accordance with existing state laws.

Health benefits for work-related injuries and illnesses continue to be defined by states. Health plans and providers are not allowed to balance bill patients with work-related injuries or illnesses for additional charges beyond those covered by the health plan. Workers will not be subject to requirements for co-payments and deductibles related to medical services as a result of workplace illness or injuries.

For regional alliances, the federal requirements related to workers' compensation become effective two years after implementation of the state health reform program. For corporate alliances and federal workers' compensation programs, the federal requirements become effective in 1998.

Compensation programs under FECA, the Jones Act and the Longshoreman's Act are subject to similar requirements.

A Commission on Health Benefit and Integration is created to study the feasibility and appropriateness of transferring the financial responsibility for all medical benefits (including those now covered under workers' compensation and automobile insurance) to the new health system. The Department of Labor and Department of Health and Human Services provide staff support to the Commission. The commission reports to the President and presents a detailed plan for integration, if it is recommended, on or before July 1, 1995.

The Department of Health and Human Services and the Department of Labor are authorized to conduct a demonstration program in one or more states related to treatment of work-related injuries and illnesses.

• The Department of Health and Human Services and the Department of Labor, in consultation with states and experts on work-related injuries and illnesses, develop protocols for the appropriate treatment of work-related conditions.

• The Department of Health and Human Services and the Department of Labor enter into contracts with one or more alliances to test the validity of protocols.

• The demonstration may include the development of per-case capitation payments to health plans for the treatment of work-related injuries and illnesses.

INTEGRATION OF AUTOMOBILE INSURANCE

Individuals receive treatment from health plans for injuries sustained in automobile accidents.

In cases in which an automobile insurance carrier is responsible for the costs of treatment (based on current law), the automobile insurer reimburses the health plan for services provided. Reimbursement is based on a fee schedule or on an alternative arrangement established by the alliance or negotiated between the automobile insurer and the health plan.

To obtain state certification, a health plan demonstrates its ability to provide or arrange for (through contracts with appropriate health care providers) medical benefits for automobile injuries.

• Health plans provide or arrange for the full range of services commonly reimbursed by automobile insurance carriers for the treatment of automobile injuries, including long-term rehabilitation and long-term care services.

• Health alliances may enter into contracts with centers of excellence or with certain specialists for the purpose of providing all health plans with access to providers of specialized treatments for automobile injuries.

Health providers may not bill patients injured in automobile accidents for charges in excess of payments made by health plans. Health plans may negotiate different fees with automobile insurance carriers.

For regional and corporate alliances, the federal requirement for automobile insurance is effective two years after the state health reform program is implemented.

13

Budget Development
and Enforcement

THE AMERICAN Health Security Act organizes the market for health care and creates mechanisms to control costs through enhanced competition, consumer choice, administrative simplification, and increased negotiating power through health alliances. A national health care budget serves as a backstop to that system of incentives and organized market power. The budget ensures that health care costs do not rise faster than other sectors of the economy.

The national health care budget centers on the weighted average premium for the nationally guaranteed benefits package in regional health alliances, establishing a target for how much that average premium may increase each year. The federal government assumes responsibility for enforcing alliance budgets.

Covered Expenditures

Health care expenditures covered by the budget include premiums paid to cover the guaranteed comprehensive benefit package whether paid by employers, employees, or individuals. Medicare and Medicaid expenditures are included under separate budgets.

Supplemental benefits beyond the comprehensive benefit package, as well as workers' compensation and auto insurance benefits, are not included in the budget. Premiums for insurance policies providing coverage for cost sharing are not included.

Annual Increases

Allowed increases in Medicare and Medicaid spending are described in the table called Growth Rate of Health Care Spending at the end of the plan. The growth in premiums in regional alliances is also limited through a national inflation factor. Regional alliance inflation factors are as follows:

- Projected increase in the Consumer Price Index (CPI) plus 1.5 percentage points for 1996
- Projected 1997 increase in the CPI plus 1.0 percentage points
- Projected increase in the CPI plus 0.5 percentage points in 1998
- Projected increase in the CPI for each year thereafter

Health expenditures for the guaranteed benefits package increase at these rates plus increases in population.

Projected inflation factors are detailed in the table called Growth Rate of Health Care Spending at the end of the plan.

The National Health Board adjusts the inflation factor for each alliance to reflect unusual changes in the demographic and socio-economic characteristics of the population covered by the alliance. The National Health Board develops a methodology for making such adjustments using commonly accepted actuarial principles. Demographic changes considered include, at a minimum, age and gender.

The Board consults with states and alliances prior to the establishment of the annual inflation factor.

National per Capita Baseline Target

The National Health Board calculates a national per capita premium target based on:

• Current per capita health expenditures for the guaranteed benefits package trended forward to 1996 based on projected increases in private sector health care spending.

• With adjustments for expected increases in utilization by the uninsured and under-insured and to recapture currently uncompensated care.

First Year Bidding and Negotiation Process

In the year prior to implementation, each alliance conducts a bidding and negotiation process with health plans. The Board provides alliances with information and technical assistance to aid in the bidding process. The bidding is conducted either by providing plans with the alliance's budget target prior to bidding, or by inviting blind bids followed by negotiations and re-bidding.

Once an alliance is satisfied with the negotiated health plan premiums, it submits them to the National

Health Board for review. The first-year bidding process occurs earlier than in subsequent years to allow time for a more thorough review by the National Health Board and possible re-negotiation of premiums.

National Board Review

The Board calculates for each alliance a per capita premium target, using the national per capita baseline target as a reference point. For each alliance, the Board adjusts the national target for current regional variations in health care spending and for rates of under-insurance and underinsurance. To measure regional variations in health care spending, the Board uses such factors as:

- Variations in premiums across states based on surveys and other data.
- Variations in per capita health spending by state, as measured by the Health Care Financing Administration.
- Variations across states in per capita spending under the Medicare program.
- Area rating factors commonly used by actuaries.

The Board establishes the premium targets for alliances so that the weighted average of the alliance targets equals the national per capita baseline target.

In states establishing regional alliances after 1996, alliance targets increase annually by the national inflation factor. Targets are not, however, enforced until alliances are formed.

The Board calculates an estimated weighted-average premium for each alliance, using the proposed premiums submitted by the alliance and a projection of the distribution of enrollment across plans. If the estimated weighted average premium for an alliance is greater than the alliance's premium target, then the Board notifies the alliance and allows it to renegotiate premiums. If an alliance chooses to re-negotiate premiums, it submits the revised premiums to the Board and proceeds with enrollment.

First Year Budget Enforcement

The Board calculates an estimated weighted-average premium based on the final bids submitted by the alliance. If the estimated weighted-average premium for the alliance exceeds the alliance's premium target, an assessment is imposed on each plan whose bid exceeds the target, and on the providers receiving payment from that plan. Revenues from assessments on plans are used to reduce required employer premium contributions. The assessment on the plan is equal to a portion of the percentage amount by which the alliance target is below the bid. The "portion" is calculated so that the weighted average of premiums after assessments equals the alliance's premium target. Payments to providers by that plan are assessed at the same percentage, with revenues from the assessment retained by the plan.

Establishing a Baseline Budget for Each Alliance

Following the first open enrollment period, the Board calculates for each alliance the weighted average premium, using actual premiums and enrollment figures.

The first year weighted average premium becomes the baseline per capita budget for the alliance.

In each subsequent year, an alliance's per capita budget equals its budget for the previous year, increased by the inflation factor.

Adjusting the Premium Inflation Factor

In general, as described above, the premium inflation factor is the increase in the Consumer Price Index. If, however, an alliance's actual weighted-average premium in a given year exceeds its premium target, then the inflation factor for that alliance is reduced for the following two years to recover excess spending.

Process for Making Adjustments in Targets over Time

The National Health Board appoints an advisory commission to recommend adjustments to the methodology for calculating premium targets. The Board provides states and alliances with information about regional differences in health care costs and practice patterns. The commission explores methods to reduce variations in budget targets across states due to differences in practice patterns, physician supply, population characteristics, and other appropriate factors. Adjustments to targets may not be made without Congressional action.

Enforcement of the Budget

The federal government is responsible for enforcing the health care budget. By October 1 of each year—

beginning in 1996—alliances submit to the National Health Board for approval their proposed health plan premiums.

Based on proposed premiums, the Board calculates the anticipated weighted average premium for each alliance. The anticipated weighted average premium is the average of the proposed premiums weighted by current enrollment in each plan, with special rules in cases of plans entering or leaving the alliance.

If an alliance's anticipated weighted-average premium exceeds its per capita budget target, an assessment is imposed on each plan whose premium increase (adjusted upward to reflect the previous year's assessment) exceeds the alliance's premium inflation factor. Revenues from assessments on plans are used to reduce required employer premium contributions. The same assessment is imposed on providers receiving payment from that plan. The assessment on the plan is equal to a portion of the difference between the plan's premium increase and the alliance's budget inflation factor (adjusted upward to reflect the previous year's assessment). The "portion" is calculated so that the weighted average of premiums after assessments equals the alliance's per capita budget target. Payments to providers by that plan are assessed at the same percentage, with revenue from the assessment retained by the plan.

Tools to Meet Premium Targets

In addition to creating a well-structured marketplace for health coverage, alliances have the ability to control costs through premium negotiations and the authority to refuse contracts with health plans whose premiums are too high. Tools available to states to contain costs include:

- Premium negotiation and regulation.
- Limiting enrollment in high-cost plans by:
  — Freezing new enrollment in high-cost plans.
  — Surcharging high-cost plans or paying rebates to consumers who enroll in low-cost plans.
- Setting rates for health providers.
- Controlling health care investments through planning.

Budgets for Corporate Alliances

A large employer may operate a corporate alliance rather than purchasing health coverage through a regional alliance, provided it complies with cost-containment goals. Large employers whose health plans do not meet national spending goals are required to purchase coverage through regional alliances.

The allowed rate of growth for corporate alliance premiums is the same as the national inflation factor for regional alliances.

The National Health Board develops a methodology for calculating an annual premium equivalent within a corporate alliance. Beginning after the third year of implementation of health reform, each corporate alliance annually reports its average premium equivalent for the previous three years to the Department of Labor.

If the increase in the premium equivalent exceeds the allowed rate of growth during two of any three years, the Department of Labor shall require the employer to purchase health coverage through a regional alliance. An employer may petition the Department of Labor for an adjustment in its inflation factor to compensate for unusual changes in the risk profile of its workforce.

14

Quality Management
and Improvement

HEALTH REFORM transforms the current prescriptive quality assurance program into a quality-management system focused on performance measures and continuous improvement.

Quality assurance programs in the current system rely on external checks, forms and process manuals. Insurance carriers, peer review organizations, state and federal inspection agencies audit the work being done in hospitals, doctors' offices and laboratories, and penalize the providers if they fail to follow rules. Patients play a minor role, lacking reliable information upon which to compare the quality of health plans, providers or treatments.

Under the American Health Security Act, customer-focused continuous improvement assures quality improvement.

National Quality Management Program

The National Quality Management Program develops the quality information and accountability program. An advisory council under the National Health Board, appointed by the President, oversees the program.

The council consists of fifteen members representative of the population, including representatives of consumer groups, health plans, states, purchasers of care and experts in public health and quality of care and related fields of health service research.

The National Quality Management Program:

• Develops the core set of quality and performance measures and consumer survey questions and updates them over time to reflect changing goals for quality improvement in health care.

• Conducts consumer surveys that measure access to care, use of health services, outcomes and satisfaction.

As part of that effort, the program develops sampling strategies to ensure that performance reports reflect populations difficult to reach with traditional consumer-sampling methods, including consumers who fail to enroll in a health plan or resign from plans.

• Sets national goals for performance on selected quality measures.

• Establishes minimal standards of access and quality for plans on selected measures.

• Supports research, technology assessment and development of reliable tools for measuring health outcomes.

• Evaluates the impact of health reform on the quality of care.

• Reports annually on performance of the health care system.

• Reviews and recommends changes to the quality measures annually and establishes a five-year priority list for measures to be included in the future.

• Uses the national network of regional centers to obtain quality management data. (See section on Information Systems and Administrative Simplification.)

Performance Reports

The National Quality Management Program under the National Health Board develops a core set of measures of performance that apply to all health plans, institutions and practitioners. It publishes annual performance reports outlining the results of those measures for each health plan, creating a public system of accountability for quality and providing consumers with meaningful information.

It also provides annual reports to the states on the comparative performance of health plans and state quality programs. Quality reports include information on the performance of alliances and health plans on as many as 50 measures of access to care, appropriateness of care, health outcomes, health promotion, disease prevention and satisfaction with care.

It provides the results of a smaller number of quality measures for health care institutions, doctors and other practitioners if the available information is statistically meaningful. State performance reports include trends, performance on national quality measures and on goals for national performance on access, appropriateness and health outcomes.

The following criteria determine the selection of national measures of quality performance:

• The measures reflect important aspects of care in terms of prevalence of illness, morbidity, mortality or cost.

- The set is representative of the range of services provided to consumers by the entities in question.
- Measures are reliable and valid and data needed for calculation can be obtained without undue burden.
- Performance on measures included in the set vary widely among the entities on the performance report.
- When the measures are rates of process of care, these processes are linked by strong scientific evidence to health outcomes.
- When the measures are outcomes of care, performance lies within the control of providers and adequate risk adjustment can be accomplished.
- The measures incorporate minimal standard for meeting public health objectives.

State Role

As part of the Quality Management Program, states assume responsibility to:

- Develop and implement plans to meet enrollment, access and quality standards established by the federal government.
- Assure that plans and providers meet essential national standards through licensure and certification procedures.
- Monitor the extent to which plans make the full range of benefits covered in the guaranteed package accessible to all population groups.
- Prepare comparative reports on the performance of alliances, plans, providers and practitioners.

- Establish in each alliance a premium check-off system at enrollment where an annual amount—up to $1 per participant—can be designated for the purpose of supporting a consumer advocacy program.
- Establish a program of technical assistance administered through either a non-profit foundation or another organization dedicated to that purpose.
  — Eligible organizations may include public-private partnerships, consortia led by academic medical centers or other forms.
  — Technical assistance may include a variety of activities such as: fostering collaboration among health plans and providers; disseminating information about successful quality-improvement programs, practice guidelines and research findings; and providing educational courses and other forums for providers to exchange information on the valuative sciences and quality improvement activities and providing information to encourage the adoption of employee participation committees and other high-performance work practices.
  — Technical assistance is targeted at improving quality management practices and not designed to regulate or interfere with the administration of plans and providers.
  — A per capita levy on insurance premiums, with the amount established by the National Health Board, funds the program.
  — Providers and health plans are not required to use technical assistance resources as a condition of participation in the new health care system, although health plans are accountable for improving performance on national quality measures.

Role of Alliances

As part of the quality management program, health alliances:

- Resolve consumer complaints, grievances and requests to leave a health plan.
- Disseminate to consumers information related to quality and access to aid in their selection of plans.
- Prepare comparative reports on the quality of health plans, providers and practitioners and assure through their negotiations with plans that performance and quality standards are met.
- Conduct education programs to assist consumers in using quality and other information in choosing health plans.

Role of Health Plans

As part of the Quality Management Program, health plans:

- Measure and disclose performance on quality measures.
- Report on, maintain and improve the quality of care delivered by providers and practitioners.
- Meet national, uniform Conditions of Participation established for health plans by the National Health Board. (See Health Plans.)

Developing Information for Quality Management

An electronic network of regional centers containing enrollment, financial and utilization data is created, as outlined in the section on Information Systems. Health plans, providers and alliances report information required for the national Quality Management Program through the regional network; information required includes data related to enrollment, clinical encounters, consumer satisfaction and specific quality measures.

Regional centers electronically link state-level quality programs, health alliances and plans, providing quality and utilization information for each health plan and provider as well as comparative information on other health plans and states. Regional centers audit samples of data to ensure integrity.

To supplement routinely collected information, health plans gather clinical data specified by the national Quality Management Program from samples of medical records. To assure coordination with other information-gathering activities, consumer satisfaction surveys are conducted as described in the section on Information Systems. Results from consumer surveys, in combination with other information, will gauge access to health care, use of service, outcomes and satisfaction.

Dissemination of Knowledge to Improve the Quality of Care

To enhance the practice of medicine and promulgate information about best practices and effective treatment approaches, the National Quality Management Program:

• Surveys statistically valid sample populations to gather information related to consumer satisfaction, access to care and health outcomes. Survey samples include representation of populations considered to be at risk for inadequate health care. The national quality program administers the survey; states may add quality measures of local interest.

• Develops practice guidelines that assist providers in achieving quality standards and underpin national measures of quality.

• Develops methodology standards for practice guidelines, an evaluation and voluntary certification process for guidelines developed by the private sector.

• Operates a clearinghouse and dissemination program for practice guidelines.

• Disseminates information documenting clinically ineffective procedures and treatments.

• Supports research on topics central to quality management and improvement, including outcomes research, dissemination methods, ways of measuring quality and design of electronic information systems and new ways of organizing work systems.

• Establishes scientific standards and procedures for evaluating the clinical appropriateness of protocols used to manage health service utilization.

• With the advice of the national quality advisory committee, defines priorities for health-care evaluation research and recommends projects. The priorities will target diagnoses with the highest level of uncertainty in treatment decisions, widest variation in practice patterns, significant costs and incidence.

Streamlining Regulatory Activities

Minimum Standards for Health Care Institutions. The National Quality Management Programs develops uniform standards for licensing of health care institutions that focus on essential performance requirements related to patient care. As they are developed, those standards replace current regulations except in areas of fire safety, sanitation and patient rights and without undermining recent reforms in nursing home care.

When the new standards are in place, agencies charged with certifying health institutions focus their attention on institutions with problematic records, responding to complaints and randomly selected validation sites.

By January 1, 1996, the National Quality Management Program completes demonstration projects for new performance standards and revises standards according to the findings. Demonstration projects evaluate the impact of these standards in assuring quality of care, reducing cost and burdens on providers.

Current standards are retained until new ones are tested, promulgated, evaluated and implemented. In the interim, government agencies responsible for licensing and certifying health care institutions coordinate inspections, reduce paperwork and control the number of inspections.

Medicare Peer Review Organizations. The peer review organization system under Medicare continues until the new quality system is implemented and the Secretary of the Department of Health and Human Services determines that Medicare enrollees are protected adequately through National Quality Management Program. PROs will end at that time.

During the interim, the PRO program is stream-lined. (See Information Systems and Administrative Simplification.)

The Clinical Laboratory Improvement Act. Regulations of clinical laboratory testing are refocused to emphasize quality protection while reducing administrative burdens.

Regulation will continue for labs that:

a. perform a comprehensive menu of tests; or

b. perform a large volume of tests (50,000 or greater); or

c. engage in critical testing (a test is critical if an answer is needed quickly or an error can result in serious harm to an individual); or

d. conduct testing to monitor care while it is being delivered.

• **Ease regulatory burden on laboratories performing simple tests.**

Exempt laboratories performing waived tests and microscopy from all requirements under CLIA, including registration and payment of fees to the DHHS. Approximately 79,000 labs will be exempted (under review).

Add more simple tests to the list of waivered tests.

In accordance with recommendations by the Clinical Laboratory Improvement Advisory Committee (CLIAC), the physician-performed microscopy category will be expanded to include those tests performed by midlevel health care providers (e.g. nurse practitioners, physician's assistants, nurse midwives, etc.).

• **Ease regulatory burden on laboratories performing moderate complexity tests.**

Create a new category of moderately complex tests that are performed using FDA-approved, highly reliable equipment that would be subject to less stringent inspection requirements.

By January 1, 1996, the Secretary of the DHHS issues a report on the extent to which regulation of laboratories performing moderate complexity tests should continue. Within six months, the Secretary determines, based on the report, where continued regulation for these laboratories is necessary.

• **Revise personnel standards to provide needed relief in urban and rural areas.**

In accordance with recommendations by the CLIAC, all individuals who are currently engaged in laboratory testing or supervision will be able to continue to perform such testing (in the absence of evidence of demonstrated poor performance).

To address the concerns of rural and underserved areas, the DHHS will modify personnel requirements for certain laboratory positions.

• **Focus proficiency testing primarily on education.**

DHHS will only take proficiency-related enforcement actions where a laboratory's performance is extremely poor or it has failed to take corrective action when proficiency testing problems are identified.

DHHS will work with Congressional committees to develop a modified approach to cytology proficiency testing.

- **Streamline inspections.**

DHHS will target on-site inspections at high-volume, high-risk labs, and they will be announced (under review).

- **Expand information and education activities.**

To eliminate confusion and misinformation with respect to CLIA requirements, DHHS will work with professional groups to expand activities in information and education.

Information Systems and Administrative Simplification

TIMELY AND RELIABLE information represents a critical element in efforts to reform the health care system and to protect and improve the health of the nation.

Health care reform establishes a new framework for health information. Using standard forms, uniform health data sets, electronic networks and national standards for electronic data transmission, the information framework supports:

• The development of clear and useful information for consumers.
• Measurement of health status.
• Monitoring and evaluation of the health care system.
• Issuance of Health Security Cards.
• Development of links among health care records to improve patient care.
• Analysis of patterns of health care.
• Streamlined and simplified administration with associated cost savings.
• Identification of fraudulent activities.

The new information system features:

- Strong privacy, confidentiality and security protection.
- The formation of partnerships between the public and private sectors.
- National standards for clinical and administrative data.
- Appropriate links to the National Information Infrastructure programs.
- Electronic network to ensure the timely availability of reliable information.

Data and Information Framework

Every American receives a national health security card to assure access to needed health services throughout the United States. Much like ATM cards, the health security card allows access to information about health coverage through an integrated national network. The card itself contains a minimal amount of information.

The National Health Board, in consultation with state and private entities and other relevant organizations, develops and implements uniform national standards for administrative, clinical, financial and other health care related information. Standards include:

- Uniform minimum health data sets with standard data items and definitions.
- Electronic data interchange standards for transfer of information.

A comprehensive health care information privacy framework is established based on federal legislation, applicable to all states, alliances, health plans and providers. Provisions include mechanisms for management and oversight of privacy and security. Principles of the framework include:

- Uniform privacy and confidentiality rights with special emphasis on protection of highly sensitive data.
- Appropriate security measures and technology.
- Enforcement mechanisms and penalties.
- Coordination with policies established under the National Information Infrastructure.
- Creation of a national privacy panel focusing on privacy protection as applied to health care information (see discussion below).

The Board establishes national, unique identifier numbers for plans, providers and patients, selecting an identification number system at the conclusion of a process that include public hearings and formal notice and comment procedures.

Information Systems

Health plans implement and maintain core discrete electronic documentation of all clinical encounters with health providers using current information system technology as the foundation for the system. Encounter records are captured, retained and transmitted as a byproduct of the routine provision of care.

- Records may be based on insurance claims or clinical encounters (depending on the type of health delivery system).
- The record may be plan- or community-based, or shared among several plans.

• Encounter records conform to the uniform minimum administrative and clinical data sets developed by the board and transmitted as appropriate to the national network (see discussion below).

• Emphasis is placed on the goal of electronic records and electronic data interchange with associated economic efficiencies. A phase-in period, with incentives, is planned to achieve this goal. During the phase-in period, standard forms may be used.

• Current information systems technology readily supports the capture, retention and electronic data interchange of encounter records as a byproduct of the provision of care and with favorable benefit cost efficiencies.

• Development of regional encounter data systems in this fashion will also support analysis of utilization and treatment patterns, as well as quality and outcome monitoring and research as a basis for improving health care.

Within this framework, plans are encouraged to make innovations:

• It is not the intent of health care reform to mandate explicit approaches to this requirement. Rather, flexible, local solutions to local needs and conditions will be fostered. Within the broad framework of national uniform standards, health plans and alliances are free to collect data and patient-care information according to their own local needs and conditions.

• This requirement does not call for implementation of a costly, full-scale computerized patient record. It calls for using today's technology to provide information to providers.

- The framework promotes the formation of community-based health information systems that improve the quality of care and reduce cost by minimizing duplicate procedures, tests and adverse drug interactions.
- Plans, providers, states and health alliances receive federal technical assistance to enable timely conformance with these requirements and to select cost effective technical solutions.
- Federal assistance is focused on long-term goal of developing a Point-of-Service system.

A Point-of-Service Information System

The long-term strategy for health care information envisions creation of a Point-of-Service information system that brings valuable information to consumers, health providers, payers and policy makers. The envisioned system offers significant potential for more effective, continuing quality improvement. In such a system, clinical, administrative and payment data move electronically among employers, health plans, physicians' offices, hospitals, laboratories, pharmacies and other providers. The system:

- Collects information as a by-product of the delivery of care.
- Protects the privacy, confidentiality and security of information.
- Provides ready access to information for appropriate uses.

The national system will evolve from information systems established by health plans, alliances and regional centers. Accelerating its development requires additional funding from the federal government to support technology development and regional demonstration projects in health plans, communities, alliances and federal health centers.

Federal, State, Alliance and Health Plan Data Network

An electronic network of regional centers containing enrollment, financial, and utilization data is created. The network receives standardized enrollment, encounter, and related data from plans for aggregation, analysis and feedback to plans, alliances, states and the Federal Government. The network will be pilot-tested before full-scale implementation.

- The network supports analytic needs, such as monitoring of budgets, measuring access and state accountability, assessing quality, among states, health plans, health alliances and the federal government.
- States and alliances could operate their own regional centers and serve the switch function as part of the national network.
- Federal funds will assist in financing the network, which is built in collaboration with private sector, state and existing federal programs.
- Required data is entered once and is a by-product of routine administration and provision of care by health plans and alliances.

• Health plans maintain uniform electronic records of encounters or claims.

• Plans transmit encounter data, in the form of a uniform minimum data set, to the network on a regular basis. The uniform encounter data set is designed to meet a variety of data needs.

• The network records national enrollment information. Health alliances and plans maintain detailed local enrollment files and submit at least a portion of those files to the network on a regular basis.

Creation of the network does not inhibit plans and health and health alliances from being innovative in meeting the information needs discussed above.

Consumer Surveys and Public Health Surveillance

Consumer surveys of satisfaction, access to care and related measures are conducted on a plan-by-plan and state-by-state basis. The National Health Board approves a nationally standard design for the survey.

Surveys will monitor the implementation of health care reform and assess its impact on the general population, potentially vulnerable populations, states and the health care system. The integration of survey data with administrative and public health data systems provides better measures of health status, risk factors and performance measures for consumers to use in choosing health plans.

Certain public health surveillance and data systems will continue to be needed to monitor the health status of the population and to identify and address emerging threats to the public health. Public health data systems, involving the federal government, states, and local governments are strengthened and more closely integrated within the overall information systems framework.

Governance

A National Health Data Advisory Council is established. The Council, reports to the Board and oversees the information and data activities, including standard setting and privacy protection, of the federal government under health care reform. Membership includes consumers, users and providers of data developed by plans, alliances, states, public-health agencies and the federal government.

Administrative Simplification

The National Health Board enters into contracts for the development and implementation of:

- Standard forms to record enrollment, clinical encounters and insurance reimbursement.
- Automation of insurance transactions and industry-wide adoption of standard forms.
- Simplified coordination of benefits.
- The creation of "standard and unique" identification numbers for all health care providers, health plans, employers and enrolled consumers.
- Steps to streamline the administration of the Medicare program.

Standard Forms

After consultation with providers, plans, employer groups, and others, standard forms for insurance reimbursement, health plan enrollment and to record clinical encounters are adopted. Standard information requirements include coding, content and data elements.

By January 1, 1995, all health plans adopt a single, standard form for reimbursement according to the following classes of providers:

- The UB-92 for institutional providers
- The Standard Health Insurance Claim Form (similar to the HCFA-1500) for all non-institutional providers except pharmacies and dentists
- HCFA-1500 for dentists
- The Universal Drug Claim Form developed by the National Council on Prescription Drug Programs for pharmacies that seek reimbursement.

The standard claim form serves the secondary purpose of collecting information required for state monitoring, accountability and the measurement of quality outcomes.

All health plans and employers also adopt a national, standard enrollment form. In conjunction with standard claim reimbursement and encounter information, enrollment data is used for monitoring accountability and performance.

Insurance Transactions

The National Health Board oversees the development of standards for the automation of insurance transactions, including claims payments and status reports, remittance advice, eligibility, coordination of benefits and utilization management.

Standard coding and content requirements eliminate multiple, conflicting requirements on health providers for information, formats and definitions.

The National Health Board identifies and consolidates existing standards in the health care industry, working from prototypes developed by the American National Standards Institute.

The Board reviews standards in consultation with groups such as the Workgroup for Electronic Data Interchange, the American National Standards Institute, the National Institute of Standards and Technology.

Within one year of enactment, the National Health Board designates national standards that providers, plans, alliances and employers adopt as a condition of participation in the health system. The Board establishes requirements related to content, definitions and a strategy for implementation no less than six months before the requirement for standardized transactions takes effect.

All government health programs, including the Department of Defense, CHAMPUS, Department of Veterans Affairs, Medicare and Medicaid adopt national standards immediately. All private payers, including purchasers of health insurance through regional and corporate alliances, adopt national standards for electronic transactions after January 1, 1995.

Major public and private payers, hospitals, major employers and corporate alliances, as well as clinics and group practices of twenty or more professionals automate the core transaction set within six months of adoption. States may deny payments to plans that have not automated transactions by that date.

To speed implementation, the National Health Board provides technical assistance to health alliances and plans.

Unique Identification Numbers

The National Health Board undertakes a process to determine, adopt and enforce unique identification numbers for consumers in health plans.

Streamlining Medicare

The Medicare program participates in the implementation of standard forms, uniform billing, electronic claims submission, remittance notices, coordination of benefits, unique identification numbers and streamlining of utilization review as required under health reform.

In addition, the Medicare program consolidates current roster of 80 insurance companies that act as contractors; it contracts separately for different functions (e.g., claims processing using a common system across contractors, provider profiling, provider relations, audit, fraud and abuse prevention).

Medicare eliminates extra billing for Part B providers such as durable medical equipment providers, orthotic and prosthetic suppliers and ambulances. The program simplifies its claims processes by:

• Deleting information related to Medicare as a secondary payer from claim form and incorporating into national eligibility file.

The Department of Health and Human Services develops and mandate model coordination of benefit rules immediately for Medicare, workers' compensation, auto insurance and other non-alliance health coverage.

Additional coordination of benefits reforms occurs when the national enrollment file is developed and operational (January 1, 1996). After the enrollment file is operational, insurers are required to forward coordination of benefits claims to appropriate insurers, through the enrollment file if necessary.

• Deleting Medigap reporting requirement from the claim form; supplemental insurance becomes part of the national eligibility file.

The Health Care Financing Administration also:

• Gives physicians presumptive waivers from collecting or filing for beneficiary cost sharing in cases where the cost sharing would pose a financial hardship on the beneficiary or in cases of professional courtesy.

• Incorporates evaluations from physicians and their representatives into annual performance evaluations of carriers, expanding the current five-state pilot project nationally.

• Eliminates complexities caused by dual funding sources and rules for Medicare Part A and Part B claims.

Efforts already underway by HCFA eliminate some complexities. In 1996, the Health Care Financing Administration begins to implement national, standard, integrated claims processing system for all Medicare claims, with the goal of full implementation by 1998.

- Streamlines the process for settling cost reports, working through the Medicare-Technical Advisory Group on Hospital Administrative Issues.
- Eliminates the requirement for physicians to sign an acknowledgement of awareness of penalties associated with falsifying claims information on an annual basis and replaces with a single acknowledgement when granted hospital privileges.
- Eliminates pre-billing requirement for attestation by physician of diagnoses and major procedures performed in the hospital.
- Simplifies the "Important Letter to Medicare Patients" in consultation with the Medicare-Technical Advisory Group.
- Repeals legislation requiring review of at least ten surgical procedures.
- Improves upkeep of data in "Common Working File."
- Limits system changes for Medicare and Medicaid programs to once every six months and notifies health care providers 120 days in advance of any major change in billing procedures.
- Consistent with the 4th Scope of Work, the PRO program will continue to move toward analysis and improvement of patterns of health care and outcomes, and away from individual case review, as appropriate.

The National Health Board explores developing standards for a single annual inspection of health care institutions to replace multiple inspections performed by federal, state, local and private accreditation, survey and certification agencies.

16

Protection of Privacy

To ASSURE the protection of privacy, security and confidentiality in the new health care system, the federal government undertakes to:

• Establish national privacy safeguards covering all health records, based on a Code of Fair Information Practices, including
— Uniform and comprehensive privacy and confidentiality protection for individually identifiable health care information. A uniform national standard simplifies compliance for organizations that operate nationwide and provide protection for data that are linked or potentially linked to other data systems.
— Protection for all types of health care information:
• Whether it is part of the new health care system or exists outside it.
• With the same level of protection for all illnesses and diseases.
• Regardless of the form in which records are kept (paper, microfilm or electronic), location (storage, transit, archive), owner, user or repository (government, health provider, private organization).

• Establish effective mechanisms for enforcement, including significant penalties for breach of legal requirements.

• Establish a national privacy framework is founded on a Code of Fair Information Practices stipulating, for example, that individuals who are the subject of data collected:

— Have the right to know about and approve the uses to which the data are put.

— Are assured that no secret data systems are permitted to exist.

— Have the right to review and correct data about themselves.

— Have adequate assurance that data may be collected and used only for legitimate purposes.

• Establish a system of universal identifiers for the health care system:

— A unique individual identifier for participants in health plans. The unique identifier may be the Social Security Number or a newly created number limited to the health care system. (See discussion of selection under Information Systems and Administrative Simplification.)

— In either case, the national privacy policy explicitly forbids the linking of health care and other information through the identification number.

• Issue effective security standards and guidance for health care information.

Currently, no uniform, comprehensive privacy standards related to health care information exist.

The National Health Board develops and periodically revises health care information security standards with active participation by other relevant federal agencies (e.g., Department of Health and Human Services, Department of Defense, Department of Veterans Affairs, National Highway Traffic Safety Administration, Consumer Product Safety Commission, and National Institute of Standards and Technology in the Department of Commerce).

• Establish a Data Protection and Security Panel under its direction. The panel oversees and manages privacy and security by, for example:

— Setting privacy and security standards through interpretive rules and guidelines.

— Monitoring and evaluating the implementation of standards set by statute, regulations and guidelines.

— Sponsoring or conducting research, studies and investigations.

— Supporting the development of fair and comprehensible consent forms governing the disclosure and redisclosure of information to authorized persons, for authorized purposes, at authorized times.

— Developing the technology for implementing security standards and sharing information in the health care setting.

— Working with health care providers to foster development of security practices.

• Establish an education and awareness program to train personnel with access to health care information as well as to inform consumers of their rights with respect to the collection and disclosure of personal information.

17

Creating a New
Health Workforce

ENSURING QUALITY health care and access for all Americans requires adjustments to the focus of investments in health care training and education in the following areas:

• Shifting the balance in the graduate training of physicians from specialties to primary care.
• Increasing investments in the training of nurse practitioners and physician assistants.
• Recruiting and supporting the education of health professionals from population groups under-represented in the field.
• Supporting workforce planning for health professions at the state level.
• Adjusting Medicare payment formulas to increase reimbursement for primary care.

Development and Support
for Graduate Medical Education

Legislative authority establishes a new system to manage the supply of specialty training for physicians, encompassing several initiatives:

Managing the number of post-graduate training positions for physicians. After a five-year phase-in period, at least 50 percent of new physicians are trained in primary care rather than in the specific specialty fields in which an excess supply currently exists. Primary care includes family medicine, general internal medicine and general pediatrics.

To achieve the goal of bringing primary care and specialty training into balance, the number of filled primary care residency positions increases by approximately 7 percent each year over the five-year period. During the same period, the number of filled specialty training positions in specialties in which excess supply exists decline by approximately 10 percent each year.

The total number of first-year residency positions available continues to exceed the number of graduates of U.S. medical and schools in the new system. The new system also encourages the location and focus of physician training to more closely reflect community medical practice.

Determination of approved residency positions. The Secretary of the Department of Health and Human Services determines the number of training positions in each specialty acting on the recommendations of the National Council on Graduate Medical Education and allocated to regional councils. Regional councils distribute positions to individual residency programs within each area of the country.

The Secretary appoints the National Council on Graduate Medical Education, which includes medical educators, practicing physicians, consumers, hospital administrators, nurses and others.

The Council recommends the total number of training positions for each medical specialty, based on the national need for new physicians in specific specialties. The national Council apportions residency positions to regions taking into account:

• Current regional distribution and quality of training programs.
• The need to maintain access to a range of primary care and specialty training positions for members of under-represented minority groups.
• Other factors relating to specific specialties and training programs.

In developing its recommendations, the Council seeks the views of professional medical, hospital and educational associations and other appropriate organizations. Positions are allocated for each post-graduate year to account for differences among specialties in the point of training when residents enter specialty training. For example, family medicine training begins in the first year of post-graduate training, while training in internal medicine specialties begins in the fourth year.

Because the integrity and success of the Graduate Medical Education system depends on commitment to it by all programs and training institutions, programs operating in institutions that continue training slots not covered in the allocation under the Graduate Medical Education system become ineligible for GME funding.

Allocation of residency positions. The Secretary of the Department of Health and Human Services appoints ten regional councils to allocate training slots among individual residency training programs.

Regional councils include representatives of academic institutions training physicians in the region, as well as representatives of regional health alliances and health plans, consumers and others.

Regional councils receive applications from training institutions in each area for residency positions in each specialty. Positions are allocated to accredited residency programs based on such factors as:

- Program quality.
- Relevance of the training program curricula to the future practice of physicians.
- Participation of under-represented minority groups.
- Participation of locally coordinated education programs.

The Secretary of the Department of Health and Human Services reviews regional council decisions and retains the right to amend allocations for good cause. To ensure continuity, allocations to programs are available for periods of up to three years and are made at least one year in advance of the residency training year.

Funding for residency training. Funds to support graduate medical education are pooled from all insurers to reflect the benefits that all patients and health plans receive from graduate medical education and training. Residency programs receive funds for each approved training position. Payments are based on a formula which considers the national average for resident salaries and the costs of faculty supervision and other related teaching expenses.

Funds from two sources are pooled (estimated at $6 billion for FY 1994):

• Medicare contributes to the direct medical education fund based on the percentage of hospital bed days its patients use (38 percent in 1992).
• Other payers contribute through a surcharge on health plan premiums.

Currently, Medicare pays explicitly for graduate medical education, based on historic costs. In FY-1992, Medicare payments for Graduate Medical Education totalled $1.5 billion. (Other payers currently support Graduate Medical Education implicitly through elevated hospital charges.)

Allocation of payments. Funding is provided directly to training programs approved for residency training positions, encouraging the development of non-hospital based training, particularly programs that provide a greater portion of their training in ambulatory and primary-care settings, such as health maintenance organizations and community clinics.

Transition payments. Transition payments are provided to teaching hospitals which are required to reduce their residency training programs. Hospitals receive transition payments to offset a portion of the costs associated with hiring replacement staff and maintaining services.

Payments phase out over a five-year period, beginning at the rate of 150 percent of the national average for direct medical education payments for an equivalent position under the new payment system. Payments decline by 25 percent each year.

Loan Forgiveness Program for Primary Care

A national "loan forgiveness" program for medical students is established to encourage physicians to devote their first years of practice to primary care.

Retraining Physicians in Primary Care

In order to further expand the availability of primary care physicians, support is provided for the development of programs to retrain mid-career specialists to serve as primary care physicians. Areas to be explored include the use of incentives, the type and length of effective retraining programs and the development of certification criteria.

Community-Based Training of Primary Care Physicians

Health reform supports community-based undergraduate and graduate medical training, continuing education and faculty development in primary care, broadening the impact of existing public support, which is limited to programs at the pre-doctoral and residency levels in family medicine and general internal medicine and general pediatrics.

Support for Training of Minorities and Disadvantaged Persons

To increase the diversity of the health care workforce, support is provided to programs that increase the number of health professionals among racial minority groups and disadvantaged persons. The goal of these programs is to double the level of underrepresented minorities enrolled in the first year of medical school to a level of 3,000 students by the year 2000.

Strategies include:

• Continuing financial assistance for under-represented minorities and disadvantaged students entering health professions training programs.

• Increasing support for recruitment and retention of under-represented minority and disadvantaged students in medicine, dentistry, nursing, public health and other health professions.

• Maintaining efforts to foster interest in health careers among under-represented minorities at the pre-professional and professional levels.

• Supporting programs to increase the number of minority faculty in the health professions, minority health services researchers and minority basic scientists.

Training for Nurse Practitioners, Nurse Midwives and Physician Assistants

Expanded training. Current funding for training of nurse practitioners and physician assistants will be amended to

• Increase current funding levels to double the number of graduates produced annually, giving priority to the expansion of existing programs, and

• Establish long-term goals and a funding strategy to maintain the supply of practitioners.

A similar program is implemented to support nurse midwives.

Barriers to practice. To remove inappropriate barriers to practice, the Secretary of the Department of Health and Human Services develops and encourages the adoption of model professional practice statutes for advanced practice nurses and physician assistants.

Rural Health Provider Grants

A rural health provider grant program supports a wide range of activities, including new community training programs for rural practitioners, the development of rurally oriented health education curricula, and the improvement of medical communications technology.

Priority Projects

A health professions special projects and demonstration training authority is established to support the transition to the new health system, including support for the following new projects:

• Training of providers in mental health, substance abuse treatment and prevention, geriatrics, and developmental disabilities.

• Training for school-based health providers in immunization, reduction of substance abuse, dealing with teen pregnancy, control of violence, and linking students and families with the community health system.

• Students in baccalaureate-level nurse training programs preparing for careers in teaching, community health service, and specialized clinical care.

- Training related to managed care, cost-effective practice management, continuous quality improvement practices, and provision of culturally sensitive care.
- Training of lower-level administrative and clerical workers in the health care field for higher-wage, higher-skill positions as technicians, nurses and physician assistants.
- Demonstration programs to develop more open occupational career ladders in health care institutions.

Programs also support Priority Health Training Programs designed to improve the supply, distribution, and quality of providers, including those in areas with inadequate health systems, especially rural areas and inner-city areas.

Support expands for:

- Service-linked regional educational networks; e.g., AHECs, geriatric education centers
- Health administration, public health training positions, special projects and preventive medicine
- Professional nurse clinician and nurse anesthetist training positions and nursing special projects

Primary care loans are provided for students in nursing and targeted allied health professions; e.g., occupational health and physician therapy.

Federal support for development of information related to the health care workforce expands, including research on primary care training practices in such areas as: relationship between education and practice patterns, effective use of practitioners and development of skills to meet future needs in health care.

INCENTIVES FOR PHYSICIANS TO PROVIDE PRIMARY CARE

In addition to refocusing federal support for physician education to focus on primary care, the Medicare programs increases its rates of reimbursement for primary care physicians.

Rate Increases

Reduce rates for office consultations to equal office visits and use savings to increase fees for all office visits: Office consultations are reduced to the same level as other office visits. The relative values for office consultations are redistributed to office visits without increasing total spending.

Because office consultations currently pay more than office visits, the change has the effect of increasing fees for office visits. Because primary care physicians perform consultations less often than sub-specialists perform them, it increases payments for primary care without increasing Medicare spending.

Increase the relative value of allowances for office visits to reflect time spent before and after visits. Currently, the relative values for procedures, including medical visits, account for physician time spent immediately prior to an office visit for preparation and immediately after an office visit for chart work, patient instructions, etc. Increasing the work component under primary care services by 10 percent increases spending for those services; the increase is offset by reducing relative values for all non-primary care services.

Establish a resource-based method to pay for the physician overhead component of the physician fee-schedule. The Secretary develops a methodology and data sets for implementing a resource-based system for determining practice expense relative value units for each physician's service. In addition, primary care practice expense RVUs increase 10 percent.

The current physician-fee schedule includes a work component that accounts for the physician's activities and a practice expense component that accounts for overhead (other than malpractice). The work component is based on resources used; the practice expense component is based on historic charges.

Because primary care services occur more often in office settings, actual overhead costs are higher than for surgical services. Under the current system, surgical services are assigned a higher overhead fee than primary care services. Collecting data on actual overhead costs and developing an allocation method for assigning overhead to individual procedures increases the relative value primary care services and decreases it for many non-primary care services.

Provide a higher expenditure target rate of growth for the separate primary care services target. Increasing the target for primary care services to GDP per capita plus 5 percentage points for FY-1995 decreases the target for other services.

Bonus payments. The 10 percent bonus payment for non-primary care services in urban Health Professional Shortage Areas will be eliminated. This will increase the bonus payment to 20 percent for primary care services in rural and urban HPSA's.

Reduce outlier intensity procedures. Reducing the work component of services with "outlier intensity" values allows the application of savings to increase the work component of the relative value of primary care services.

18

Academic Health Centers

THE AMERICAN Health Security Act creates a national pool of funds to support costs associated with the institutional costs of research, development of new medical technology, treatment of rare and unusually severe illnesses and provision of specialized patient care.

Medicare payments and a surcharge on private health insurance premiums flow into the pool (estimated at $6 billion for FY 1994). Funds are allocated to academic health centers and affiliated teaching hospitals through a fixed percentage added to hospital payments.

Academic health centers, including affiliated teaching hospitals, receive a new, separate payment as reimbursement for costs incurred over and above the cost of routine patient care. Only institutional costs not covered by typical fees for patient care, and which can be analytically justified, are included in the formula.

This approach represents a revision of the current Medicare indirect medical education payment formula to factor in the impact of universal health insurance coverage. The revised system reduces Medicare payments to teaching hospitals for the cost of caring for uninsured patients and disproportionate share of low-income patients because such payments will no longer be required once universal coverage exists.

In Fiscal Year 1992, Medicare Indirect Medical Education payments totalled $3.6 billion, including the cost of bad debts, charity care and other costs not related to medical education. As these costs decline, Medicare IME costs are reduced accordingly, and Medicare payments reflect the program's proportionate share of the total remaining costs. All private payers also contribute explicitly to the national fund on a proportionate basis.

Financing Clinical Research

The American Health Security Act expands investment in clinical investigations and research related to the delivery of health services and outcomes. Health plans also are required to provide coverage for routine patient care associated with approved clinical trials. (See Guaranteed National Benefit Package.)

Ensuring Access to Academic Health Centers

To ensure that all patients receive the specialized services available through academic health centers when appropriate (see Health Care Access Initiatives):

• The Department of Health and Human Services, in cooperation with states and health alliances, identifies rare diseases, specialized procedures and treatments for which health plans are required to establish contractual relationships with academic health centers.

• Health alliances monitor contractual relationships between health plans and academic health centers to assure appropriate coverage for severity of illness and to prevent anti-competitive pricing.

• Health alliances oversee quality management and patient grievance mechanisms to ensure appropriate detection, referral, morbidity and mortality of illnesses eligible for referral and specialized treatment.

• Health alliances provide health professionals and consumers with information regarding potential eligibility for clinical trials of relevant investigational treatments.

Ensuring Rural and Urban Access to Academic Health Centers

To secure appropriate access to academic health centers for patients in rural and urban areas with inadequate health care systems:

• Grants to academic health centers assist in the development of an information and referral infrastructure to support rural health networks.

• Grants to establish health-care networks in inner-city areas build on existing urban charity hospitals and affiliated neighborhood clinics.

• Health alliances institute additional protection to ensure access by rural and urban underserved populations to special services.

19

Health Research Initiatives

THE AMERICAN Health Security Act encourages cost-conscious choices on the part of consumers and health care providers through explicit financial incentives. At the same time, expanded investments in health research represent integral features of cost control and quality goals under health reform. The assessment of costs and effectiveness of new procedures and technologies will be increased through expanded funding and refocusing of clinical trials on more common conditions, high cost procedures, and highly variable treatment patterns.

Advances in medical science, development of new medications and technology, as well as innovations in the organization and delivery of personal and public health services hold the promise of increased efficiency in the health care system, longevity and improved quality of life.

New funding for health research focuses on two areas:

• **Prevention research** related to biomedical and behavioral aspects of health promotion and prevention of disease.

• **Health services research** related to the development of quality and outcome measures, access and financing and cost effectiveness, as well as research related to consumer choice and decision making, primary care and evaluation of health reform.

Priority Areas for Prevention Research

The National Institutes of Health expands prevention research in priority areas including:

• Child health, including perinatal health, birth defects and diseases of childhood, unintentional injuries, learning and cognitive development, and adolescent health.

• Chronic and recurrent illnesses, including research on Alzheimer's disease, cancer, cardiovascular diseases, bone and joint diseases, and other chronic diseases and conditions.

• Reproductive health, including contraceptive development and use, sexually transmitted diseases, adolescent pregnancy, and pregnancy-related complications.

• Mental health, including research in the area of mental disorders in children and adolescents, child abuse and neglect, women's mental health, mental disorders in the elderly and their caregivers, severe mental disorders, and violence.

• Substance abuse, including targeted research related to vulnerable populations, such as high-risk youth, the development of medications and prevention of dependence on tobacco, alcohol, and drugs.

• Infectious diseases, focusing on new and emerging infectious diseases, vaccine development and basic vaccine research, as well as infectious diseases including:

— HIV infection and AIDS—Research on behavior, vaccines, transmission of HIV, and prevention of disease progression to AIDS.

— Tuberculosis—Research on new vaccines to prevent TB, early diagnosis, and preventing disease progression.

- Health and Wellness Promotion including:
  — Nutrition—Includes defining optimal diets, dietary links to disease, and obesity.
  — Physical activity—Includes an emphasis on fitness for all ages, and fitness and aging.
  — Environmental health—Includes an emphasis on identifying health hazards and their effects, and disorder-specific research.
- Prevention research and infrastructure resource development including basic science development providing foundations for prevention efforts across a range of diseases and disorders, encompassing behavioral and social approaches, and genetics.
- Resource development including support for prevention research training and enhancement of statistical and epidemiologic techniques.

Coordination and Funding of Prevention Research

The National Institutes of Health distributes funds using three mechanisms: grants, contracts, and NIH intramural research.

The NIH Associate Director for Prevention coordinates the prevention research programs of the national research institutes and will report annually to the NIH Director and the Secretary on the status and progress of prevention research activities.

In consultation with the national research institutes, the NIH Associate Director will develop an ongoing plan for prevention research activities conducted by the NIH.

Prevention research findings are translated into, or appropriately integrated with, personal health services and public health programs to maximize the impact of prevention research on disease reduction and improved health status.

Priority Areas for Health Services Research

This research provides the knowledge to increase the cost effectiveness, appropriateness and quality of care in a reformed health care system. The health services research program includes research designed to improve the effectiveness and appropriateness of clinical practice through several interrelated activities, including:

- Effectiveness research
- Quality and outcomes research
- Development and dissemination of clinical practice guidelines
- Research and evaluation related to administrative simplification under health care reform
- Research on consumer choice and information resources
- Evaluation of health care reform
- Workplace injury and illness prevention research and demonstration programs

A new generation of health services research intended to answer critical questions on the effectiveness of treatments for common clinical conditions is initiated. Patient-outcomes research and the development of clinical practice guidelines form a central part of the health services research agenda.

Examples of specific areas of health services research:

- Effectiveness research which examines the appropriateness and effectiveness of alternative strategies for the prevention, diagnosis, treatment, and management of clinical conditions, in terms of patient outcomes. The Medical Treatment Effectiveness Program research focuses on conditions that meet one of more of the following criteria:
  — Large number of individuals are affected.
  — Uncertainty or controversy regarding effectiveness of treatment exists.
  — Associated risks and/or costs of treatment are high.
- Patient outcomes research teams (PORTs) are five-year grants that include elements of formal literature synthesis, data acquisition and analysis, development of clinical recommendations, dissemination of findings, and evaluation of the effects of findings on change in clinical practice.
- The development of clinical practice guidelines improves the quality, appropriateness, and effectiveness of health care. The guidelines also represent standards of quality, performance measures, and medical review criteria through which health care providers may assess or review the provision of health care. Guidelines assist in the determination of how diseases, disorders, and other health conditions can most effectively and appropriately be prevented, diagnosed, treated, and managed clinically.
- Research and evaluation regarding computerized medical records and information systems simplifies the administration of health care.
- Studies assess the impact of barriers to access, utilization, and continuity of health care services on health care reform.

• Research and analytic work contributes to efforts to devise, implement, maintain, and evaluate the new system of health care budgets, at the national, state and alliance levels.

• Expanded research into risk adjustment facilitates efficient measurement of health care needs.

• Long-term care research and demonstrations focused on new program models expand the range of financing and administration for those services.

• Research into service organization and structure include examination of the relationship of continuity, accessibility, and comprehensiveness of primary care to cost, quality, and access.

Evaluation of Health Care Reform

The introduction of comprehensive health reform affects every aspect of American health care. To support implementation of the American Health Security Act, evaluation research includes:

• Short-term research—Evaluate the responsiveness of the system to health care reform, including its effects on institutions, health care professionals, and specific population groups.

• Long-term monitoring—Examine the effect of reforms on cost, quality and access. Longitudinal studies using databases developed through the augmentation of national and regional surveys and analyses of secondary data are needed.

• Demonstrations and evaluations—Address critical issues in health care reform, such as quality assurance and medical liability.

Consumer Choice and Decision-Making Research

Research aimed at improving information resources that enable purchasers to make health care choices based on their relative value and quality assumes top priority. This research contributes to improved decision making by consumers, resulting in more cost-effective service delivery and health plan selection. Prospective research efforts include:

- Consumer awareness of benefit plans, availability of supplemental coverage, cost-sharing, and utilization.
- Effect of consumer knowledge on the selection of health plans including the relationship between health status and choice of plan.
- Types of information and form of media most effective in assisting consumers in selecting health plans and providers, including information on costs and quality of care.
- Impact of improved information on consumer satisfaction, access to care, quality of care and cost of services.
- Patient choice and decision making related to treatment alternatives.

Coordination of Health Services Research

The Agency for Health Care Policy and Research in the Public Health Service and the Office for Research and Demonstrations in the Health Care Financing Administration assume administrative responsibility for research related to the impact of health care reform. Research activities are conducted through intramural and extramural programs using the mechanisms of grants, contracts, and cooperative agreements.

20

Public Health Initiatives

THE PUBLIC health system and the reformed health care delivery system share a common purpose: to improve the health of the American population at an affordable cost.

While health reform strengthens the personal care delivery system, an enhanced public health system also plays an essential role to:

• Protect Americans against preventable, communicable diseases, exposure to toxic environmental pollutants, harmful products and poor quality health care.
• Identify and control outbreaks of infectious disease and patterns of chronic disease and injury.
• Inform and educate consumers and health care providers about their roles in preventing and controlling disease and the appropriate use of medical services.
• Define and validate new prevention and control interventions.

The public health initiative builds on the capability of health alliances and plans to reach out to their participants, providing them with information about prevention and appropriate use of medical services. The initiative promotes readiness and flexibility in the public health system by strengthening core functions at the local, state, and federal level. It also focuses attention on specific health problems of regional and national significance to consolidate categorical programs into an integrated health system, reducing administrative burdens.

The public health initiative repairs, strengthens and consolidates essential federal, state and local public health functions through three approaches:

• Improving the performance of the core functions of public health.

• Authorizing a flexible pool of resources to address priority health problems of regional and national significance.

• Expanding federal support for unified data systems, technical assistance and information networks.

Because dealing effectively with public health problems requires the coordinated involvement of multiple parties, the initiative is designed to foster inter-agency collaboration and public-private partnerships, including close working relationships between public health, community groups, alliances, and plans.

Core Public Health Functions

Health reform clears the way for the emphasis of public health activities to shift away from the direct delivery of health services. It positions public health to maintain a strong defense against preventable diseases and conditions that affect local communities and to work with the health delivery system to address them. The following essential functions are supported:

- **Health-related data collection, surveillance, and outcomes monitoring.** The basic tool for the health care system as a whole, providing for regular collection and analysis of information on key dimensions to ensure timely awareness, decisions, and interventions related to epidemics, emerging patterns of disease and injury, prevalence of risks to health, and outcomes of personal health services.
- **Protection of environment, housing, food, and water.** Enforcement functions related to air pollution (including indoor air), exposure to high lead levels, water contamination, handling and preparation of food, sewage and solid waste disposal, radiation exposure, radon exposure, noise levels and abatement, consumer protection and safety.
- **Investigation and control of diseases and injuries.** Identification, containment and provision of appropriate emergency and treatment resources for community-wide health problems, including emergency preparedness and control of violence.
- **Public information and education.** The mobilization of communities and motivation of individuals to reduce risks to health, such as tobacco use, abuse of alcohol and other drugs, sexual activity that increases vulnerability to HIV infection and sexually transmitted diseases, inadequate nutrition, physical inactivity, and childhood immunization.
- **Accountability and quality assurance.** Enforcement functions to ensure that providers, clinics,

hospitals, long-term care facilities, laboratories, and allied health providers meet established standards through licensure, certification, and inspection.

• **Laboratory services.** The provision of individual testing and pathology services, including the system of state laboratories that screen for metabolic diseases in newborns, provide toxicology assessments of blood lead levels and other environmental toxins, diagnose sexually transmitted disease and tuberculosis requiring partner notification, test for cholera and other infections or food-borne diseases, and monitor the safety of water and food supplies.

• **Training and education.** Ensuring adequate training with special emphasis on public health professionals such as epidemiologists, biostatisticians, health educators, public health administrators, sanitarians, and laboratorians.

• **Leadership, policy development, and administration.** Public health's responsibility to define health goals, standards, and policies that affect the health of whole communities; to define health issues of major importance and devise interventions to address them; to build coalitions with related public sectors such as housing, public transportation, and agriculture; and to ensure accountability for public resources devoted to health. Public health coordinates closely with the leadership of alliances and plans, mobilizing community support for public health policies and initiatives.

Funds are distributed to states using a formula based on three weighted factors that take into account population (one-third), poverty rate (one-third), and years of productive life lost (one-third). No state receives an allocation less than the State's grant in the last year preceding enactment of this initiative. To receive funds under the formula, states are required to maintain their current level of support for public health and prevention activities at no less than the average of the past two years' funding level.

Funds are used to develop and strengthen public health core functions at the state and local level, including county, district and municipality levels. Accountability for effective use of state formula grant funds are monitored through reporting progress in achieving health improvements using a common data set of health outcomes developed as a part of the *Healthy People 2000* initiative.

Priority Health Problems of Regional and National Significance

Additional funds support a federal program to develop innovative strategies for addressing priority health needs of regional and national significance. The purpose of this program is to address specific issues in ways that are responsive to the needs of populations served by alliances and plans and that consolidate rather than proliferate authorities, management structures, and funding and reporting requirements.

Congress establishes some priorities for funding through dedicated appropriations. The Secretary of the Department of Health and Human Services identifies other areas of priorities relying on recommendations of a national advisory board representing the perspective of the Public Health Service, states and local public health agencies, as well as regional health alliances and plans.

The Secretary solicits proposals for innovative interventions that link public health agencies and the delivery system to achieve measurable reductions in the incidence of illness and injury. Grants are made through competitive awards to state and local government agencies, not-for-profit organizations and research institutions. As effective interventions from these projects are identified, information is disseminated to facilitate their adoption in other communities.

The following are examples of the types of regional and national priority health issues to be addressed:

- **Infectious diseases**

Immunization. Education and outreach to ensure the broadest possible immunization coverage against childhood vaccine-preventable infectious diseases, as well as influenza, pneumonia, hepatitis B, and tetanus among adults.

HIV/AIDS. Education for prevention, confidential screening programs, and partner notification programs particularly in urban areas with special focus on minorities, women, children, and adolescents.

Tuberculosis. Case location, targeted education, and training for providers regarding treatment and control measures, with special attention to its spread among homeless people.

- **Chronic and environmentally related diseases**

Diabetes. Community-oriented diabetes education and control programs, directed especially to minority and low-income populations at highest risk, appear to offer economies of scale to complement individually provided medical services.

Violence and injury control. The leading cause of years of potential life lost among Americans and the leading cause of death among children, adolescents, and young adults, this category requires close collaboration among several systems, including law enforcement, education, transportation, and recreation and parks. It is linked to alcohol misuse and requires an integrated multi-faceted set of interventions.

- **Health-related behavior and other priority issues**

Tobacco prevention. The increasing incidence of smoking among adolescents and women poses future risks for heart disease and cancer, as well as low-birth-weight babies and infant morbidity.

Comprehensive school health. Furthering development of links between health and education in a nascent program of comprehensive school health program.

Maternal, child health, and family planning. With continued special attention is needed to provide education and outreach to prevent infant mortality and morbidity. In addition, the persistent and intractable incidence of adolescent and unwanted pregnancy calls for targeted education and outreach in support of family planning services. Closely linked to social services, interventions include targeted public education, programs of home visiting, case management for children with special needs, and child and spouse abuse services.

Enhancement of Federal Capacity to Support Public Health

In support of federal assistance for core public health functions and categorical activities, additional funds improve direct federal capacity, including:

• **Federal surveillance and health statistics, laboratories, and epidemiologic services.** Whether fighting the "old" diseases such as tuberculosis and cholera or "newer" ones such as Lyme disease or antimicrobial-resistant infections, public health's basic tools are data collection and biostatistical analysis, laboratory capacity, and epidemiologic expertise. An effective and efficient central capacity at the Federal level provides for economies of scale in addressing many of these health problems.

An essential part of reinventing public health is the consolidation of currently fragmented public health data systems and the integration of these systems with the regional and national data network described in the Information Systems chapter. The need for separate public health data systems is minimized to the extent that the elements included in the regional and national data network support public health functions. The unified health information system provides timely information to support health policy development, budget formation, efficient program administration and general improvement of the public's health and does so at the lowest cost and burden.

• **Technical assistance and national health information networks.** To support the refocus of public health at local, State, and Federal levels and the application of findings from priority health programs described above, technical assistance and information networks are needed to link Federal, State, and local public health agencies and various grant-supported programs carried out by State, local, and not-for-profit agencies. Information from these networks and the health data system provide the basis for regular reports to the President and the Congress for purposes of monitoring the effectiveness of this initiative.

21

Long-Term Care

A NEW LONG-TERM care program, created through Title XV of the Social Security Act, encompasses five components:

- Expanded home and community-based services.
- Improvements in Medicaid coverage for institutional care.
- Standards to improve the quality and reliability of private long-term care insurance and tax incentives to encourage people to buy it.
- Tax incentives that help individuals with disabilities to work.
- A demonstration study intended to pave the way toward greater integration of acute and long-term care.

Home and Community-Based Services

The American Health Security Act increases federal authority to provide home and community based services to individuals with severe disabilities without regard to income or age.

The expanded home and community-based service program is a federal/state partnership. The federal government provides most of the funding. The state contribution is set roughly equal to current state Medicaid and some state-only spending on the severely disabled. When fully implemented, federal funding is capped based on the estimated cost of serving the eligible population.

The Home and Community Based Services program supplements other coverage for care. It does not reimburse for services to which the individual is entitled under the nationally guaranteed, comprehensive benefit package, Medicare or private insurance.

Each state submits for federal approval a plan outlining the implementation of expanded home and community-based services.

Eligibility. The Secretary of the Department of Health and Human Services issues regulations establishing uniform eligibility criteria, which states implement using a standard instrument developed by the Department. To be eligible, an individual meets one of the following conditions:

• Requires personal assistance, stand-by assistance, supervision or cues to perform three or more of the following five activities of daily living (ADLs): eating, dressing, bathing, toileting and transferring in and out of bed.

• Presents evidence of severe cognitive or mental impairment as indicated by a specified score on a standard mental status protocol developed by the Secretary of the Department of Health and Human Services or

— A score specified by the Secretary on the standard mental status protocol described above, as well as evidence of the need for constant supervision because the applicant poses a significant danger to self or others, has multiple and significant behavior problems, or is unable to administer prescribed medications, or

• Has severe or profound mental retardation as indicated by a score of 36 or less on a standard intelligence test.

• For children under the age of six, is dependent on technology and otherwise requires hospital or institutional care.

Benefits. At a minimum, States provide to each eligible individual a standardized assessment and an individualized plan of care. Personal assistance services are available throughout all states for every category of eligible participant. Personal assistance services are defined as "assistance (including supervision, standby assistance, and cuing) with activities of daily living." Both agency-administered and consumer-directed personal assistance services are available. Consumer-directed services are those provided by individuals who are hired, trained and managed by the person receiving the services.

States have the flexibility to design and define their community based services system and to provide any other community based long-term care service including: case management, homemaker and chore assistance, home modifications, respite services, assistive technology, adult day services, habilitation and rehabilitation, supported employment and home health services not otherwise covered under Medicare, private insurance or through the basic health plan. Room and board are not covered services.

Services other than those listed above may also be covered; they may be delivered in a person's own home, a range of community residential arrangements, or outside the home, except in licensed nursing homes or intermediate care facilities for the mentally retarded (ICFs/MR).

States may also elect to offer vouchers or cash directly to eligible individuals or to capitate benefits to health plans or other providers.

Consumer choice regarding services and providers is honored by states to the extent possible.

Co-insurance. Eligible individuals pay co-insurance to cover a portion of the cost of all services they receive according to a sliding scale. Income may be adjusted downward to take medical expenditures into account.

- Individuals with incomes between 150 and 249 percent of the federal poverty standard contribute 10 percent of the cost of services; between 250 and 399 percent of the federal poverty standard they contribute 25 percent, and over 400 percent of the federal poverty standard individuals pay 40 percent of service cost.

- States have the option of imposing nominal cost sharing on individuals with incomes below 150 percent of the federal poverty standard.

- Co-insurance is calculated based on the amount paid by the program. Providers must accept the combined program reimbursement and co-insurance as payment in full.

State Administration. To implement the program, the state plan:

- Designates an agency or agencies to administer the program.

- Specifies benefit and payment policies.
- Defines services included in the state program in addition to personal care/personal assistance and any limits on those services.
- Specifies how the state determines eligibility, develops care plans (including responding to consumer choice), allocates resources, coordinates services (including how case management will be used in the program and for whom), administers co-insurance requirements, reimburses providers, administers voucher/cash payments (including compliance with applicable Social Security and unemployment insurance laws), ensures quality (including safeguarding the health and safety of consumers), defines (as applicable) licensure or certification requirements for provider agencies, obtains consumer input in services monitoring (including measuring consumer satisfaction with services).
- Specifies how states will comply with federal requirements for claims processing and information to be specified by the Secretary of HHS.
- Describes how the program will be managed and resources allocated during the phase in.

States hold public hearings on the community services plan to solicit input from individuals in the state with disabilities and their representatives. The state plan reflects input from these hearings.

Administrative Costs. The costs of administering the program (including the eligibility determination process and care planning) are included under the national budget ceiling. The Secretary of HHS defines administrative costs and specifies limits on the proportion of expenditures that may be used for such costs.

Funding. The Department of Health and Human Services allocates funds for the program to the states.

The Department of Health and Human Services establishes a national budget for home and community based services. States may claim federal matching funds up to maximum budgeted amount, which is based on the average estimated cost of serving individuals eligible for the program when the program is fully implemented.

The maximum budgeted amount (or national expenditure ceiling) increases annually consistent with the rate of increase allowed in the national budget for health care and changes in the number of people over the age of 75. The Secretary determines a formula to allocate funds to the states based on:

- Estimated number of individuals with severe disabilities.
- Age and gender distribution in the population.
- Prevalence of poverty.
- Average wage for individuals in service occupations in the state.

Federal Matching Rates. The Secretary of the Department of Health and Human Services determines federal matching rates for allowable costs according to a formula that reflects the total estimated cost of fully funding the program for the eligible population minus the amount spent by states under Medicaid and state only programs on community long term care services for the eligible population.

The federal matching rate is approximately 30 points higher than the current Medicaid FMAP rate, but is in no case lower than 75 percent or higher than 95 percent.

States are prohibited from using other federal dollars to match the federal share under the new program. Current restrictions under Medicaid on use of donations and taxes apply.

Funding phases in beginning in fiscal year 1996. In that year, states receive 20 percent of their allocation under the national budget, 40 percent in FY-1997, 60 percent in FY-1998, 80 percent in FY-1999 and 100 percent in FY-2000. Minimum benefit requirements do not take effect until the program is fully implemented. States specify how they will phase in the program; however, income cannot be used as a criteria for allocating resources during the phase in.

Treatment of Medicaid Community Long-Term Care

The new program of community-based services for people with severe disabilities is available to *all* people, regardless of income—including low income people previously served under the Medicaid program. Some people now receiving Medicaid community LTC services, however, do not meet the functional eligibility requirements of the new program. To avoid reductions in service for this population, current Medicaid programs for those who do not meet the eligibility criteria of the new program are replaced with a new community-based LTC program for low income people.

The Medicaid community LTC services which are combined into the new low income program are: personal care, home and community based waiver services, frail elderly, Community Supported Living Arrangements, the long term care portions of Medicaid home health, targeted case management, clinic services and rehabilitation services.

Eligibility. States must continue to serve all individuals currently receiving Medicaid community LTC services. Beyond current recipients, states set functional eligibility standards for the low income program and use the same intake and assessment process that is used for the new program for people with severe disabilities. States set financial eligibility at a point that is no lower than Supplemental Security Income (SSI) eligibility and no higher than the federal poverty standard or the State Supplemental Payment level, whichever is higher.

• States set resources limits, but they cannot be lower than $2,000 or exceed $12,000 per individual.

• States have the option to apply asset transfer prohibitions.

Benefits. Eligible individuals are assessed and receive a plan of care. There is no further entitlement to community services. States define the services to be included in their program and can incorporate at their discretion any community long term care services previously funded under Medicaid.

State Administration. To implement the program, states develop a state plan which is a component of the state plan for the new LTC program for people with severe disabilities, addressing:

• the definition of functional and financial eligibility requirements.

• the designation of an agency or agencies to administer the program and clarification of how the low income program will be integrated with the new program for people with severe disabilities.

• specification of the benefit and payment policies and definition of services.

• specification of how the state develops care plans, allocates resources, coordinates services and assures quality.

States may distribute grants through medical vendor payments to providers, through vouchers or cash payments to individuals, or through capitated payments to providers such as HMOs.

Funding. Funding for the low income program is based on each state's FY 1993 Medicaid expenditures. Until full implementation, this amount increases according to HHS projections of the growth rate that, if Medicaid had been left unchanged, would have occurred in Medicaid community-based LTC expenditures on behalf of low income people who are disabled but do not qualify for the new LTC program for people with severe disabilities.

At full implementation, expenditures under the low income program are pooled with the funds for the new LTC program for people with severe disabilities and are subject to the national budget ceiling.

Administrative Costs. Administrative costs for the low income component of the program are treated in the same manner in which they are treated under the new LTC program.

Match Rates. The current Medicaid FMAP rate applies to all expenditures for eligible individuals served in the low income program.

Maintenance of Effort. In the combined program, states must continue to serve at least the same number of low income individuals as they served in their FY 1993 Medicaid community LTC program.

Optional Combined Cap for Community and Institutional LTC

At state option, states may combine into a single capped program the new community LTC program expenditures, former Medicaid community funding, *and* Medicaid institutional expenditures for any or all categories of recipients of LTC, and create a new, separate program.

If a state elects to operate this new combined capped community/institutional LTC program, the state has increased flexibility to set financial or functional eligibility standards.

The Secretary of HHS will specify in regulation the formula for developing the cap for this program, and the formula for growth rates in the cap.

Improvements to Medicaid Coverage for Institutional Care

The American Health Security Act amends Title XIX of the Social Security Act to provide the following improvements in coverage for institutional care under Medicaid:

- States establish a medically needy program for all residents of a nursing home or an intermediate care facility for the mentally retarded.

• States permit residents of nursing homes and intermediate care facilities for the mentally retarded to retain $100 per month as a living allowance.

That amount is excluded from calculation of an individual's obligation to spend down private assets to qualify for Medicaid coverage.

• States allow single residents of nursing homes and intermediate care facilities for the mentally retarded to retain up to $12,000 in personal assets in determining eligibility for Medicaid coverage.

Regulation of and Tax Incentives for Private Long-Term Care Insurance

A long-term care insurance policy is any insurance policy, rider, or certificate advertised, marketed, offered, or designed to provide coverage for not less than twelve consecutive months for each covered person on an expense incurred, indemnity, prepaid, or other basis for diagnostic, preventive therapeutic, rehabilitative, maintenance, or personal care services provided in a setting other than an acute-care hospital.

Long-term care insurance policies include:

• Group and individual annuities and life insurance policies, riders or certificates that provide directly or indirectly, or that supplement long-term care insurance.

• Policies, riders or certificates that pay benefits based on cognitive impairment or loss of functional capacity.

Long-term care insurance excludes any insurance policy, rider or certificate that primarily offer supplemental coverage for Medicare, hospital expenses, medical and surgical expenses, hospital confinement indemnity coverage, major medical expense coverage, disability income or related asset protection, accident coverage, coverage in the case of specified diseases or specified accidents, or limited health insurance coverage.

The definition of long-term care insurance also excludes life insurance policies that provide accelerated payment of benefits and a lump-sum payment and in which neither the benefits nor eligibility are based on the need for long-term care services or the standard eligibility triggers.

Any other product advertised, marketed, or offered as a long-term care insurance policy, rider, or certificate is considered a long-term care insurance policy subject to these limitations.

Consumer Education. The federal government establishes a grant program to states and organizations for fiscal year 1996–98, providing grants for consumer information, counseling and technical assistance to educate consumers about long-term care insurance.

Regulation. Minimum long-term care insurance product and business standards and requirements for monitoring and enforcing insurance industry practices and state regulatory systems are established. States may exceed these minimum standards. The Department of Health and Human Services awards grants to states to establish demonstration programs to improve enforcement of long-term care insurance.

A Long-Term Care Insurance Advisory Council is appointed by the Secretary of HHS to advise and assist the Secretary on matters relating to long-term care insurance and to monitor the development of the insurance market. The Council consists of five members chosen for their expertise in provision and regulation of long-term care insurance.

The Secretary of the Department of HHS, after considering recommendations of the Council, promulgates federal regulations for long-term care insurance offerings within two years of enactment of the American Health Security Act. At a minimum, Federal regulations require that policies:

- Provide for nonforfeiture of benefits in the event of policy lapse.
- Offer inflation protection at an annually compounded benefit rate.
- Do not limit payment of benefits based on pre-existing conditions that are not documented at the time of sale.
- Require third-party notification of pending lapse and reinstatement for up to five months after termination if lapse was due to incapacitation.
- Clearly define covered services, benefit eligibility triggers, premiums and expected increases, and the tax treatment of the long-term care insurance policy.
- Define eligibility for benefits based on an independent professional functional assessment.
- Contain requirements concerning continuation and conversion of group policies and other regulations for group policies.

Federal regulation of business practices related to long-term care insurance include, but are not limited to:

- Requirements for states to establish an appeals process for beneficiaries.
- Mechanisms for timely resolution of consumer complaints.
- Provisions regarding adequate responses to claim denials.
- Training and certification of agents.
- Limits on commissions paid to agents.
- Requirements for premium approval and pricing assumptions.
- Prohibitions against improper sales practices.
- Association endorsement or sale of policies.

The Secretary of the Department of Health and Human Services also may regulate the long-term care insurance aspects of Continuing Care Retirement Communities.

States implement and enforce standards for long-term care insurance. Within two years of enactment of the American Health Security Act, states submit to the Secretary of the Department of Health and Human Services a plan describing the implementation and enforcement.

If a state fails to submit a plan or its plan is not approved, no long-term care insurance policy may be sold in the state until it submits an acceptable plan. Penalties apply for agents and insurers who fail to comply with these requirements.

States submit annual reports; the Department of Health and Human Services conducts periodic audits of state performance.

Tax Treatment of Premiums for Long-Term Care Insurance. The Internal Revenue Code is amended to provide for:

• The exclusion from taxable income of amounts paid for services or as cash payments under a qualified long-term care policy.

Requirements for a policy to qualify for tax purposes, including criteria that trigger eligibility for benefits, shall be developed by the Secretary of HHS in consultation with the Treasury Department.

• The maximum daily benefit excluded is $110 in 1994 with annual adjustments based on increases in the wage price index or an alternative selected by the Treasury Department in consultation with the Department of Health and Human Services.

• The cost of qualified long-term care policies as defined in this section may be included as an itemized medical expense deduction.

• The definition of medical expenses is clarified to include qualified long-term care services.

• Employer-paid premiums for long-term care insurance are treated as deductions for employers and excluded from taxable income for employees.

Tax Incentives for Individuals with Disabilities Who Work

Employed individuals who require assistance with activities of daily living and who purchase personal care and personal assistance services may obtain a tax credit for 50 percent of their costs, up to a maximum of $15,000 per year.

The Internal Revenue Service issues regulations defining personal care/personal assistance services eligible for the tax credit, including:

• Personal services, including, but not limited to, those appropriate to carrying out activities of daily living in or out of the home.

• Home services, including meal preparation and shopping.

• Assistance with life skills, including money management.

• Communication services.

• Security services, including monitoring alarms.

• Mobility services.

• Work-related support services.

• Service coordination.

• Assistive technology services, including evaluation and training of family members.

• Emergency services, including substitute services.

Demonstration Study of Acute and Long-Term Care Integration

The Secretary of the Department of Health and Human Services conducts a demonstration program for integrated models of acute and long-term care services for individuals with disabilities and chronic illnesses. The demonstration:

• Defines organizational arrangements to integrate models of acute and long-term care services.

• Assesses the operational and financial viability of the integrated models developed and tested.

• Evaluates the impact of integrated models.

• Determines the appropriateness of including these models as program options in the managed competition structure.

The Secretary of the Department of Health and Human Services establishes minimum benefit specifications. Sponsors of integration models include the following services:

- Comprehensive medical benefits.
- Specialized transitional benefits.
- Long-term care benefits.
- Specialized habilitation services for participants with developmental disabilities.

The Secretary of the Department of Health and Human Services establishes eligibility criteria for the demonstrations including one or more of the following groups:

- Individuals with disabilities covered under the basic health insurance program.
- Medicare beneficiaries who qualify for Part A and participate in Part B.
- Medicaid beneficiaries eligible for Medicare or otherwise eligible for long-term care services under the SSI program.

The Secretary of the Department of Health and Human Services establishes criteria for sponsor participation. The criteria assesses financial controls, commitment to the goals of the demonstration, information systems and compliance with applicable state laws.

Demonstration sponsors provide enrollment services, client assessment and care planning, simplified access to services, on-going integrated acute- and chronic-care management, continuity of care across settings and services, quality assurance, grievance and appeal procedures, member services and strong consumer participation.

LTC System Performance Review

The overall performance of the new program will be assessed in terms of quality, access, and availability of long-term supports for individuals with disabilities. Five years from the date of implementation of the long-term care reform plan, or by the year 2000 (whichever is sooner), the Secretary of HHS will submit to the Congress an interim assessment of the effectiveness of the new package of long-term care reforms.

The assessment will include the following components:

• An evaluation of access to long-term care services (both community based and residential) for individuals with disabilities of all ages representing diverse disability groups, levels of disability, income levels, minorities, and rural areas.

• A review of the quality of services.

• An evaluation of the performance of the private sector in offering affordable insurance products that provide adequate protection against the high cost of nursing home care. This component of the assessment will also entail a review of the adequacy of the standards for private long-term care insurance and an assessment of how well the standards are being enforced.

• An evaluation of the system's effectiveness in containing long-term care costs.

• An evaluation of the impact of the program on individuals with lower incomes.

• An evaluation of the system's performance with regard to coordination and integration of services, and providing services in the least restrictive environment to the degree possible.

• The Secretary will submit a final report on the assessment to Congress by the year 2002, or two years after the interim assessment, whichever is earlier.

22

Malpractice Reform

REFORM OF THE dispute resolution system for medical malpractice in the American Health Security Act encompass both changes in tort law and the development of alternative approaches to resolving patients' claims against providers. Reforms are:

• Creation of Alternative Dispute Resolution Mechanisms

Each health plan establishes an alternative-dispute resolution process using one or more of several models developed by the National Health Board. Potential model systems include early offers of settlement, mediation and arbitration.

Consumers who have a claim against a health care provider are required to submit the claim through the alternative dispute system. At the completion of the alternative dispute system, if the consumer is not satisfied with the outcome, he or she is free to pursue the complaint in court.

• Requirement for Certificate of Merit

Lawsuits claiming injury from medical malpractice include submission of an affidavit signed by a medical specialist practicing in a field relevant to the claimed injury. The affidavit must attest that a specialist examined the claim and concluded that medical procedures or treatments that produced the claim deviated from established standards of care.

- **Limits on Attorney Fees**

Attorneys' fees for malpractice cases are limited to a maximum of 33⅓ percent of an award. States may impose lower limits, as many have.

- **Repeat Offenders**

The Department of Health and Human Services establishes rules for public access to information contained in the National Practitioner Data Bank, which tracks health care providers who incur repeated malpractice judgments and settlements.

All malpractice awards and settlements must be reported to the National Practitioner Data Bank, initiated in 1990 and administered by the Department of Health and Human Services. The Data Bank collects information concerning malpractice awards, along with other information about adverse professional actions, but the information is not available to the public.

- **Collateral Sources**

New rules require reduction of the amount of any award in a medical malpractice case by the amount of recovery from other sources, such as health insurance payments, disability, workers compensation, or any other programs that compensate an individual for an injury.

- **Periodic Payment of Awards**

Consistent with the relevant portions of the Uniform Periodic Payment of Judgements Act proposed by the National Conference of Commissioners on Uniform State Laws, either party to a malpractice case may request that an award be made payable in periodic installments as appropriate to reflect the need for medical and other services.

- **Enterprise Liability Demonstration Project**

Federal funds support states demonstration projects to establish enterprise liability. Projects are designed to determine whether substituting physician liability with liability on the part of the health plan leads to improvements in the quality of health care, reductions in defensive medicine and better risk management.

- **Standards Based on Practice Guidelines**

Based on a five-year program underway to determine the effect of using practice patterns in three specialty areas (anesthesia, emergency medicine and gynecology), the Department of Health and Human Services will develop a medical liability pilot program based on practice guidelines adopted by the National Quality Management Program.

Under such a system, a physician able to demonstrate that his professional conduct or treatment complied with appropriate practice guidelines is not liable for medical malpractice.

The Department of Health and Human Services has authority to work with states to invest practice guidelines with the force of law for physicians and other health care providers participating in the pilot program. After the first practice guideline is available, the Department reports annually to Congress on the results of the pilot program and makes recommendations about whether changes in malpractice law should follow.

23

Antitrust Reform

THE ANTITRUST laws serve an important function in the new health care system, enforcing rules of competition critical to the efficient operation of the new system.

While the vigorous enforcement of the antitrust laws is important, in several areas legitimate concerns exist about the need for greater clarity concerning enforcement policy and the ability of some health care providers to be sure their conduct comports with antitrust rules.

Hospital Mergers

Hospitals smaller than a certain size, as measured, for example, by number of beds or patient census, require certainty that they will not be challenged by the federal government if they attempt to merge. Such hospitals often are sole community providers that do not compete with other hospitals.

The Department of Justice and the Federal Trade Commission publish guidelines that provide safety zones for such mergers and an expedited business review or advisory opinion procedure through which the parties to such mergers can obtain timely (i.e., within 90 days) additional assurance that their merger will not be challenged. Guidelines also will provide the analysis the agencies use to evaluate mergers among larger hospitals.

Hospital Joint Ventures and Purchasing Arrangements

Hospitals may enter into joint ventures involving high technology or expensive equipment and ancillary services, as well as joint purchasing arrangements involving the goods and services they need.

The Department of Justice and the Federal Trade Commission publish guidelines that provide safety zones for such joint ventures and arrangements, examples of ventures that would not be challenged by the agencies, and an expedited business review or advisory opinion procedure through which the parties to joint ventures can obtain timely (i.e., within 90 days) advice and assurance as to whether ventures that do not fall with the safety zones will be challenged.

Physician Network Joint Ventures

Physicians and other providers require additional guidance regarding the application of the antitrust laws to their formation of provider networks that would negotiate effectively with health plans.

The Department of Justice and the Federal Trade Commission publish guidelines that provide safety zones for physician network joint ventures that do not possess market power (below 20 percent) and that share financial risk, examples of networks that would not be challenged by the agencies, and an expedited business review or advisory opinion procedure through which the parties to networks that do not fall within the safety zones can obtain timely (i.e., within 90 days) advice and assurance as to whether their network will be challenged.

Within the safety zones physicians may bargain collectively with health plans about payment, coverage, decisions about medical care, and other matters without fear of federal enforcement of the antitrust laws.

Provider Collaboration

During the transition to the new health care system, physicians and other providers may require some protection to negotiate effectively with health plans and to form their own plans. To protect physicians and other providers from the market power of third party payers forming health plans, providers are provided a narrow safe harbor to establish and negotiate prices if the providers share financial risk. The financial risk may not be simply fee discounting.

Physicians who provide health services for the benefit package may combine to establish or negotiate prices for the health services offered if the providers share risk and if the combined market power of the providers does not exceed 20 percent. This safe harbor does not apply to the implicit or explicit threat of a boycott.

State Action Immunity

The Department of Justice and the Federal Trade Commission publish guidelines that apply the "state action doctrine" where a state seeks to grant antitrust immunity to hospitals and other institutional health providers.

If a state establishes a clearly articulated and affirmatively expressed policy to replace competition with regulation and actively supervises the arrangements, the hospitals and other institutional providers involved will have certainty that they will not face enforcement action by the federal government.

Provider Fee Schedule Negotiation

The Department of Justice and the Federal Trade Commission publish guidelines that describe under existing law the ability of providers to collectively negotiate fee schedules with the alliances.

Alliances, as established and supervised under state law, are required under federal law to establish a fee schedule for fee-for service plans, and providers in order to participate in the negotiation process need certainty that their actions will not violate the antitrust laws.

McCarran-Ferguson

The current exemption from the antitrust laws enjoyed by health insurers is repealed, eliminating the ability of health plans to collectively determine the rates they charge, and other terms of their relationship with providers.

24

Fraud and Abuse

THE AMERICAN Health Security Act establishes an all-payer health care fraud and abuse enforcement program, increases funding for and coordinates activities of various branches of government for enforcement against fraud and abuse in the health care system.

Improved Coordination

The fraud and abuse enforcement program coordinates federal, state and local law enforcement activities aimed at health care fraud and abuse. The Department of Justice and the Department of Health and Human Services jointly direct the program.

Trust Fund

Fines, penalties, forfeitures and damages (other than restitution) for fraud or abuse in health care delivery are deposited in a trust fund to supplement federal efforts to combat health care fraud and abuse.

Exceptions are made to the extent that current law directs that the money be given to other parties (such as the states) or deposited in other trust funds (such as the Medicare Trust Fund).

Control Kickbacks

The American Health Security Act expands the scope of the current anti-kickback statute from covering only Medicare and Medicaid to covering all health payers. The new provision calls for punishment for the payment or receipt of any item of value as an inducement for referral of any type of health care business (subject to the exceptions described below).

The federal government is authorized to seek civil remedies in U.S. District Court, including: civil penalties, injunctive relief to halt kickback schemes and ability to secure assets in appropriate cases. The statute provides a new administrative remedy involving civil monetary penalties for kickback violations.

Exceptions to the kickback provision include payments for items or services furnished to patients paid for on an at-risk basis to that provider furnishing the items or service, such as capitated payments. Also included are payments made on an "at risk" basis to a health plan ("at risk" would include capitation, global fees, and perhaps other bundled payment arrangements). The exception covers all "downstream" payments made to providers by such an "at risk" plan, even fee-for-service payments. Similarly, if a provider network is paid by a plan on an "at risk" basis, any downstream payments for ancillary items and services made by the network are covered by the exception. In addition, the statutory and regulatory ("safe harbor") exceptions under the current kickback statute apply to an expanded kickback statute that applies to all payers.

End Self-Referrals

Payment to an entity for any item or service is prohibited (subject to the exceptions discerned below) in which the physician ordering services has a financial relationship with the entity and in which the physician does not render that item or service.

Self-referral limitations carry an exception in which items or services are paid for on an at-risk basis to that provider, such as capitated payments. The exception to the anti-kickback prohibitions for "at risk" payments to plans and networks, described above, also applies to self-referral prohibitions. The exceptions in section 1877 are retained except that:

- The exception for group practices is narrowed to prevent the creation of sham groups.
- Exceptions for investments by large entities require that the company hold $100 million in shareholder equity.

Toughen Penalties for Wrongdoers

Current federal authority is amended to allow forfeitures of proceeds derived from health care fraud. The forfeiture remedy allows the federal government to use either criminal or civil remedies to seize assets derived from fraudulent or illegal activities.

A new health care fraud statute, modeled after existing mail and bank fraud statutes, sets penalties for schemes to defraud either public or private health care programs. The existing mail fraud statute is amended to address schemes that use private delivery services in addition to the United States mail system.

A new federal criminal statute prohibits deliberately making false statements to health plans, health alliances or state health care agencies.

A new federal criminal statute prohibits the payment of bribes, gratuities or other inducements to administrators and employees of health plans, health alliances or state health care agencies.

The federal government is authorized to assess civil monetary penalties against individuals who engage in any of the following prohibited activities:

- **False Claims**
  — Submitting a claim for an item or service not provided as claimed. (See section 1128A(a)(1)(A) of the Social Security Act. All references in this section are to the Social Security Act unless otherwise specified.) (Many of these actions are already the basis for civil monetary penalties with respect to Medicare and Medicaid.)
  — Submitting a false or fraudulent claim for an item or service. (See section 1128A(a)(1)(B).)
  — Submitting a claim for a physician's service provided by a person who was not a licensed physician, whose license was obtained through misrepresentation or who improperly represented to a patient that he or she was a certified specialist. (See section 1128A(a)(1)(C).)
  — The routine waiver of co-payments if co-payments are required under a health plan.

— Claiming a higher health-service code in order to obtain higher reimbursement for a health service.

— Unbundling or fragmenting charges as part of a bundled-payment scheme. (See section 1866(g).)

— Engaging in practices such as unnecessary multiple admissions to a hospital or other health care institution or engaging in other inappropriate medical practices in order to circumvent a bundled payment scheme.

- **False Statements**

— Failing to report information or reporting inaccurate information that is required to be submitted to a data bank. (See section 421(c) of the Health Care Quality Improvement Act.)

— Submitting false or fraudulent statements to the National Health Board, a health alliance or a plan. (See section 1876(i)(6)(A)(v).)

- **Violations Specific to Plans**

— Failing substantially to provide medically necessary services, items or treatments required (under law or contract) to be provided to an individual. (See section 1876(i)(6)(A)(1).)

— Acting to cancel the enrollment of or refusing to enroll an individual in violation of the law. (See section 1876(i)(6)(A)(iii).)

— Engaging in any practice that reasonably could be expected to have the effect of denying or discouraging enrollment by eligible individuals whose medical condition or history indicates a need for substantial future medical services. (See section 1876(i)(6)(A)(iv).)

— Employing or contracting with any individual or entity excluded from participation in the health care system for the provision of services, utilization review, medical social work or administrative services or employing or contracting with any entity for the provision (directly or indirectly) through such an excluded individual or entity of such services. (See section 1876(i)(6)(A)(vi).)

- **Miscellaneous**

  — Failing to cooperate with quality program or utilization review.

  — Paying or receiving unlawful kickbacks (subject to exceptions).

  — Submitting a claim for an item or service submitted by an excluded person. (See section 1128A(a)(1)(D).)

  — Failing to report violations of federal criminal law. Whistleblowers are protected against adverse employment actions through mechanisms similar to section 7 of the Inspector General Act.

The penalty amount is $10,000 per item or service claimed (consistent with the Civil False Claims Act (31 U.S.C. § 3729) and an assessment of no more than triple the amount claimed. The law provides for prejudgment interest or penalties and assessments imposed by an administrative law judge.

The standard of knowledge in these cases is "knows and should know."

The basis for exclusion from Medicare and state health programs serves as the basis for an exclusion from all other health programs.

The following actions represent the basis for exclusion from health care programs. The exclusion from the programs is mandatory:

- Criminal conviction relating to fraud, theft, embezzlement, breach of fiduciary responsibility or other financial misconduct in connection with the delivery of a health care item or service. (See section 1128(a)(1) and (b)(1).)
- Criminal conviction relating to the neglect or abuse of patients in connection with the delivery of a health care item or service. (See section 1128(a)(2).)

With respect to the following bases for exclusion, the Department of Health and Human Services determines whether, given the facts of the case, an individual should be excluded:

- Criminal conviction relating to fraud, theft, embezzlement, breach of fiduciary responsibility or other financial misconduct in connection with an act or omission in a program operated by or financed in whole or in part by any federal, state or local government agency. (See section 1128(b)(1).) (This would cover convictions for fraud against any non-health related government program.)
- Criminal conviction relating to the unlawful manufacture, distribution, prescription, or dispensing of a controlled substance. (This would not include convictions for simple possession.) (See section 1128(b)(3).)
- Revocation, suspension, or loss of a license to provide health care for reasons of professional competence, performance, or financial integrity or the surrender of a license pending a formal disciplinary proceeding for allegations of professional competence, performance or financial integrity. (See section 1128(b)(4).)

- Exclusion from Medicare or other federal or state health care programs (e.g., CHAMPUS, VA). (See section 1128(b)(5).)

- Furnishing or causing to be furnished items or services to patients that fail to meet professionally recognized standards in a gross and flagrant manner or in a substantial number of cases. (See section 1128(b)(6)(B).)

- Commission of an act described in the federal criminal laws specifically related to health care or civil monetary penalty laws specifically related to health care. (See section 1128(b)(7).)

- Entities controlled by an excluded individual. (See section 1128(b)(8).)

- Individuals who have a majority ownership interest in or hold significant control over the operations of an entity convicted of an offense related to the delivery of a health care item or service.

- Failure to disclose required information regarding ownership, controlling interests or convictions of individuals with ownership or controlling interests, officers, directors, agents or managing employees. (See section 1128(b)(9).)

- Failure to provide access to documentation or to provide documentation related to the health care claims submitted to a health benefit plan, a health alliance or the government. (See section 1128(b)(11).)

- Failure to grant physical access, with reasonable notice, to appropriate authorities for on-site reviews and surveys. (See section 1128(b)(12).)

- Defaulting on repayment of scholarship funds or loans in connection with health professions education made or secured in whole or in part, by the Secretary of the Department of Health and Human Services. (See section 1128(b)(14).)

The current procedure under which the Department of Health and Human Services may exclude an individual or entity prior to a hearing continues conditional on the prior determination of another tribunal, such as a criminal conviction or action by a federal or state administrative body.

All other exclusions take effect after a hearing and administrative law judge decision regarding the exclusion.

Anti-Fraud Standards for Electronic Media Claims

A requirement for standards to safeguard against fraud and abuse in an electronic media environment (i.e., to assure the identity of those submitting claims electronically, and impose provider responsibility for such claims) is included.

25

Health Care Access Initiatives

IN THE EXISTING health care system, major financial and non-financial barriers reduce access for a number of population groups in American society. Population groups that particularly confront barriers to care include:

- Low-income groups and individuals who have little education.
- Members of certain racial, cultural and ethnic groups and those who speak languages other than English.
- Residents of central cities, rural and frontier communities.
- Individuals who lack a stable residence, such as migrant workers and homeless individuals or families.
- Adolescents.
- Individuals with certain severe health problems, such as HIV infection, AIDS, chronic mental illness, substance abuse or serious disability.

As a result, members of those population groups often experience reduced health status and quality of life. Health care reform will significantly improve access to care by providing all Americans with comprehensive coverage for treatment services, clinical preventive services, mental health and substance abuse services.

However, universal insurance coverage and market reforms alone will not eliminate all barriers to care or ensure quality. In order to meet their obligations to provide comprehensive health care benefits, health plans will require assistance and financial incentives to expand into low-population areas and to ensure that hard-to-reach populations have access to quality care.

In order to fulfill the promise of health reform, other inadequacies requiring attention include: the supply of providers and health plans in both rural and low-income urban areas; poor integration and coordination of care between primary care and specialized services; cultural and linguistic barriers; transportation and hours of service; lack of understanding among consumers about the availability of services; and resistance to the use of services. Many health care providers who are skilled and committed to serving populations most affected by access barriers also will require special assistance to prepare for and ensure their effective participation in the reformed system.

Goals and Strategy of the Public Health Service Access Initiatives

The programs described in the following section are designed to reduce disparities in health status by ensuring access to needed services for low-income, underserved, hard-to-reach, and otherwise vulnerable populations. They build on the strengths of the reformed delivery system, the expertise and experience of current public health providers, and the enhanced capacities of state and local public health agencies.

The Public Health Service access initiatives are designed to:

- **Expand capacity** by increasing the supply of practitioners, practice networks, clinics, and health plans in underserved areas.

- **Assist alliances and health plans** to deliver culturally sensitive care to vulnerable segments of their populations.

- **Achieve accountability** by assuring that health plans enroll vulnerable populations and meet their personal health care needs.

- **Assist organizations and professionals supported by public funding** to adapt to the reformed system. Integration of these providers into practice networks or health plans will ensure that they receive payment for covered services from plans. It will provide critical support services (administration, information systems, telecommunications, specialty services) to improve the delivery and coordination of care.

- **Shift the emphasis of existing public funding** away from the delivery of services covered in the standard benefit package and toward:

  — Activities designed to enable, enhance and ensure access to care by addressing persistent barriers, especially hard-to-reach populations.

  — Services not covered in the benefit package but essential to prevent morbidity and mortality among certain populations;

- **Integrate and coordinate current programs** to provide the federal government, states, health departments and community-based organizations flexibility to tailor their activities to the varied health needs and problems of different populations and geographic regions.

— Reduce the current administrative burden of multiple grant application procedures, management structures, funding requirements, and reporting systems.

Access Initiative Programs

• **The National Health Service Corps** expands to reduce the shortage of primary care practitioners in underserved areas.

• **Categorical Programs and Formula Grants** continue to pay for personal health services for specific populations that confront barriers to care (such as community and migrant health centers, family planning clinics, health care for the homeless program, and portions of the maternal and child health block grant) continue.

However, as reform is implemented, with the exception of the Ryan White HIV/AIDS program, funding shifts from clinical services to expansion of health care capacity in underserved areas in order to ensure access for vulnerable populations (see discussion below).

• **New Grants and Loans** support capacity expansion undertaken by a new federal authority with the mission of ensuring adequate choice of providers and health plans in underserved areas, supporting the development of networks of care providers, and overseeing the integration of federally funded providers into the new system.

Flexible grants provide start-up and operating funds and guaranteed loans to community-based providers and public and non-profit health care institutions. Funds also provide capital infrastructure development to expand access in underserved areas for low-income, hard-to-reach, or otherwise vulnerable populations.

New funds allocated for this purpose are supplemented by development and expansion funds transferred from existing programs. The federal government determines the allocation of funding among states and types of programs. A specific portion supports initiatives such as school-based clinics. States have expanded input into the decision-making process.

• **New Formula Grants** to states provide funds to ensure access to health care for low-income, underserved, hard-to-reach, and otherwise vulnerable populations. Grants cover:

— Outreach and enabling services (e.g., transportation, translation/interpretation, child care).

— Supplemental services.

— The development of linkages between health plans and providers through improved information and referred systems.

— Integration of health services with community health and social services.

— Advocacy and follow-up services.

States become eligible for formula grants as they implement reform, using funds to reduce disparities in access and health status among population groups and monitor access for vulnerable populations. (Programs designed to build state capacity are described in the section on public health initiatives.)

To assure accountability, state and local public health agencies follow local indicators measuring access as well as health status measures closely linked to access. To participate in the formula-grant program, states must demonstrate improvement over time.

State allocations are based on demographic and need factors. To encourage states to implement reform and encourage enrollment of vulnerable populations, the program will not include a matching requirement other than maintenance of effort in state and local funding for services to vulnerable populations. After reform is fully implemented, a state matching formula will be developed.

• **Designation of Essential Community Providers** assures access and continuity of care during the first five years of reform by requiring health plans to contract with and reimburse established community-based providers. Independent health professionals and health care institutions operating in underserved areas may apply to the Department of Health and Human Services for designation as essential providers.

Plans are required either to contract with essential providers at a capitated rate no less than that paid to other providers for the same services or to reimburse them at rates based on Medicare payment principles.

By the end of five years, providers either become integrated into health plans or join together to create new, community-based health plans. At that time, health plans must either demonstrate their capacity to provide access for all participants or continue contracting arrangements with essential providers.

• **Adolescent and School-Aged Youth Initiative** supports the delivery of clinical services through school-based or school-linked sites (consistent with goals of health reform and Goals 2000) and comprehensive health education in high-risk schools.

Dedicated funds in the capacity expansion program (see above) support school-based clinics targeted at middle schools and high schools. Clinics provide physical and mental health services and counseling in disease prevention and health promotion as well as in individualized risk behavior reduction.

School-based clinics established under the program are automatically designated as essential community providers.

Authorized as a formula grant to states funded jointly by the Department of Health and Human Services and the Department of Education, health education focuses on the reduction of risk behaviors among adolescents and adults. The curriculum is linked to *Healthy People 2000* objectives and will target those areas of health risk where research suggests that health education can reduce risk-taking behavior and improve health outcomes.

Grantees have flexibility in determining what services and what service delivery mechanisms are most appropriate for their community.

Mental Health and Substance Abuse Services

Mental health and substance abuse initiatives refocus existing formula grants to encourage development of community-based programs by:

• Restructuring Existing Formula Grants

As states implement reform, funding through Community Mental Health and the Substance Abuse Prevention and Treatment Formula Grant is required only for treatment in excess of the comprehensive benefit. Funds shift from support for direct treatment to service system development, supplemental services, and population-based prevention services.

State Systems Development Program and Mental Health Systems Improvement Program continue to be funded with the five percent technical assistance set aside from formula grants.

• Maintenance of Effort

States are required to maintain support for mental health and substance abuse treatment activities, although they may obtain a waiver to assist in the development of community-based systems of care to promote the eventual integration of the public and private systems for the treatment of mental and addictive disorders.

• Special Initiatives

Competitive project grants to states support pilot projects related to integrating the private and public mental health and substance abuse systems. Funds support linkage of treatment and prevention for substance abuse with a broad array of health services and systems management for seriously emotionally disturbed children.

• Research and Demonstration Projects

Funds support the development of improved outreach strategies for AIDS and HIV-infected drug abusers, the homeless, individuals involved in the criminal justice system, and populations with co-morbidity, including mechanisms for sharing information about the applicability of promising approaches to prevention within specific populations and service-delivery settings and the effectiveness of prevention and early intervention services in reducing health costs.

Funds also support development of systems that link substance abuse and mental health treatment with primary care, target rural and remote areas and culturally distinct populations, and facilitate the transfer of knowledge.

• Training and Staff Development

The Department of Health and Human Services expands its curriculum development and health education efforts in clinical prevention within schools of medicine, nursing, and social work as well as its information services for current health professionals and provides primary care professionals with information and training to screen and identify mental health and substance abuse problems and risk factors.

• Capital Assistance

Direct loan and loan-guarantee programs support the development of additional non-acute, residential treatment centers and community-based ambulatory clinics, particularly in medically underserved areas.

American Indians and Alaska Natives

Supplemental financing and services provide access to health care for American Indians and Alaskan Natives populations with diverse language and cultural needs, many of whom live in remote and underserved reservation areas. Supplemental services include transportation, outreach and follow-up, community health representatives, public health nurses, non-medical case management, child care during clinic visits, health education, nutrition, home visiting, and supplemental mental health and substance abuse prevention and treatment services.

The Indian Health Service also expands population-based public health and prevention activities. Under new authority, it covers all residents, Indian and non-Indian, living on reservations in addition to populations living near reservations.

Population-based public health and prevention activities include surveillance and monitoring of health status, medical outcomes, threats to public health, public health laboratories, community-based control programs, community health protection and public health information.

Health Workforce

To increase the recruitment, preparation, and retention of American Indians and Alaska Natives into medical, nursing, public health and other health professions, existing programs are expanded.

The Indian Health Scholarship Program and Loan Repayment Program expands to fund all eligible applicants under the current authorities of sections 104 and 108 of P.L. 94-437. Additional financial assistance increases the number of American Indians and Alaska Natives entering training programs under current authorities of sections 103 and 105 of P.L. 94-437.

Sanitation and Environmental Health

Additional funding expands construction of water, sewer, and other sanitation and environmental health facilities, as well as provide for training and technical assistance to tribes that wish to operate tribal facilities under P.L. 86-121 and Section 302 of P.L. 94-437.

26

Medicare

State Integration

The Secretary of the Department of Health and Human Services has authority to permit states to integrate Medicare beneficiaries into health alliances under specified conditions that ensure:

- Beneficiaries have the same or better coverage as standard Medicare benefits
- Federal financial liability is not increased.

Alliances must offer at least one fee-for-service option that offers the Medicare benefit package at no greater cost to the beneficiary than traditional Medicare. If only an enhanced benefit package is offered, the cost to the beneficiary still can be no greater than under traditional Medicare.

Transition

After a state establishes health alliances and enrolls its population in them, states can request inclusion of Medicare beneficiaries in the population covered under health alliances. States submit proposals to the Secretary of HHS describing:

- The state plan for integration of Medicare and providing evidence regarding compliance with standards related to access, quality of care and cost containment
- The state's capacity to ensure equity for Medicare beneficiaries and providers
- Administrative capacity to carry out the option
- Ability to ensure that the financial and fiduciary interests of the federal government are served by the proposal.

States are permitted to discontinue a Medicare integration program at the end of any fiscal year with sufficient notice to the federal government, beneficiaries and health providers.

The federal government assumes administration of Medicare in a state if assurances are not met and the state is not operating an effective Medicare program.

Assurances

To approve a waiver, the federal government requires assurance that Medicare beneficiaries have:

- Access to the same, or higher, level of benefits as standard Medicare.
- Access to care that is substantially comparable to standard Medicare. The state must demonstrate adequate risk adjustment methodologies to assure that plans have sufficient compensation to provide appropriate access to care.
- Assurance of at least one fee-for-service option with out-of-pocket expenses no higher than under traditional Medicare program for comparable or better benefit.

- Assurance of equal, or better, protection against balance billing.
- Protection under comparable, or better, quality assurance mechanisms.
- Assurance of the same, or better, appeal rights in the event of disputes, including right to an administrative law judge hearing and judicial review when applicable.

States operate within a capitation rate consistent with budget limits on growth of federal spending for Medicare. No cost-shifting to the Medicare program occurs as a result of Medicare integration in a state. Savings accruing to the state are shared with the federal government and/or Medicare beneficiaries (savings may be used to reduce the Medicare Part B premium in the state).

States assume additional administrative costs (e.g., special processing of claims by out-of-state carriers and intermediaries for claims received from residents of states in which Medicare is integrated). The federal government retains the right to evaluate, directly or through contractors, the state's program and audit records to determine compliance with assurances.

Individual Election at Age 65 to Remain in the Health Alliances

After establishment of health alliances, individuals have the right to elect to remain in an alliance when they reach age 65. If they remain in the alliance, they continue to receive the nationally guaranteed comprehensive benefit package with the full range of options available to individuals younger than age 65.

Plans negotiate rates with alliances for participants over age 65 choosing to remain in the alliances; these rates are separate from those covering younger participants. Any plan providing coverage through an alliance must bid to cover the older population to continue operating through the alliance.

Alliances make risk adjustments to premiums among plans using methods prescribed by the National Health Board. Medicare pays a fixed contribution to alliances equal to the costs that Medicare would be projected to bear—under the new budget constraint—for the same beneficiary population in the alliance. Beneficiaries pay the difference between Medicare's payment and the plan's premium.

During the annual enrollment period, beneficiaries over age 65 may return to Medicare or choose a new plan through the alliance.

Medicare Managed Care

Changes in payment methodology improve and strengthen the Medicare managed care program:

• A research initiative focuses on the development and demonstration of health-status adjustors.
• Interim measures improve the current payment methodology, including:
— Making adjustments to reflect payments currently not captured in the payment methodology because of coordination of benefits or services received through VA or DOD.

— Seeking discretionary authority to establish a ceiling and floor for payments and to create a special pool for high-cost cases.

For the longer term, demonstrations of alternative payment methodologies (such as competitive bidding, new risk sharing arrangements and cost reimbursement subject to limits) are implemented.

Coordinated open enrollment promotes managed care. Medicare establishes an annual open enrollment period for Medicare managed care plans and Medigap plans. Medicare develops and distributes comparative materials on all managed care and Medigap plans, with the plans paying the cost. A third party coordinates enrollment to reduce the possibility of favorable selection. One-year enrollment replaces current month-to-month commitment.

Medigap insurance practices conform with the new requirements for open enrollment and other new insurance reform standards for supplemental insurance under health care reform.

Medicare offers beneficiaries greater choice of managed care options through the following changes:

• Expanding choice of managed care plans: Within three years of enactment, all health plans capable of qualifying for a Medicare contract are required to enter into a cost contract as a condition for participation in health alliances.

• Medicare Point-of-Service option: A non-enrollment based Point-of-Service option is created within fee-for-service Medicare. Medicare contracts with for the creation of comprehensive preferred provider networks in major metropolitan areas. Beneficiaries not enrolled in a capitated health plan choose whether to use the network of preferred providers on a service-by-service basis.

MEDICARE OUTPATIENT PRESCRIPTION DRUG BENEFIT

Two years from the date of enactment of the plan, but no later than July 1, 1996 benefits offered under the Medicare program expand to cover outpatient prescription drugs. Thus, assuming enactment in December 1993, the new drug benefit would be in effect beginning in January 1996.

Any Medicare beneficiary who elects to enroll in the Part B program (97 percent of the Medicare population) automatically enrolls in the new prescription drug benefit.

As with other Part B benefits, the Medicare prescription drug benefit is funded by both general revenues and beneficiary premiums. The Part B premium increases to cover the new benefit. Premiums currently finance 25 percent of the cost for Part B coverage. Thus, beneficiaries would pay 25 percent of the cost of the new drug benefit. Other rules related to enrollment in Medicare Part B also apply to the prescription drug benefit.

Coinsurance, Deductibles and Caps

The new drug benefit carries a $250 annual deductible. Once the deductible has been met, beneficiaries pay 20 percent of the cost of each prescription with an annual limit on out-of-pocket expenditures of $1,000.

Both the annual deductible and out-of-pocket cap are indexed each year to assure that the same percentage of beneficiaries continue to receive benefits as did with the initial $250 deductible and $1000 out-of-pocket cap.

Coverage

The Medicare drug benefit covers all drugs, biological products and insulin approved by the Food and Drug Administration (FDA) for their medically accepted indications as defined in at least one of the three compendia which are the American Medical Association Drug Evaluations, the American Hospital Formulary Service and the United States Pharmacopeia, or other authoritative compendia identified by the Secretary or as determined by the carrier based on evidence presented in peer reviewed medical literature.

The Medicare drug benefit includes coverage of home IV drugs. In addition, the current limited coverage of outpatient drugs under Medicare such as immunosuppressive drugs are incorporated into the drug benefit.

The Secretary of Health and Human Services has the discretion not to cover certain pharmaceutical products listed in Section 1927(d) of the Social Security Act. Examples include fertility drugs, medications used to treat anorexia and drugs used for cosmetic purposes. However, benzodiazepines and barbiturates would be covered under the Medicare drug benefit. Further, the Secretary has the authority to establish maximum quantities per prescription or limit the number of refills in order to discourage waste.

The Secretary may require physicians or pharmacists to obtain approval before prescribing or dispensing certain medications based on evidence that they are subject to clinical misuse or inappropriate use or because the Secretary determines that they are not cost effective.

Cost Containment

As a condition of participation in Medicare and Medicaid, drug manufacturers must sign rebate agreements with the Secretary. Rebates are paid to the Secretary on a quarterly basis.

For single source and innovator multiple source drugs, manufacturers pay a rebate to Medicare for each drug based on the difference between the average manufacturer price (AMP) to the retail class of trade and the weighted average of the prices of the drug in the non-retail market, or 15 percent of the AMP, whichever is greater. The Secretary has the authority to verify the AMP.

For single source and innovator multiple source drugs, an additional rebate is required on a drug-by-drug basis for manufacturers who increase prices at a higher rate than inflation. The baseline indexed price is the average manufacturers price from April through June 1993.

In the case of new drugs that the Secretary determines are excessively or inappropriately priced, the Secretary has the authority to negotiate a special rebate with the manufacturer. Such a determination by the

Secretary would be based on such factors as the prices of other drugs in the same therapeutic class, cost information supplied by the manufacturer to the Secretary, prices of the drug in other comparable countries, and other relevant factors. If a manufacturer refuses to negotiate or the Secretary is unable to negotiate a price that the Secretary determines to be reasonable, the Secretary may exclude the new drug from coverage under Medicare.

In the case of dual eligibles, to prevent manufacturers from paying rebates to Medicare and Medicaid, Medicare will be the recipient of the rebate.

A manufacturer is the entity holding legal title to or possession of the new drug code (NDC) for the covered outpatient drug.

The new program provides incentives to encourage the use of generic drugs. The benefit only covers generic drugs unless the physician indicates that a brand name medication is required. The Secretary may require that physicians obtain prior approval before prescribing specific brand-name products if a generic substitute is available.

Reimbursement

For brand name drugs, reimbursement is the lower of the 90th percentile of actual charges in a previous period, or the estimated acquisition cost (EAC) plus a dispensing fee.

For generic drugs, Medicare pays the lower of the pharmacist's actual charge or the median of all generic prices (times the number of units dispensed) plus a dispensing fee.

For participating pharmacies, the dispensing fee is $5, indexed to the Consumer Price Index (CPI). Participating pharmacies are required to accept assignment on all prescriptions. Non-participating pharmacists receive $2 less per prescription.

Changes in Private Insurance Requirements

The National Association of Insurance Commissioners (NAIC) will be instructed to make the necessary adjustments to Medigap policies to reflect the prescription drug coverage under Medicare. Private insurance plans may cover Medicare deductibles and co-payments for prescription drugs.

Subsidies

Low-income Medicare beneficiaries receive the same financial assistance for out-of-pocket costs associated with the drug benefit as provided for other cost-sharing amounts.

Reviews

The Medicare DUR program parallels the program established in OBRA 1990 for Medicaid. Participating pharmacists are required to offer counseling to Medicare customers on the use of medications.

The Secretary establishes a national system of Electronic Claims Management as the primary method for determining eligibility, processing and adjudicating claims, and providing information to the pharmacist about the patient's drug use under the Medicare drug program.

Equal Access for Purchasers to Pharmaceutical Discounts

As a condition of participation under Medicare and Medicaid, manufacturers of prescription pharmaceutical products sold in interstate commerce would have to offer discounts to all purchasers of pharmaceuticals on equal terms. This provision would not prohibit pharmaceutical manufacturers from offering differential discounts to purchasers in return for differential economic advantages realized by the manufacturer, such as volume buying, prompt payment, prompt delivery, or other mechanisms that can influence physician prescribing behavior.

Under this provision, pharmaceutical manufacturers would be precluded from providing discounts to purchasers based solely on the class of trade to which the purchaser belongs. Sales to federal health care programs that directly purchase pharmaceuticals, such as the Departments of Veterans Affairs and Defense, would be exempt from these provisions.

These provisions would become effective two years after the date of enactment Medicare Cost Savings.

Medicare Cost Savings

Growth in Medicare expenditures will be budgeted (see Budget Section). The following changes in the Medicare program will reduce the rate of growth in the Medicare program and allow Medicare to operate within the constraints of the budget:

• Reduce the Hospital Market Basket Index (HMBI) update by a further 0.5 percent in FY 1997 and 1 percent in FY 1998–2000.

• Reduce IME Adjustment to 5.65 percent in FY 1995 and 3.0 percent in FY 1996 and thereafter.

• Reduce payments for hospital inpatient capital.

• Phase down the Disproportionate Share Hospital (DSH) adjustment by 1998.

• Establish cost limits (similar to SNFs) fee long-term care hospitals.

• Expand centers of excellence.

• Lower home health cost limits to 100 percent of Median by July 1, 1999.

• Delete volume and intensity from the Medicare volume performance standard (MVSP) formula.

• Establish cumulative expenditure goals for physician expenditures.

• Reduce the Medicare fee schedule conversion factor by 3 percent in 1996, with primary care services exempt.

• Establish prospective payment for hospital outpatient radiology, surgery, and diagnostic services.

• Contract competitively for all Part B Laboratory Services, except in rural areas.

• Competitively bid other Medicare Part B services.

• Extend the Medicare Secondary Payor (MSP) data match with SSA and IRS.

• Establish a threshold of 20 employees for MSP for the disabled.

• Extend Medicare Secondary Payor Provisions for ESRD patients.

• Improve HMO payment.

- Increase Part B premiums for individuals with incomes above $100,000 and for couples with incomes above $125,000.
- Require a 10 percent coinsurance on home health visits for visits more than 20 days after a hospital discharge.
- Establish a 20 percent coinsurance for laboratory services.
- Phase down the coinsurance paid by beneficiaries to 20 percent of the total payments to hospitals for all outpatient surgery, radiology and diagnostic services.
- Subject all state and local employees to hospital insurance tax.
- Set Part B premium into law.

27

Medicaid*

___

Guaranteed Benefits for Non-Cash Recipients

• Under-65 Medicaid recipients who are not receiving either AFDC or SSI cash payments will no longer receive insurance through Medicaid. They will enter regional and corporate alliances based on their employment status.

• An exception to this policy is that undocumented persons will continue to receive Medicaid coverage for emergency services.

Guaranteed Benefits for Recipients of AFDC and SSI Cash Payments

• The Medicaid program will continue to make payments on behalf of AFDC and SSI recipients. For services covered in the comprehensive benefit package Medicaid will make capitated payments to regional alliance health plans (instead of making fee-for-service

___

* Long-term care policy is described in the chapter on Long-Term Care.

payments directly to providers at Medicaid specific rates, as is currently the norm).

• Cash assistance recipients, just like other members of the alliance, will choose from among plans participating in the regional alliance. Medicaid recipients can choose any plan at or under the weighted average premium without making an additional payment. Just like other members of the alliance, AFDC and SSI recipients with incomes below 150% of poverty will receive subsidies for copayments and deductibles if no plan with low cost sharing is available at or below the weighted average premium.

• In many regions of the country, organized delivery systems have little experience providing care to severely disabled persons. During a transition period it is important that disabled Medicaid recipients have access to a fee-for-service plan, and additional subsidies will be made available to secure this access. If no fee-for-service plan is available at or below the weighted average premium, an additional premium subsidy will be provided for Medicaid disabled so that they can join the lowest priced fee-for-service plan without additional payment. Further, deductibles and copayments will be subsidized for disabled Medicaid recipients in fee-for-service plans.

• The National Board will assess the extent to which organized delivery systems are capable of providing high quality care to disabled persons. At such time that the National Board determines that access to freedom of choice plans is not necessary to assure high quality care for the disabled, these additional premium and cost sharing subsidies will be phased out.

Supplemental Services

• Supplemental services for cash recipients (e.g., non-emergency transportation, vision care) will remain as in current law. Under consideration is conversion of supplemental services payments for cash and non-cash recipients into a block grant and providing states greater flexibility in targeting and delivering these services.

• Medicaid benefits and payments will continue to supplement Medicare as under current law.

Payments to Plans

• Per capita payments from Medicaid to regional alliances for the coverage of AFDC and SSI recipients will be equal to 95 percent of:

— Each state's per capita Medicaid spending on behalf of the recipient group to pay for services provided in the comprehensive benefit package;

— In the year prior to implementation of reform;

— With annual rates of increase subject to the national health care budget (see chapter on Budgeting).

• The federal and state shares of these and other Medicaid costs continue as under current law.

• Health plans submit premium bids to alliances for the non-AFDC, non-SSI population. Following negotiations with the alliance, as described in the budget chapter, premiums are adjusted, if necessary, to comply with the requirements of the budget. Required employer and employee payments are calculated based on the premiums negotiated between alliances and plans.

• For each health plan and policy type, the alliance computes a 'blended premium.' The blended premium for each plan is the weighted average of the plan's private sector premium and the Medicaid capitations, where the weights are the alliance wide proportion of private sector, AFDC and SSI persons. The blended premium for each health plan will depend on the private sector premium for the plan, but will not vary with the proportion of welfare recipients in the plan.

• Employers and employees continue to make payments into the alliance based on the private sector, not the blended rate.

• Alliances pay health plans based on the blended premium for all enrollees. In other words, a health plan receives the same payment for a person of a given risk class regardless of that person's welfare status.

• Payments from the alliance to health plans are risk adjusted, as described in the chapter on risk adjustment. If the risk adjustment is sufficiently refined, the risk adjuster will be blind to the welfare status of enrollees.

• However, if the risk adjustment system is not sufficiently refined, payments to plans on behalf of welfare recipients might actually be below the level of total dollars contributed for such persons by the Medicaid program. To prevent such an outcome, the risk adjustment system may include receipt of AFDC or SSI as a risk adjustment factor.

• If the National Board determines that, even with the risk adjustment system, plans that serve disproportionately large numbers of Medicaid recipients are paid less for the care of these recipients than they would be paid if the same recipients were not AFDC or SSI enrollees, then the Board creates a payment transfer system in which plans within an alliance that serve disproportionately low numbers of SSI and AFDC enrollees pay money to plans within the alliance with disproportionately high numbers of such enrollees.

Employed Recipients of AFDC or SSI

• Employers of AFDC or SSI recipients make payments to the alliance as specified in the financing chapter.

State Maintenance of Effort

States maintain spending for the acute-care portion of health coverage under Medicaid at a level equal to its share of total Medicaid spending for services covered in the nationally guaranteed benefit package in the year prior to implementation of reform. That figure is projected forward by the budgeted growth in the State's weighted-average premium for the state population not covered by Medicaid.

These expenditures pay health insurance premiums in alliances on behalf of individuals eligible for Medicaid and, if additional resources exist, other population groups. The Board makes adjustments as necessary in the amounts required of individual states so long as the total Medicaid maintenance of effort remains constant. The Board may increase the payments for "low effort" states (i.e., those with spending that is substantially below their revenue base).

Disproportionate Share Payments

Under health reform hospitals and other providers will receive insurance payments for virtually all patients they serve, and the need for disproportionate share payments will be eliminated. Therefore, DSH payments will be eliminated. The implementation schedule for this proposal is under review.

Implementation

With the possible exception of the elimination of DSH payments, provisions go into effect on the same date that states implement health reform.

28

Government Programs

Department of Defense

The Secretary of Defense supports coordinating the military health system with national health reform, and the Department will develop a plan for implementation.

The Department of Defense maintains the readiness capabilities of the military health care system as its critical priority and carries out commitments to beneficiaries in the military health care system at the time that national health reform is enacted.

To develop and implement the specific elements of a plan for the military health care system, the Secretary establishes ongoing consultation with the branches of the armed services and with appropriate committees of Congress.

Chapter 55 of Title 10 is amended to permit implementation when the Secretary decides to coordinate the military system with national health reform.

• Establishment of Plans

The Secretary may establish military health plans covering broad regions in which military medical treatment centers play a central role. Military health plans may contract with civilian health providers to deliver services to military beneficiaries.

Military health plans conform to requirements and standards for all health plans. Military plans may be offered within the regional alliance in which the military medical center is located.

Since military plans may also be subject to federal regulation under Chapter 55, however, military plans may not be rejected from participation in regional alliances because of a conflict between health plan requirements and federal law or regulations applicable to military health plans.

- **Eligibilty**

In areas in which a military health plan is established, active-duty personnel automatically enroll in the military health plan. Under current rules for priority described in Chapter 55 of Title 10, dependents of active-duty personnel, military retirees, dependents of retirees and survivors are eligible to enroll. Individuals who are not currently eligible for care in the military system, are not eligible to enroll in a military health plan.

- **Benefits**

Military health plans provide the nationally guaranteed benefit package. Under regulations issued pursuant to section 1112(a), supplemental services may be provided.

- **Appropriations and Reimbursement**

Payment responsibilities of the Department of Defense, military beneficiaries and others are established by regulations issued pursuant to section 1112(a).

Regulations provide that each category of enrolled beneficiaries who have continuously been beneficiaries under sections 1079 or 1086 (without regard to the exclusion of subsection (d) of section 1086) since

December 31, 1993, do not pay higher costs than under the current military system.

Employers of all military beneficiaries enrolled in a military health plan pay the employer contribution to the plan. Military health plans may receive capitated payments from Medicare for services to Medicare beneficiaries enrolled in military plans (under review).

Each military health plan establishes a financial account for receipts from military beneficiaries and others on behalf of military beneficiaries enrolled in the plan. These funds are used for the delivery and financing of care under the plan.

Veterans Affairs

The Department of Veterans Affairs may organize its health centers and hospitals into health plans or allow them to function as health providers contracting with health plans or other providers to deliver services.

Health plans organized within the VA system conform to the requirements and standards for all other health plans. If the VA plan meets requirements for health plans, it is offered as an enrollment choice within the regional health alliance that serves the area in which the VA plan is based.

Because VA health plans may also be subject to federal regulation under Title 38 of the United States Code, however, health alliances may not reject VA health plans from inclusion within the alliance because of a conflict between health plans requirements and federal law or regulations applicable to VA health centers.

Eligibility

All veterans are eligible to enroll in a VA health plan if one exists in their area. If capacity in the health plan is limited, veterans are eligible to enroll in the following order of priority:

- Veterans with service-connected disabilities
- Veterans meeting the income criteria set forth in 38 U.S.C. § 1722(b) ("low-income veterans")
- Veterans with higher incomes who do not have service-connected disabilities ("higher-income veterans").

Americans who are not veterans are not eligible to enroll in a VA health plan or to receive services on a contract basis from a VA health plan. However, dependents of veterans currently eligible under the Civilian Health and Medical Program—Veterans Affairs (CHAMPVA) may receive care through a VA health plan. The Secretary of Veterans Affairs may determine if a VA health plan offers family coverage to the dependents of veterans.

Benefits

VA health plans provide the nationally guaranteed comprehensive benefit package to every eligible person who enrolls. VA health plans may contract with other VA health centers or non-VA health providers or health plans to deliver the comprehensive benefit package.

Veterans who enroll in non-VA health plans may not receive care at VA centers for services in the comprehensive benefit package, except that non-VA health plans may contract with the VA to provide services in the comprehensive benefit package to veterans enrolled in non-VA plans.

Veterans with service-connected disabilities and low-income veterans will continue to be eligible for supplemental benefits not included in the comprehensive benefit package, such as treatment for post-traumatic stress disorder and certain dental services, at no cost to those individuals. The VA may offer these supplemental benefits to higher-income veterans at an additional premium.

Appropriations and Reimbursement

Federal appropriations for the VA health system cover actual costs of delivering the comprehensive benefit package for which the VA health plan is not reimbursed by other sources of revenue on behalf of veterans with service-connected disabilities and low-income veterans who enroll in a VA plan. Appropriations also cover the actual cost of supplemental benefits for veterans with service-connected disabilities and low-income veterans.

Higher-income veterans who select the VA plan pay their share of the premium and any applicable co-payment or deductible. Employers of all employed veterans enrolled in a VA health plan pay the employer contribution.

The VA has the right to retain all premiums, deductibles, co-payments or other cost sharing paid to the VA by individuals or employers as well as revenue obtained as reimbursement by third-party payers.

Medicare may reimburse VA health plans and centers for services to higher-income veterans eligible for Medicare. The Secretary of the Department of Veterans Affairs and the Secretary of the Department of

Health and Human Services will undertake negotiations to determine the application of Medicare rules and rates of reimbursement for VA services (under review).

VA centers that provide health services on a contract basis to veterans and their dependents enrolled in other health plans have the right to retain reimbursement from these plans.

Regulatory and Management Changes

Restrictions on the Secretary's authority to contract for services are eliminated if contracting is more cost effective than providing services at VA centers. Redundancies in oversight activities also are removed.

The Secretary may waive current requirements capping travel funds and restricting use of personnel funds.

Transition

The provisions of Chapter 17 of Title 38 governing VA health care remain in effect at any VA health center not functioning as a health plan.

National health reform establishes a revolving fund (with an appropriation to seed the fund) for investment in the start-up costs of VA health plans. VA health plans may borrow funds from the revolving fund and obtain multi-year authority to re-pay the fund with interest. The fund continues without fiscal-year limitations.

Indian Health Service

Indian Health Service clinics and hospitals, tribal health centers and urban Indian programs operate outside regional health alliances. National health reform does not limit options currently available to tribes to control and operate health facilities under the Indian Self-Determination and Education Assistance Act. Public Health Service programs for American Indians and Alaska Natives continue and expand as described under public health programs.

Eligibility

American Indians and Alaska Natives and their dependents currently eligible to receive services at Indian Health Service are eligible to enroll. All eligible American Indians/Alaska Natives choosing to receive care through the Indian Health Service must enroll.

American Indians and Alaska Natives may enroll in a health plan offered through the alliance but receive no federal subsidies for health care costs on the basis of their status as an American Indian or Alaska Native. American Indians and Alaska Natives, whether enrolled in a health plan in an alliance or enrolled with the Indian Health Service, are eligible for financial subsidies on the same basis as other Americans. American Indians and Alaska Natives who enroll in a health plan in the alliance may receive care through the Indian Health Service if the health plan contracts with the Indian Health Service.

An Indian Health Service center may serve non-Indians enrolled in health plans in the regional alliance on a contract basis.

Benefits

After a five-year transition during which the Indian Health Service renovates and expands its clinics, Indian

Health Service centers begin to deliver the full array of services guaranteed in the comprehensive benefit package. Indian Health Service centers may contract with other providers or health plans in order to provide the comprehensive benefit package.

Indian Health Service centers continue to provide the broad range of supplemental benefits currently available, such as public health nursing and health education, outreach services, environmental surveillance, health promotion and injury prevention, technical assistance, training and construction of sanitation infrastructure.

Appropriations and Reimbursement

The portion of premiums paid by employers on behalf of individual American Indians and Alaska Natives enrolled in an Indian Health Service center is paid into a fund that supplements appropriations to the Indian Health Service. If the employer is a tribal government, the employer is exempt from contributing the employer portion of the premium.

American Indians and Alaska Natives enrolled in an Indian Health Service center are not required to pay individual contributions for health insurance premiums.

These provisions do not alter the authority of the Indian Health Service to bill Medicare, Medicaid and other third-party payers for services provided in Indian Health Service clinics and permit the Indian Health Service to bill those payers for contract care delivered outside the Indian Health Service.

An Indian Health Service clinic receives reimbursement for non-Indians enrolled in a health plan in the regional alliance.

Federal Employee Health Benefits Plan

As health reform is implemented, federal employees purchase coverage through regional health alliances that serve the area in which they live, choosing from among health plans offered by the alliance much as they choose among Federal Employee Health Benefit Plans in the current system.

Coverage of federal employees and their dependents under FEHBP ends as regional health alliances begin operation in the area in which a beneficiary resides. The transition to new coverage occurs on a specified date or the last day of the first pay period beginning after January 1 of the first full year that a regional health alliance is fully operational in the area in which the federal employee resides.

If any covered family member resides outside the health alliance area, family enrollment may continue in FEHBP until all covered family members live in an area served by a health alliance and reciprocal arrangements to provide coverage outside the area are in place.

Enrollees who move out of the enrollment area of an FEHBP plan into an area served by a regional health alliance change their enrollment to a health plan offered through the health alliance. The transition occurs as a non-open season FEHBP enrollment change.

Eligibility

Enrollees and covered family members are no longer eligible for FEHBP on the date that transfer to the new system is complete in the region in which they reside. Temporary employees retain existing eligibility rights.

Restored employees and survivor or disability annuitants retain the rights they had until such time as they become eligible for coverage through a health alliance.

Any person losing coverage under the FEHBP, except for voluntary cancellation by them, gross misconduct, or because they are eligible for coverage through a health alliance is entitled to continued coverage under the FEHBP. Enrollees covered under this provision pay the entire premium plus a 2 percent administrative fee.

Coverage continues for federal employees working abroad. Annuitants without Medicare obtain insurance through regional alliances; annuitants with Medicare obtain coverage through an OPM-administered Medigap plan. In both cases, OPM pays a premium contribution sufficient to prevent an increase in annuitants' costs over current fees.

Transition

During phase-out, health plans offered on the date of repeal are offered as long as a contract continues between the Office of Personnel Management and the sponsoring carrier. The office continues to conduct annual open seasons and makes plan information available to individuals covered by the FEHBP to the maximum extent feasible.

Carriers continue to offer the same scope of benefits being offered on the effective date of repeal. Benefit levels are subject to annual negotiations until the FEHBP phases out entirely.

The office may continue to contract with carriers that have a signed contract in place on the effective date of repeal. Contract provisions in effect for the contract term ending on the date of repeal remain in effect unless OPM and the carrier agreed to modifications during the annual negotiations for the new contract term and signed contract amendments are in place.

The office may not enter into contracts during the phase-out period with carriers not already participating in the FEHBP on the effective date of repeal.

The Office of Personnel Management may terminate contracts at the end of a contract term at the convenience of the government. Generally, decisions to terminate are based on significant loss of enrollment resulting in a non-viable risk pool or other such phase-out problems. Enrollees and covered family members in terminated plans are automatically enrolled in the Standard Option of the government-wide Service Benefit Plan.

Contributions During Transition

During the phase-out period, the employer contribution continues at current levels. Employees pay the remainder of the premium. Postal employees eligible for a higher employer contribution than the new system requires continue to receive that benefit.

Both the employer and the participant contribution are funded, collected and distributed in accordance with existing mechanisms.

The phasing-out of FEHBP occurs on a state-by-state basis, as regional alliances take over FEHBP's function and role. When phase-out is complete, the FEHBP office continues to receive annual appropriations, to be made available until expended to pay the required employer contribution to premiums for annuitants as provided under provision of national health reform legislation.

The employer contribution for federal enrollees covered through a health alliance are made directly by the employing office to the health alliance. The Office of Personnel Management has no further functions relative to the health insurance coverage of federal enrollees covered through health alliances.

Employee Health Benefits Fund

The Employee Health Benefits Fund continues to operate as a reserve fund until phase-out is complete. When phase-out is complete, and all allowable claims for covered services are provided, any funds held in accounts held by participating carriers, except for monies in the contingency reserve accounts of community rated plans, are divided in the ratio of 72 percent to the employer and 28 percent to individuals enrolled in a fee-for-service plan on the date of repeal of federal employee health insurance.

Funds remaining in the contingency reserve accounts of community rated plans will be pooled and distributed in the same proportion as above to the government and those enrolled in community rated plans on the date of repeal.

Administration

Regulations prescribed by the Office of Personnel Management to carry out Chapter 89 of Title 5 of the United States Code remain in effect unless amended or unless they conflict with the provisions of this statute. In addition, the federal office may prescribe any regulations necessary to implement the provisions of this statute.

The Office of Personnel Management and the General Accounting Office retain the rights to audit provided in prior statute and under regulation and the provisions of the carrier contracts.

29

Transition

Schedule for Phase-in of States

States begin implementation of the new system as early as January 1, 1995.

Implementation involves enactment of a statute adopting federal program standards, formation of regional health alliances, and imposition of requirements for employers and individuals to obtain coverage.

At the time of state implementation, federal support systems and reforms take effect, including:

• Subsidies to assist low-income individuals and small, low-wage employers in purchasing health insurance.

• Limitations on balance billing by health care providers.

All states have implemented plans approved by the National Health Board by January 1, 1997. The Board may extend the deadline for six months for states that have made a good faith effort to begin implementation of the new system.

Incentives are offered for states implementing reform prior to January 1, 1997. The incentives include:

- Access to special start-up funds
- Access to subsidies
- Expedited federal consideration, with federal disapproval of state plans only if failure to comply with statutory requirements.

Medicaid Maintenance of Effort

States maintain current levels of financial support for the Medicaid program.

Federal Support for Implementation

States become eligible for federal support for administrative costs related to implementation of health reform in three phases:

Phase 1: Within one month of the passage of federal legislation, each state receives a planning grant to aid in the development of health care reform plans and alliances. Planning grants total $100 million and are distributed based on a formula specified in federal law.

Phases 2 and 3: Following passage of state statutes implementing health reform, the federal government provides financial support for start-up of the regional alliance system.

Funds provided under this provision support start-up costs only; after implementation of the new system, health insurance premiums absorb administrative costs associated with regional alliances.

The National Health Board develops the formula for distribution of federal funding for implementation. The formula takes into account projected start-up costs for administration and the development of the regional alliance system in each state. States are required to match federal financial support.

States receive one-third of their total allocation of federal funding for start-up costs upon passage of legislation implementing health care reform. The National Health Board releases funds following a determination that the state law conforms with federal requirements.

The remaining two-thirds of federal funds are released upon submission to the National Health Board of a state plan of operation. The board forwards funds after determining that the state plan of operation conforms with federal requirements.

Technical Assistance

The federal government assists states during the transition by drafting model legislation for state consideration, drawing up regulations and requests for proposals.

Federal funds support technical assistance provided by non-governmental entities in areas such as contracting, development of automated information exchange system, data collection and analysis.

Rulemaking

Rapid implementation of the American Health Security Act is vital to assure access to health care for millions of Americans to reduce the runaway growth in health care spending. To expedite implementation, the National Health Board, the Department of Labor and the Department of Health and Human Services are authorized to issue any regulations by the Act on an interim and final basis.

Implementation of Corporate Alliances

Large employers and other entities eligible to form corporate alliances must form an approved corporate alliance or join regional health alliances by January 1, 1997. Corporate alliances can be formed earlier.

If a state implements universal coverage prior to the date an eligible employer or other entity forms a corporate alliance, the eligible employer or other entity must form and maintain an employee benefit plan for its employees and their dependents who reside in the state. The plan must cover at least the benefits in the comprehensive benefit package. The eligible employer or other entity must contribute at least 80 percent of the cost of the comprehensive benefits.

Insurance Reform

To reduce the potential for disruption in the health insurance industry during the transition to the new health system, the American Health Security Act imposes interim insurance regulations.

States enforce the regulations; the Department of Health and Human Services enforces them in states that default on the requirement to enforce reforms.

Partially self-funded groups, self-funded multiple employer welfare arrangements (MEWAs), HMOs and other health plans are subject to the same regulatory requirements as insurers.

Requirements to Keep Coverage in Force. Insurers are prohibited from terminating or failing to renew health insurance coverage for any insured person, except for non-payment of premiums or other strictly defined cause.

Insurers are required to accept all newly hired, full-time employees and dependents added to groups currently insured. Rates charged coincide with rates set according to a state-approved rate table.

Restrictions on Premium Increases. Premium increases during the transition to health reform are subject the following requirements:

• Each insurer divides its business in each state into three sectors:
— Individual contracts
— Contracts covering groups with less than 100 participants
— Contracts covering larger groups.
• Any increases in premium rates must apply equally to all covered groups and individuals:
— All small groups and individuals receive the same percentage increase in rates.
— For larger groups, a portion of any increase could be based on group credibility as long as the total average increase equals the increase charged to individuals and small groups.

To address changes in group composition, each insurer is required to develop a single rate manual for each segment of its market in compliance with guidelines set forth in federal law or emergency regulation. Base rates in the manual are fixed at the average costs in each segment.

Changes in premium rates for groups due to changes in the demographic composition of the group are calculated from the manual. New additions to groups and groups applying for new coverage are accepted at rates established in the manual.

States with existing statutes reforming the market for health insurance may modify rules related to premium increases to accommodate the goal of rate compression. The Department of Health and Human Services, in consultation with states (e.g., the National Association of Insurance Commissioners), issues guidelines for state modifications.

Premium increases that exceed a prescribed percentage are subject to prior approval by state insurance regulators. An administrative process provides a channel for appeal by insurers damaged by this requirement.

Portability. To increase portability of coverage during the transition to the new health insurance system:

• Insurers and self-insured employer plans are prohibited from applying exclusions for pre-existing medical conditions to new employees and their dependents who were insured within the 90-day period immediately prior to current employment.

For new employees and their dependents previously not insured, exclusions for pre-existing conditions may not extend beyond six months.

These rules apply both to individual and group insurance policies.

• Self-funded health plans and employers with insured health plans are prohibited from imposing waiting periods for coverage on any employee otherwise eligible under the terms of the plan.

Reductions in Benefits. To ensure that employers and insurers do not impose caps or exclusions on coverage for specific medical conditions during the transition, employers and insurers are prohibited from reducing existing coverage for any medical condition or course of treatment if the anticipated cost is likely to exceed $5,000 in a year.

As under current law, employers may impose overall caps or reduce coverage as long as these changes are applied equally to all participants in a health plan.

Access to Coverage. To assure that health insurance is available during the transition for individuals who lose coverage or are unable to obtain coverage because of health status, the Secretary of Health and Human Services may organize a national risk pool.

The Department of Health and Human Services administers the pool which contracts with one or more private insurance firms to act as its intermediaries and administrative agents.

The risk pool provides coverage to any uninsured person or group unable to obtain coverage in the private insurance market. Premiums are set in a manner similar to existing state high risk pools. Because the pool is voluntary, it operates under traditional insurance rating methods. Premiums vary according to age, gender and place of residence. Premiums and assessments against all insurers support the pool, with assessments calculated based on market share in the health insurance market. Self-funded health plans also contribute to the pool through an assessment.

If premiums are not sufficient to pay claims incurred by the pool, additional assessments against insurers and self-funded health plans make up the difference.

The pool reimburses providers who treat participants based on Medicare payment rates; providers may not bill patients for the balance of any fee covered under the pool.

States with existing risk pools continue their operation or enroll individuals currently insured through pools in the federal pool. A state that transfers participants in its risk pool to the federal pool must continue its financial support at the same level.

The Department of Health and Human Services may enter into contracts with risk pools in states to administer the federal pool.

Short-Term Voluntary Cost Containment

Upon introduction of the reform plan, the President announces a program urging all sectors of the health care system, hospitals, physicians, laboratories, drug manufacturers, and all others, to limit price and expenditure increases to a specified amount.

The Secretary of the Department of Health and Human Services begins a program to monitor prices and expenditures in the health care system. The Secretary reports periodically to the President on the extent to which each sector is conforming to the voluntary restraints.

The Secretary has the authority to obtain information on prices and expenditures. All individual information is confidential. The Secretary periodically issues public reports on the levels of compliance in each sector.

30

Financing Health Coverage

OVERVIEW

Contributions for Health Coverage

Payments for health coverage will be divided into two shares: contributions by individuals and families and contributions by employers.

Individuals who work less than a full year, as well as families whose members jointly have less than one full year's employer contributions, are also responsible for any unpaid employer share to the extent they have non-wage income.

Individual and Family Contributions

Each individual and family is guaranteed health coverage through the alliance in which they are enrolled. Where families have workers at firms in two different corporate alliances or in one regional and one corporate alliance, they may choose coverage through either alliance.

Alliances offer consumers a choice of health plans. All consumers receive the same schedule of premiums for enrollment.

Premiums vary according to four family types: single individual, couple without children, single-parent family, and two-parent family.

Employer contributions pay for 80 percent of the average priced plan in the alliance for each family type.

Families and individuals pay the difference between 80 percent of the average priced premium and the actual cost of the plan they select.

The following example illustrates the choices that might face a single individual in an alliance where the average individual premium is $1,800. The employer contribution is 80 percent of $1,800, or $1,440.

Subsidies for Low-Income Families and Individuals

Families and individuals with incomes below 150 percent of poverty in a regional alliance may apply to their alliance for help in paying their premium. The subsidy will depend on their family income and the average premium for that family type in the alliance. If, for

Example: Premiums and Payments for Single Individuals

	Total Annual Premium	Annual Employer Payment	Annual Employee Payment	Monthly Employee Payment
Plan A	$1,500	$1,440	$60	$5.00
Plan B	$1,700	$1,440	$260	$21.66
Plan C	$1,800	$1,440	$360	$30.00
Plan D	$2,100	$1,440	$660	$55.00

example, a family qualified for a subsidy of $460, they could apply $460 toward the cost of any plan. If that family chose a plan costing less than $460 because of its quality or convenience, their subsidy would be limited to the actual cost of the plan.

Subsidy costs are borne by the federal government.

Employer Contributions

The contributions of employers total 80 percent of average premiums for each family status in an alliance.

Firms in the regional alliance pay a fixed per-worker contribution for each employee according to his or her family status.

The per-worker employer contribution depends on the average number of workers per family within each family status in the alliance. For example, if two-parent families in a region have an average of 1.5 workers per family, the per-worker contribution for a two-parent family is 80 percent of the average family premium divided by 1.5. In an alliance where 80 percent of the average family premium is $3,360, the per-worker contribution is $2,240 ($3,360 per family divided by 1.5 workers per family). Thus, each employer pays a flat $2,240 premium for each family worker, and total employer contributions for all family workers cover 80 percent of family premiums.

The following chart shows the relationship between premiums and per-worker contributions in an alliance where the average individual premium is $1,800, the average family premium is $4,200, and the average number of workers per family is as listed:

**Example: Average Premiums, Workers per Family,
and Premiums per Worker for Employers
by Family Status of Worker**

Type of Policy	Total Average Premium	80 Percent of Average Premium	Average Number of Workers per Family	Employer Contribution per Worker
Single individual	$1,800	$1,440	1.0	$1,440
Two-parent family	$4,200	$3,360	1.5	$2,240

Premiums and the number of workers per family will vary from one alliance region to another.

Subsidies for Employers

No employer in a regional alliance will be required to pay more than 7.9 percent of payroll for health coverage annually. Firms with fewer than 50 employees will be eligible for caps varying from 3.5 to 7.9 percent of payroll, depending on the employer's average wage.

PREMIUMS IN REGIONAL ALLIANCES

Families and employers pay premiums for coverage under the new system. Separate premiums are calculated for four categories:

- Single individuals.
- Couples.

- Single-parent families.
- Two-parent families with children.

Health plans submit premium bids to alliances, which review the bids and either accept them or negotiate lower amounts.

Premium bids are made on the basis of community rating, with rate variation allowed only for family category. Premiums are not adjusted for geographic area within an alliance.

Premiums are divided into two shares: the employer share and the family share. In general, employer contributions are calculated to equal 80 percent of the weighted average premium in the alliance for each premium category. A weighted average premium (hereafter referred to as an average premium) is the average premium bid for each category, weighted by plan enrollment. Families contribute the difference between 80 percent of the average premium and the price of the plan they choose.

To assure equity across all employers, employers make a contribution for each worker ("per-worker contribution") based on the family status of the worker. Because some workers have working spouses, the employer per-worker contribution rates for couples and two-parent families will be less than 80 percent of the average premium. The employer contribution rates for each category are calculated so that their total contributions equal 80 percent of the average for that category.

The alliance collects and aggregates all employer contributions and credits each working individual or family with an amount equal to 80 percent of the appropriate (based on family status) weighted average premium in the alliance. The family pays the difference between the credit and the premium of the plan that they choose.

INDIVIDUAL AND FAMILY CONTRIBUTIONS

Paying for Coverage in Both Regional and Corporate Alliances

All individuals and families in an alliance are charged the same community rates to enroll in a health plan.

• Individuals and families pay the difference between 80 percent of the average premium in their alliance for their family status and the premium of their chosen plan.
• Those who select a plan costing the average pay 20 percent of the premium. They pay the full difference for a plan costing less than or more than the average.

Working individuals and families may pay their share of premiums in one of several ways:

• Withholding from wages by one employer.
• Withholding from sources of non-wage income.
• Directly to the alliance in annual, quarterly, or other installments, as the alliance may arrange.

Alliances may require employee withholding to avoid bad debt.
Employers may pay part or all of the individual or family share of the premium.

• Employers that do so must make the same dollar contribution for all employees with the same family status, unless a bona fide collective bargaining agreement requires otherwise.

• Any additional employer contribution may not vary according to the health plan selected by the employee, and the employer must provide a rebate to the employee if the contribution exceeds the employee's share of the premium. Such a rebate is taxable income to the employee.

Individuals and Families in Regional Alliances

Premium Subsidies for Low-Income Persons

During the annual open enrollment period conducted by alliances, each regional alliance publishes a table showing subsidies available to individuals and families toward the cost of premiums by income level. Subsidies are available to individuals and families with incomes up to 150 percent of poverty.

An individual or family eligible for a subsidy pays the difference between: (1) Their plan's premium and (2) The sum of their subsidy and 80 percent of the average premium in the alliance.

Subsidized individuals and families may sometimes be unable to enroll in a plan at or below the average premium because none is available or enrollment is limited. In such cases, the alliance raises the subsidy to permit them to enroll in the lowest-cost plan above the average.

**Example: Premiums, Subsidies, and Payments
for a Family with Subsidy**

	Total Annual Premium	*80 Percent of Avg. Premium*	*Annual Subsidy*	*Annual Family Payment*
Plan A	$3,600	$3,460	$460	$0
Plan B	$4,000	$3,360	$460	$180
Plan C	$4,200	$3,360	$460	$380
Plan D	$4,500	$3,360	$460	$680

Cost-sharing Subsidies
for Low-Income Persons

In areas not served by a plan or network with low cost sharing and a premium at or below the average premium in the alliance, individuals with family incomes less than 150 percent of the poverty level qualify for subsidies to cover co-payments and deductibles. Subsidies reduce cost sharing to the level charged by a low cost sharing plan. Alliances determine whether such a plan is available. The same process used for determining eligibility for premium subsidies is used for determining eligibility for cost-sharing subsidies.

Administration of Subsidies
for Low-Income Persons

Individuals and families may apply for premium and cost-sharing subsidies during any open enrollment period, at the same time of transfer to a new alliance, or after a change in life circumstances, such as unemployment or divorce.

Alliances distribute applications for subsidies directly to consumers and through employers, banks, and designated public agencies. Consumers forward completed applications to alliances or an agency designated by the state.

Determination of eligibility is based on family income. When applying for a subsidy, eligible individuals and families submit a declaration of estimated annual income. After the end of the year, the alliance or another agency designated by the state checks self-declared estimates of income against income tax returns and other data presented by the beneficiaries and reconciles estimates with final income for the year.

Beneficiaries receive notice of any additional payment or rebate due following a year-end reconciliation. Subsidies are conditional until a year-end determination that the individual or family qualified for the subsidy.

Individuals and Families in Corporate Alliances

Employees of corporate alliance employers pay the difference between 80 percent of the average premium in the corporate alliance and the premium of their chosen plan. Employees who select a plan costing the average pay 20 percent of the premium. They pay the full amount less for a plan costing less than the average; they pay the full amount more for a plan costing above the average.

For low-wage full-time workers, the employer contributes an additional amount. If the worker earns annualized wages of $15,000 or less, the employer contributes the greater of 80 percent of the average premium of 95 percent of the premium for the lowest cost plan available to the employee in the corporate alliance.

Family Choice

Alliances may establish procedures for spouses to enroll in separate health plans.

Choice of Alliances

A family in which one full-time worker is eligible for coverage through a corporate alliance and one full-time worker is eligible for coverage through a regional alliance may choose one alliance in which to enroll.

If the entire family enrolls in a plan through the regional alliance, the family may qualify for a subsidy based on income. If the family enrolls in the corporate alliance, subsidies are not available.

A family with full-time workers eligible for coverage in different corporate alliances may also choose one alliance in which to enroll.

EMPLOYERS IN THE NEW SYSTEM

Regional Alliances

For each of their eligible full-time employees, employers participating in a regional alliance contribute 80 percent of the appropriate per worker contribution for the employee's family status.

The per worker contribution paid by the employer varies only by the alliance area in which the employee lives and the family status of the employee. There are per worker contributions for:

- A single worker.
- A couple.
- A single-parent worker.
- A worker with a spouse and children.

Employers receive subsidies that cap total premium contributions for employees at 3.5 percent to 7.9 percent of the firm's payroll.

Contributions for employers with 50 or fewer employees are capped at a lower level, based on the average wage of the firm. Caps vary as follows:

Employers with more than 50 employees pay no more than 7.9 percent of payroll.

Small Employer's Average Wage per Full-Time Equivalent Worker	Cap on Employer Contributions as a Percentage of Total Payroll
Less than $12,000	3.5%
$12,000 to $15,000	3.8%
$15,000 to $18,000	4.4%
$18,000 to $21,000	5.5%
$21,000 to $24,000	6.5%
Greater than $24,000	7.9%

Corporate Alliances

For each of their eligible full-time employees, employers in corporate alliances contribute a minimum of 80 percent of the weighted average premium among the health plans they offer to employees. The employer contribution varies according to the type of policy chosen by the worker—single, couple, single-parent family, or two-parent family.

For low-wage full-time workers in corporate alliances, the employer contributes an additional amount. If the worker earns annualized wages of $15,000 or less, the employer contributes the greater of 80 percent of the average premium or 95 percent of the premium for the lowest cost plan available to the employee in the corporate alliance.

No subsidies are available for corporate alliance employers.

If a large employer chooses to join the regional health alliances, the rules are the same as for other employers, except that the per worker premiums contributed by the employer are adjusted for the risk profile of its employees. Risk is measured based on the industry classification of the employer and the demographic characteristics of its workforce.

For the first four years after choosing to join regional alliances, the employer pays the greater of the community rated per worker premiums or its risk adjusted per worker premiums. The risk adjustment uses a national formula developed by the Department of Labor, but is calculated separately for each alliance area in which the firm's employees live.

The employer contribution for each regional alliance area is adjusted over the four subsequent years until it reaches the level of the community rated per worker premium:

- In the fifth year, the employer's payment is equal to 75 percent of the risk adjusted employer share of the per worker premium plus 25 percent of what the employer would pay under a community rated per worker premium.
- In the sixth year, the employer's payment is equal to 50 percent of the risk adjusted employer share of the per worker premium plus 50 percent of what the employer would pay under a community rated per worker premium.
- In the seventh year, the employer's payment is equal to 25 percent of the risk adjusted employer share of the per worker premium plus 75 percent of what the employer would pay under a community rated per worker premium.
- In the eighth year, the employer begins paying on the basis of community rated per worker premiums.

Subsidies to which an employer is entitled are similarly phased in over several years. The employer receives no subsidies in the first four years. It receives 25 percent of the subsidies to which it would normally be entitled in the fifth year, 50 percent in the sixth year, 75 percent in the seventh year, and 100 percent beginning in the eighth year.

Employer Contributions for Families with Workers in Multiple Alliances

For families where two full-time adult workers are eligible for coverage through different alliances, the family chooses an alliance through which to enroll in a health plan.

The employer in the chosen alliance makes a premium contribution as it normally would. The employer in the alliance that is not chosen contributes 80 percent of the appropriate per worker premium for the regional alliance area in which its employee lives. The employer in the alliance that is not chosen makes this payment regardless of whether it participates in a regional alliance or corporate alliance. The employer payment is forwarded to the chosen alliance to pay for a portion of the family's coverage.

Employer Contributions for Part-Time Employees

Regional alliances cover part-time workers, whether they work for a regional alliance or corporate alliance employer. A part-time worker who is the spouse or child of a full-time worker covered through a corporate alliance is an exception, and is instead covered through the corporate alliance.

For part-time workers, all employers—regardless of whether they participate in a regional or corporate alliance—contribute a pro-rated portion of the regional alliance's appropriate per worker premium (varying by the worker's family status). The contribution is pro-rated based on the ratio of hours worked to a thirty hour work week.

All employer payments for part-time workers are forwarded to the regional alliance.

Administration

When an employee begins a new job, employers collect the following information and forward it to the appropriate health alliance:

• Registration information, including: name, address, identification numbers, family status, and names and Social Security numbers of spouse and dependent children.
• Choice of health plan, if the employee is new to the area or newly hired by a corporate alliance.

Employers forward the information to the alliance within 30 days. Pending notice by the alliance, employers make contributions according to the premiums provided by the alliance.

Employers are required to make premium contributions to alliances at least monthly, but may make them more frequently. Alliances may require electronic payment of premiums for employers already required to do so under the federal tax system, and may create disincentives for paper transactions.

When making premium contributions, employers cap their total contributions at the relevant percentage of total payroll for the period. If an employer is making contributions to multiple regional alliances, its payments—capped, if relevant—are distributed across alliances based on the proportion of uncapped premiums due to that alliance. With its last premium payment for a year, each employer reconciles its total premium payments for the year capped at the relevant percentage of its total annual payroll, and reports the information used for this reconciliation to the alliance.

Employers maintain records for auditing purposes that document premium contributions. The regional alliance that covers the largest share of an employer's workforce has responsibility for auditing the employer's records. Other alliances abide by that alliance's audit determinations. The employer or another alliance may appeal the result of an audit to the Department of Labor.

SELF-EMPLOYED, NON-WORKERS, PART-TIME AND SEASONAL EMPLOYEES

Self-employed individuals, part-time and seasonal employees, and non-working single individuals and families pay premiums based on their family status.

Self-Employed Individuals

Self-employed people pay the employer share and the individual share of the appropriate premium (e.g., individual, couple, single parent family, or two-parent family). Contributions are made to alliances at least quarterly.

The employer share paid by the self-employed person is equal to the amount employers contribute for workers in the alliance with the same family status. The contribution is capped as a percentage of self-employed income, using the percentage caps applied to small businesses in the alliance.

If a self-employed person also works for another employer, any amount contributed by that employer—prior to any employer subsidies—reduces the person's premium obligation as a self-employed person.

The self-employed person and his or her family are also responsible for the family share of the premium. Subsidies are provided to families whose income is below 150 percent of poverty.

All premium payments made by self-employed persons are fully tax deductible.

Non-Workers and Part-Time Workers

All part-time workers and non-workers without a spouse working full-time for a corporate alliance employer are covered through a regional alliance.

Non-working and part-time single people and families make contributions based on their unearned income. Non-workers and part-time workers pay towards the employer share and the family share of the appropriate premium for their family status.

Single people and members of families who work only part-time or part of the year owe one per worker contribution for the appropriate family status minus any employer contributions (before subsidies) made on their behalf. The required payment is reduced for families whose family income is less than 250 percent of poverty.

Non-workers make such payments to the alliance at the end of the year.

Non-workers also are responsible for family share of the premium. Subsidies are provided to families whose income is below 150 percent of poverty.

Retirees [under review]

Retired people not yet eligible for Medicare who are over 55 years of age and who meet the Social Security requirements for quarters of work are eligible for a subsidy for the employer share of their premium.

If a retiree has a working spouse, the contribution from the retiree subsidy program covers only the unpaid portion of the employer share of the premium. The retiree subsidy equals one per worker contribution for the appropriate family status minus the amount contributed by the spouse's employer.

If the retiree works part-time, the amount contributed by the retiree subsidy program is reduced by any employer contributions due to the part-time work.

Alliances administer the retiree subsidies. To be eligible for a subsidy, the person must submit an application to the alliance. The alliance verifies compliance with the prior work requirement with the Social Security Administration. Information received from SSA is held strictly confidential.

The retiree and his or her family are also responsible for the family share of the premium. Subsidies are provided to families whose income is below 150 percent of poverty.

Where an agreement exists for employers to pay retiree health benefits, the employer's responsibility will shift to paying the 20 percent family share on behalf of the retiree.

Employers who realize a reduction in retiree health costs may be assessed a one-time payment for the extra cost associated with induced early retirements due to the retiree subsidy program. [Under review.]

Students

A full-time student covered under a family's policy receives coverage through the alliance where he or she attends school. The alliance receiving premium payments from the family and its employer transfers a portion of the family's premium payments to the alliance providing coverage.

MANAGEMENT OF REGIONAL ALLIANCE FUNDS AND RECORDS

Federal Payments to Alliances for Subsidies

Alliances will periodically request payments from the Department of Health and Human Services to make up shortfalls as a result of employer and family subsidies. Alliances will maintain records justifying subsidy payments, which may be verified and audited by HHS. Federal payments for subsidies are net of state Medicaid maintenance of effort payments made to alliances.

Alliance Management Standards

States set standards for procedures, policies, due diligence, and good faith in the management of alliances. These standards are required, at least, to meet federal minimums. These standards will include record-keeping, budgeting, credit and collections, internal controls and internal audit, bonding, and general board oversight.

Alliances are required to publish periodic financial statements, including year-end audited statements prepared in accordance with generally accepted auditing standards and bearing an unqualified opinion from an outside, independent auditor.

Failure to Pay Premiums

Federal guidelines require that regional alliances exercise due diligence in collecting unpaid employer and consumer premium contributions, including the imposition of interest charges and late fees for non-payment and other credit and collection procedures. Premium contributions owed to regional alliances are privileged compared to other corporate or personal obligations in bankruptcy proceedings.

Alliances recover for unpaid premium contributions through a premium assessment paid by employers and consumers. This bad debt premium assessment is not included in the alliance's weighted average premium for the purposes of budget enforcement, and is in excess of any capped employer or consumer premium payments.

State Maintenance of Effort Payments

States make Medicaid maintenance of effort payments to offset subsidy costs. Maintenance of effort payments are made to regional alliances by states, and reported and documented to the Department of Health and Human Services.

Alliance Management of Funds

Regional alliances are required to safeguard premium and subsidy payments held in alliance accounts. Operating funds are held only in banks meeting the Basel capital standards, and are transferred into investment accounts at least daily. Investment funds, which are those held longer than one day, are held in instruments or in separate accounts collateralized by instruments that qualify as collateral for U.S. Treasury funds held in banks.

ERISA standards continue to apply to corporate alliances in their management of funds representing employee premium contributions.

Standardization of Information

The Departments of Labor and Health and Human Services develops standardized forms—and, in the case of electronic submissions, standardized data fields—for use by alliances, employers, and consumers. DOL and HHS also develops standards for minimum frequency of information submission to alliances and for alliance record keeping responsibilities.

Privacy

Federal guidelines ensure the confidentiality of financial and other records submitted to alliances by employers and consumers, and restrict the merger of information held by alliance and health status information held by plans.

Power to Borrow

Alliances have the power to borrow to cover short-term cash flow shortages created by mismatching of required payments to plans and receipts of premium payments and subsidies.

TAX SUBSIDIES

Employer contributions toward the premium and toward cost sharing for the nationally guaranteed comprehensive benefit package and for additional benefits phased in by the year 2000 are tax deductible to the employer and not counted as income to the employee.

Any premium payment by a self-employed person for the comprehensive benefit package is fully tax deductible.

Once alliances are established, contributions continue to be tax-preferred only if made through an alliance.

Benefits that exceed the fully phased in benefit package are taxable to the employee, however they continue to be fully tax preferred for ten years after enactment if they were provided as of January 1, 1993.

How Reform Is Financed
($ billion, 1994–2000)

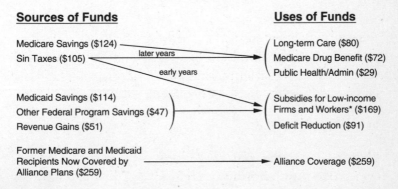

Sources of Funds

Medicare Savings ($124)
Sin Taxes ($105)

later years
early years

Medicaid Savings ($114)
Other Federal Program Savings ($47)
Revenue Gains ($51)

Former Medicare and Medicaid Recipients Now Covered by Alliance Plans ($259)

Uses of Funds

Long-term Care ($80)
Medicare Drug Benefit ($72)
Public Health/Admin ($29)

Subsidies for Low-income Firms and Workers* ($169)
Deficit Reduction ($91)

Alliance Coverage ($259)

To qualify for the continued tax exclusion, employers must register their benefit plans with the Department of Labor prior to December 31, 1994.

If a benefit exceeds an employer's registered plan as well as the guaranteed benefit package in the year 2000, employers may continue to deduct the cost as a business expense. However, employer payments for such benefits are counted as taxable income to the employee.

Section 125 plans (so-called cafeteria plans) are amended to exclude employee contributions for health benefits.

Employers submit annual reports to the Internal Revenue Service and list on employee W-2 forms the amount of taxable and tax-exempt contributions to health insurance.

Growth Rate of Health Care Spending
(Growth Rates in Percent)

Calendar Years	1994	1995	1996	1997	1998	1999	2000
GDP Growth Rate	5.4	5.3	5.0	4.6	4.3	4.1	4.2
CPI Inflation Rate	2.7	2.7	2.7	2.7	2.7	2.7	2.7
Population Growth	1.0	0.9	0.9	0.9	0.8	0.8	0.8
Private Sector	baseline	baseline	cpi+pop+1.5	cpi+pop+1	cpi+pop+0.5	cpi+pop	cpi+pop
Medicare and Medicaid*	baseline	baseline	cpi+pop+2.4	cpi+pop+1.9	cpi+pop+1.4	cpi+pop+0.9	cpi+pop+0.4
Private Sector							
Baseline	7.4	7.6	7.7	7.6	7.2	6.8	6.4
Reform	7.4	7.6	5.2	4.7	4.1	3.6	3.5
Medicare (Fiscal Years)							
Baseline	11.6	11.2	11.1	9.5	9.1	9.0	9.0
Reform**	11.6	11.2	7.4	5.7	5.1	4.6	4.1
Medicaid (Fiscal Years)							
Baseline	16.5	14.3	11.7	11.6	11.2	11.0	11.0
Reform**	16.5	14.3	7.5	5.7	5.1	4.6	4.1

* Assumes differential growth of 0.9 percent in the public sector.
** Reform estimates are on a fiscal year basis for public programs.

Budgetary Effects of Health Care Reform
(billions of dollars)

Fiscal Years	1994	1995	1996	1997	1998	1999	2000	1994–00
Total New Spending	1	7	45	64	71	79	83	350
Subsidies Net of Offsets	0	5	25	33	34	33	30	160
Self-Employed Tax Deduction (100%)	0	0	1	2	2	2	2	9
Long-Term Care	0	0	5	10	15	22	28	80
Medicare Drug Benefit	0	0	10	14	15	16	17	72
New Public Health Spending	0	1	3	3	3	4	4	18
Administration	1	1	1	2	2	2	2	11
Total Savings	−12	−15	−36	−59	−81	−104	−134	−441
Medicare Savings	0	0	−7	−15	−23	−33	−46	−124
Medicaid Savings	0	0	−7	−15	−22	−30	−40	−114
Other Federal Program Savings	0	0	−5	−8	−10	−11	−13	−47
Revenue Effects of Mandate	0	0	−2	−6	−10	−14	−19	−51
Sin Taxes and/or Corporate Assessment	−12	−15	−15	−15	−16	−16	−16	−105
Change in Deficit	−11	−8	9	5	−10	−25	−51	−91

* Estimates are preliminary and do not incorporate interactive effects.

Detail of Subsidy Costs
(billions of dollars)

Fiscal Years	1994	1995	1996	1997	1998	1999	2000	1994–00
Subsidies Net of Offset	0	5	25	33	34	33	30	160
Gross Subsidies	0	14	58	80	86	89	92	419
Total Offsets	0	−9	−33	−47	−52	−56	−62	−259
State Offset for Medicaid in Alliance	0	−3	−10	−14	−15	−15	−16	−73
Federal Offset for Medicaid in Alliance	0	−4	−15	−22	−25	−28	−31	−125
Federal Offset for Medicare in Alliance	0	−?	−8	−11	−12	−13	−15	−61

* *Estimates are preliminary and do not incorporate interactive effects.*

Budgetary Effects of Health Reform
(billions of dollars)

Fiscal Years	1994	1995	1996	1997	1998	1999	2000	1994–98	1996–00
Changes in Outlays for Existing Programs	0	−5	−28	−53	−73	−94	−123	−159	−371
Medicaid	0	−4	−21	−36	−46	−57	−70	−107	−230
Liberalized Long-term Care Eligibility	0	0	1	1	1	1	1	3	5
Offset for Medicaid-eligibles in Alliances	0	−4	−15	−22	−25	−28	−31	−66	−121
Savings Due to Cap	0	0	−7	−15	−22	−30	−40	−44	−114
Medicare	0	−2	−5	−12	−20	−30	−44	−39	−111
Cost of Drug Benefit (with Rebate)	0	0	10	14	15	16	17	39	72
Offset for Employed Beneficiaries	0	−2	−8	−11	−12	−13	−15	−33	−59
Savings Due to Cap	0	0	−7	−15	−23	−33	−46	−45	−124
Veterans	0	0	−1	−2	−2	−2	−2	−5	−9
Defense Department Health	0	0	0	0	0	0	−1	0	−1
Federal Employees Health Benefits	0	0	−2	−4	−5	−6	−7	−11	−24
New Public Health Initiatives	0	1	3	3	3	4	4	10	17
Public Health Savings	0	0	−2	−2	−3	−3	−3	−7	−13
Added Outlays for New Programs	1	12	52	76	86	95	103	227	412
Long-term Care (Net of Premium)	0	0	3	8	13	19	25	24	68

Subsidies (a)	0	14	58	80	86	89	92	238	405
Less State Offset for Medicaid in Alliance	0	−3	−10	−14	−15	−15	−16	−42	−70
New Administrative Costs	0	0	1	2	2	2	2	5	9
Start Up Costs	1	1	0	0	0	0	0	2	0
Total Outlay Changes	1	7	24	23	13	1	−20	68	41
Receipts Changes	12	15	15	18	23	26	31	83	113
Sin Taxes/Corporate Assessment	12	15	15	15	16	16	16	73	78
Tax Incentives for Long-term Care	0	0	−1	−1	−1	−2	−2	−3	−7
Expanded Deduction for Self-Employed	0	0	−1	−2	−2	−2	−2	−5	−9
Effects on Other Taxes of the Mandate (b)	0	0	2	6	10	14	19	18	51
Deficit	−11	−8	9	5	−10	−25	−51	−15	−72

(a) From Urban Institute using HCFA premiums.

(b) Unofficial estimate.

* Estimates are preliminary and do not incorporate interactive effects.

National Health Expenditures
(billions of dollars)

Calendar Years	1994	1995	1996	1997	1998	1999	2000
CBO Baseline	998	1,089	1,185	1,288	1,395	1,510	1,631
% GDP	15.1	15.7	16.3	16.9	17.5	18.2	18.9
% change	9.4	9.1	8.8	8.6	8.4	8.2	8.0
Reform	999	1,112	1,237	1,314	1,376	1,438	1,495
% GDP	15.1	16.0	17.0	17.2	17.3	17.4	17.3
% change	9.4	11.3	11.2	6.2	4.7	4.5	4.0
Change in Spending:							
New Alliance	0	19	71	83	86	90	93
Other New Spending	1	4	13	20	25	33	38
Savings	0	0	−32	−77	−130	−195	−267

* *Estimates are preliminary.*